100
classic
backcountry
Ski and Snowboard Routes
in Washington

100

classic
backcountry

Ski and Snowboard Routes

in Washington

Rainer Burgdorfer

THE
MOUNTAINEERS

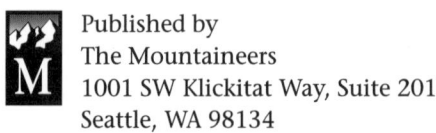

Published by
The Mountaineers
1001 SW Klickitat Way, Suite 201
Seattle, WA 98134

© 1999 by Rainer Burgdorfer

First edition, 1999

Published simultaneously in Great Britain by Cordee, 3a DeMontfort Street, Leicester, England, LE1 7HD

Manufactured in Canada

Edited by Susan Hodges
Maps by Jacqui Weber
Cover and book design by Kristy L. Welch
Book layout by Margarite Hargrave

Cover photograph: Gary Brill crashing through the powder. © Mark Kroese
Frontispiece: Snowboarder Luke Edgar (Photo by William C. Shigley)

Library of Congress Cataloging-in-Publication Data
Burgdorfer, Rainer, 1948–
    100 classic backcountry ski and snowboard routes in Washington / by Rainer Burgdorfer. — 1st ed.
        p. cm.
    Includes bibliographical references and index.
    ISBN 0-89886-661-8 (paperbound)
        1. Cross-country skiing—Washington (State)—Guidebooks.
    2. Snowboarding—Washington (State) Guidebooks. 3. Cross-country ski trails—Washington (State) Guidebooks. 4. Washington (State) Guidebooks. I. Title II. Title: One hundred classic backcountry ski and snowboard routes in Washington
    GV854.5.W33 B85 1999
    796.93'2'09797—dc21   99-6535
                                                                      CIP

☻ Printed on recycled paper

Contents

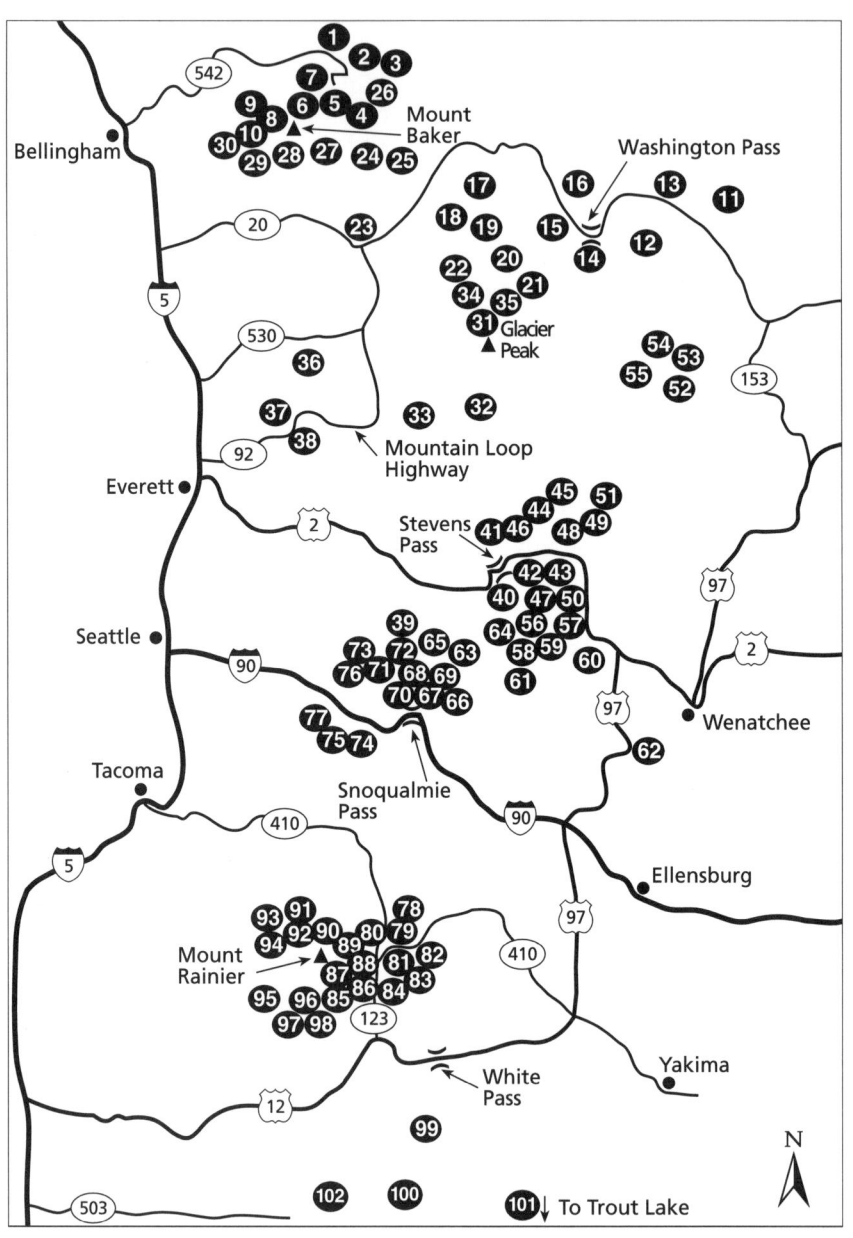

KEY TO TOUR MAPS

Main Approach Road	— — — — -
Secondary Approach Road	— — — — -
Main Route	————
Alternate or Optional Routes	··················
Avalanche Zone	
Good Camping	▲
Gate	=
Good Skiing	⚡

Mount Rainier, Spirit Lake, and the caldera and rim of Mount Saint Helens (Photo by Craig Miller)

This book is dedicated to Doug Walker,
who, by his example,
sets a standard for community service,
and whose friendly support made this book possible.

Preface

Backcountry skiing has never been easier or more fun—and it's never been more challenging. This guide is intended to help you maximize your fun while minimizing your exposure to risk. Some of the destinations described in these pages will be familiar to readers of other backcountry guidebooks. However, the tours in *100 Classic Backcountry Ski and Snowboard Routes in Washington* differ substantially from those described in other guides. They feature alternative, steep descent routes, making them suitable for skiers who seek great downhill runs, spectacular views, and an alpine experience. Many make wonderful summer hikes, too. Recognize that the tours mentioned in this book represent only a tiny sampling of the skiing available in Washington's Cascades.

Recreational users continue to flock to the Cascade Mountains in unprecedented numbers and are finding unprecedented political and economic obstacles to their formerly free playground. For a party of three people to visit all of the places described in this guide would cost more than $250.00 in user fees. The issues of user fees and access must be addressed by those who want to resume enjoying snow tours and access in general to public lands. Write to your representatives! It is essential that backcountry skiers make their voices heard to secure access for themselves and for future generations. On a regional level, I encourage all skiers to urge their state legislatures to secure full funding for the Northwest Avalanche Center.

Acknowledgements are due to Gary Brill, whose expertise complemented the avalanche section, and to Jeff Renner, who helped me to understand Cascade weather.

Harry Hendon's encouragement helped me launch the original project. Special thanks are due to Debbie Yardley, without whose technical assistance and personal support this project would not have been completed in a timely manner. The following people helped by offering photos or useful suggestions: Joe Catellani, Luke Edgar, Sue Harris, Harry Hendon, Jens Kieler, Craig Miller, Brian Povolny, Donal O'Sullivan, Ron Proper, Ken Ritland, Bryan Scott, Bill Shigley, Lowell Skoog, Brian Sullivan, and Scott Wicklund. Thank you all.

The tours described in this book are suitable, in varying degree, for snowboarders, snowshoers, hikers, and skiers. As literary shorthand, I will use the old-fashioned term "ski" or "skiing" to describe the mode of travel on these tours.

Rainer Burgdorfer

Introduction

Why bother, anyway? Why would anybody hike five miles (or more) to ski the equivalent of five lift-served runs? Imagine untracked snow, stunning views not available to lift-bound skiers, and the look of envy on your friends' faces when you tell them you got face-shots of powder—in May! Use this guide and find 100 more reasons.

A decade ago, the revolution in Cascade ski touring was in full swing. Lightweight equipment, greater knowledge of alpine travel and skiing skills, and an influx of new talent from other areas made backcountry skiing practical for more people than ever before. Then a strange invention turned skiing upside down—the snowboard came into its own, offering a new way to ski backcountry runs. On other fronts, improvements in navigational tools and avalanche survival equipment and information, not to mention clothing and skis, have tremendously increased safety and touring power.

Safe backcountry skiing requires more than gear, however. It demands skill, local knowledge, judgment, and a safety-conscious attitude. This guide provides *some* of the necessary local knowledge. The skill, judgment, and attitude are up to you.

HOW TO USE THIS GUIDE

Selecting a tour is easy with this guide. Use the Seasonal Cross-Reference Table, Appendix C, to pick a tour based on the season, or turn to the Table of Contents to choose a tour in a specific area. Now match your choice with the current weather forecast, and bingo! Pay the user fee and go.

Each tour description consists of a summary, a map, and a written description. The summary should help you match a tour to your circumstances. The following is a guide to the tour summaries in this book.

Start Point is where you leave your vehicle. This location may vary, depending on road conditions, snow levels, or closures.

High Point is the highest elevation reached on the tour. Elevations are approximate, due to the limitations of civilian GPS data.

Best Time suggests a good season for the tour, taking road approaches into consideration. Road access can be improved by the judicious use of snowmobiles or mountain bikes. (This is now common practice in some parts of the Cascades.) Weather and snow conditions will vary from month to month, so this suggestion must be taken with a view to recent weather patterns. Successful backcountry skiers inevitably become competent amateur meteorologists!

Skill Level indicates the skiing and mountaineering skills required for the tour. *None of the tours in this book are for novice skiers. Every tour requires at least intermediate skiing skills.* Attempting a tour outside of the suggested season or in unsuitable weather will affect the difficulty rating. Be aware that snow conditions have as much, or more, to do with difficulty as any factors intrinsic to the tour.

Descending Inspiration Glacier from the summit of Eldorado (Photo by Rainer Burgdorfer)

Intermediate skiing skills imply the ability to climb up and slide down moderate slopes, turning at will. An intermediate tour will require some experience and competence with winter conditions. On intermediate tours, some experience with winter camping, survival, and alpine travel is needed. Skiers must understand the basics of avalanche hazard avoidance and navigation, especially when snow obscures trails.

Advanced skiing skills imply the ability to ascend and descend steeper slopes under varying conditions, including tree and gully skiing and travel in deep, soft, or icy snow conditions. Advanced tours require a high degree of skill in all aspects of snow climbing, including avalanche hazard avoidance. Where corniced ridges and other obstacles make travel difficult, or level areas make descents impractical for snowboarders, it is so noted.

Alpine tours are generally serious undertakings. They involve routefinding and travel over extremely steep terrain, with high avalanche potential over virtually the entire route.

Tours calling for *extreme* skiing (if you fall, you die) are not considered here.

Day Trip, Overnight, Weekend, and Extended Tour are categories that indicate the length of a tour. The approximate round-trip distance is given in miles.

Skiing Time suggests how many hours of round-trip travel may be expected for a typical party, using modern equipment, in good conditions. You can expect to take longer if, for instance, you encounter fog or deep snow, the descent leads over steep ice, or you are carrying overnight gear on a day trip. While some of the stated time estimates may seem short to those who have hiked the same routes in summer months, remember that ski descents can be significantly faster than hiking descents. Also keep in mind that sundown comes early in winter months.

Difficulties are the obstacles to be overcome on a tour. For example, Granite Mountain, although clearly an advanced descent with high avalanche potential, requires little in the way of mountaineering skills, while the Muir Snowfield can require considerable routefinding, even if the skiing is quite moderate.

Avalanche potential may be low, moderate, considerable, high, or extreme. For more on avalanche danger, see Appendix D: Sources of Weather and Snow Information.

Routefinding required indicates that a map, a compass, and possibly an altimeter or GPS are essential for reaching the tour objective in a reasonable amount of time. Where appropriate, tours unsuitable for snowboarders are identified.

Permit or fee indicates that some government agency has deemed it appropriate to require an entry permit and/or charge an entry fee to public lands, such as a "Conservation Permit" (Washington Department of Fish and Wildlife); a "Sno-Park Permit" (various agencies); a "Parking Permit" (the United States Forest Service, or USFS, may require separate permits for individual national forests); an "Alpine Lakes / Enchantment Lakes Entry Permit"; and various other entry fees and permits at national monuments and parks. These are not individually specified because of the rapidity, variety, and cupidity with which the agencies change their policies.

Maps are current versions of USGS and Green Trails, Inc.™ maps appropriate for the tour. Distances within the tour descriptions are taken from these maps; distances to key locations are rounded to the nearest tenth of a mile.

Within the **Tour Descriptions**, where there is more than one approach, the primary approach is described. Directions are given using points of the compass without accounting for declination. Landmarks, elevations, and map coordinates are provided when helpful for routefinding. **Alternative Route** indicates an optional descent or side trip.

ETIQUETTE

Customs and laws change. Ever-increasing numbers of outdoor enthusiasts place heavy pressure on the alpine and subalpine environment. Backcountry skiers must do their part to reduce the adverse impact of their passage.

▲ Defecate away from streams, lakes, and low areas. Highly motivated (f)ecophiles may even pack it out. Burn your toilet paper on dry twigs (not on the tree!). Consider using snow instead.

▲ Carry litter out.

▲ Consider leaving your dog at home. There are very real alpine hazards for pets: moats, cliffs, tree wells, avalanches, dehydration, hypothermia and frostbite, porcupines, and rangers eager to write

Hidden Lake Peak (Photo by Rainer Burgdorfer)

citations. In addition, dogs are less fastidious about toilet habits than most backcountry skiers are. At the very least, if you wear an avalanche beacon yourself, get one for your best buddy as well. On the other hand, your friend's nose just might be the one thing that finds you buried under avalanche debris. This has happened before.

▲ Step out of the way of snowmobiles or faster skiers, especially when you are skiing a defile. Etiquette demands that speedy skiers and snowmobilers steer clear of slower-moving persons; prudence suggests that you protect yourself. When climbing through a ski area, keep a low profile by staying off to one side and crossing runs cautiously. Not everyone skis in control.

▲ If you are using snowmobiles for access, minimize your potential impact on other parties.

▲ Do not cut conifer boughs for shelter or sleeping platforms. Camp on snow. Keep off fragile alpine vegetation whenever possible.

▲ Use a stove instead of building fires.

▲ Do not block other vehicles parked at trailheads. Be certain your car is parked completely off the public highway. Park on the shoulder side of the fog line, the white line at the edge of the road.

▲ When skiing in the company of others, conserve untracked snow. Start skiing a slope from the safest side and gradually work your way across. This is also the safest way to ski untracked slopes.

▲ When hiking in snowshoes, avoid damaging the tracks of skiers who have preceded you, especially on gentle logging road approaches. They will be grateful to you for easing their road ski out.

SAFETY CONSIDERATIONS

Inclusion of a tour in this guide does not guarantee its safety for you or your party.

Backcountry skiing is a risk sport. All of these tours take place in an uncontrolled, unpatrolled environment. Natural occurrences on terrain, from weather or avalanches, or mistakes on your part, may cause serious injury or death to you or members of your party.

Every traveler who uses this guide and ventures into the mountains assumes and must manage these risks, as well as take responsibility for his or her own safety. Remember that local route conditions may change rapidly, sometimes in a matter of hours. Routes that were safe in midmorning may be dangerous only hours later, due to weather or snow changes. You can minimize risks by developing a base of experience and training, by being prepared, and by fostering a safe attitude. The publications listed in Appendix B, Recommended Reading, should be considered "must read" material. Taking classes in alpine travel, avalanche skills, and first aid can be fun and may save your life.

To be prepared, you must be able to assess your resources. You must be aware of conditions including your own equipment, skiing and climbing skills,

Early-season ski tours often require a hiking approach. (Photo by Ken Ritland)

and physical ability *on the day of the tour.* Many of the springtime tours, for example, take place above timberline and involve climbing (and skiing) steep, exposed slopes. Wind, time of day, or cloud cover may make these slopes rough, soft, or icy. When planning tours in such terrain, you should develop tactical alternatives, including early departures, in case conditions don't go your way. If conditions make you uncomfortable, choose a different tour. Ask yourself, "Is this tour, or run, worth getting hurt for?"

Descend slopes within your ability, with an eye to the consequences of a fall. For instance, you might think to yourself, "I can't ski that steep ramp there; a fall would put me over that cliff band into the moat below." By scouting your descent, you can usually remove your skis or snowboard and climb down if necessary.

Be flexible. If your stated objective is to climb to, say, Camp Muir and you find a band of wonderful snow between 8,000 and 9,000 feet, consider yo-yo skiing the good stuff and forgoing the goal. It is easier and safer to ski good "hero" snow. If you're religious about the requisite number of vertical feet you must climb, simply yo-yo ski to approximate your desired vertical gain.

On backcountry trips, make sure that all members of your party carry compatible avalanche transceivers. Avalanche victims who have been buried less than 6 feet deep *and* were in parties equipped with transceivers have experienced over a ninety-five percent live recovery rate. This remarkable outcome is a powerful argument for carrying the added equipment and learning how to use it well. Practice! (For more on safety equipment, see Appendix A, Reflections on Equipment, Clothing, Accessories, and Technique.)

This guidebook is based on personal experience and should be used as an aid rather than a substitute for your own judgment. You are truly on your own. These warnings are not intended to keep you out of the backcountry. Thousands of people take safe and enjoyable tours every year. However, one aspect of the beauty, freedom, and excitement of the backcountry is the presence of risks normally hidden by the veil of civilization. When you "go wild," you assume those risks. You must exercise your own independent judgment and common sense.

Rainer Burgdorfer

A NOTE ABOUT SAFETY

Safety is an important concern in all outdoor activities. No guidebook can alert you to every hazard or anticipate the limitations of every reader. Therefore, the descriptions of roads, trails, routes, and natural features in this book are not representations that a particular place or excursion will be safe for your party. When you follow any of the routes described in this book, you assume responsibility for your own safety. Under normal conditions, such excursions require the usual attention to traffic, road and trail conditions, weather, terrain, the capabilities of your party, and other factors. Keeping informed on current conditions and exercising common sense are the keys to a safe, enjoyable outing.

The Mountaineers

Part I
LEARNING TO LOVE CASCADE WEATHER AND SNOW

If you don't learn weather basics in Washington, you'll encounter crud and ice more often than powder and corn. Worse, you might find yourself on the receiving end of an avalanche. You don't have to become a weather expert, but you do need to ask the right questions and understand their answers.

TRACKING STORMS, TRACKING GOOD SNOW

Air masses are the basic building blocks of regional weather. An air mass is a large body of air (typically extending over half a continent) that takes on some of the characteristics of the surface below it. Because the ocean warms and cools slowly, *marine* air masses tend to be mild and moist. *Continental* (over land) air masses tend to have greater extremes (and more rapid changes) of temperature and are generally drier than marine air masses. In western North America, the Cascade and Coast Ranges present a fairly effective barrier between marine and continental air masses.

The Pacific Ocean generates the frequent storms that blanket our region. Once these systems mature, they become imbedded in upper-level air currents called the *jet stream* and are carried from west to east in a path called a *storm track*.

West to Northwest

When planning your tour, be sure to watch the weather report on television (or the Internet), especially the satellite photo and the synopsis. If the storm track is coming from the northwest, it will likely bring cool air and dump dry and plentiful snow to 1,000 feet in the winter and 3,000 feet in spring and fall. Under these conditions, you can sometimes find excellent early season skiing on heather benches and permanent snowfields.

West Wind

The most common storm track in this region is from the southwest or west. In winter, freezing levels associated with this pattern vary from 3,000 to 5,000 feet, rising to 5,000 to 7,000 feet in autumn and spring. Southwest/west storm tracks tend to have less intense rainfall with breaks between showers. During these storms, you can often find good skiing on eastern or northeastern

Skiers and snowboarders can coexist amicably on the same tour. (Photo by William C. Shigley)

slopes, provided that winds are not excessive. Keep in mind that snow slabs form on lee slopes.

Pineapple Express

This storm track comes from the south-southwest, originating in the subtropical Pacific, and brings warm air and lots of moisture to the Puget Sound region. A Pineapple Express storm track tends to last for several days and can bring several inches of rain to western Washington. The freezing level usually rises to 8,000 feet or higher, resulting in avalanche activity during and after the storm, as temperatures rise. The large amounts of rain translate into deep new-snow deposits at elevations above 10,000 feet. Under these circumstances, touring is not recommended. Even at moderate elevations, large amounts of new snow will result in poor and dangerous touring conditions. Touring above timberline during storms is not recommended.

North from Alaska

Winter storms that bring snow at sea level in western Washington are most frequently the result of storm tracks coming from the north. In this weather pattern, cold air descends from the north and collides with warmer ocean air. The moist air overrides the cool air and produces snow from the Canadian border south, sometimes as far as Olympia. Often under these conditions as much snow may fall in the lowlands as in the mountains.

Storm tracks from the north sometimes bring cold continental winter weather to the Cascade region. This occurs when the boundary between the arctic continental air mass in Canada and the marine air mass over the Gulf of Alaska passes south through western Washington. A typical cycle involves a snowstorm followed by a period of clear skies and low temperatures, then snow again as the flow turns to the southwest. If the northerly winds are not too strong, skiing can be excellent during these periods, especially on sun-warmed slopes.

Snow Droughts

Even during periods of little snowfall, there is often good skiing, so long as temperatures are low enough and there is enough snow to cover rocks and stumps (wear kneepads). Snow on north-facing or tree-sheltered slopes often maintains a soft surface due to surface hoar formation. On warmer days, snow-packs on south-facing slopes sometimes soften enough in midday sun to permit beautiful skiing, but turn to boilerplate as shadows lengthen.

Local Factors

Three local phenomena that affect snowfall and skiing are *orographic lifting,* the *convergence zone,* and *easterly flow.* Orographic lifting is caused by the position and height of the mountains. As an air mass moves east, it is forced up and over the Cascades. As it gains altitude, the air expands and cools. Its water vapor condenses and drops out as precipitation on the windward side of the range. On average, the temperature drops 3.5° Fahrenheit per thousand feet of elevation. For instance, if air passed Seattle at 45°, by the time it arrived at Snoqualmie Pass (3,000 feet), it would have cooled to 32°. On its way down to eastern Washington, the air would warm on its descent, becoming drier in the process. That's why the climate is drier east of the Cascades.

Convergence zones occur where an airflow recombines after being split by a large obstacle (in our case, the Olympic Mountains and Mount Rainier). When the air converges, it is forced to rise and cool. Wherever there is a convergence zone, precipitation is usually greater than in the surrounding area. Convergence often delivers thunder, rain, and snow showers from Glacier Peak to Mount Rainier. If coastal winds approach from west-southwest or west-northwest and if there are northerly winds in the Strait of Juan de Fuca or southerly winds in South Puget Sound, better weather can usually be found either to the north or south of the convergence.

On sunny winter days when the air pressure is higher east of the Cascades and low pressure lies offshore, we often experience "easterly flow." The infamous Snoqualmie ice fog is a result of easterly flow. As the higher-pressure air spills through Snoqualmie Pass, it is lifted orographically and forms a freezing fog at the surface. People at the pass are often unaware that a few hundred feet above, or a mile to the west, the sun is shining!

WEATHER AND AVALANCHE DANGER

Avalanche danger is the likelihood of a slope releasing, and what the result will mean to you or your party. To help you plan your tour and minimize avalanche danger, contact the Northwest Avalanche Center (see Appendix D).

According to the Northwest Avalanche Center website: "Most avalanche

Lenticular clouds sometimes augur bad weather. (Photo by Rainer Burgdorfer)

accidents are caused by slab avalanches which are triggered by the victim or a member of the victim's party. However, any avalanche may cause injury or death and even small slides may be dangerous. Hence, always practice safe route finding skills, be aware of changing conditions, and carry avalanche rescue gear. Learn and apply avalanche terrain analysis and snow evaluation techniques to help minimize your risk. Remember that avalanche danger rating levels are only general guidelines. Distinctions between geographic areas, elevations, slope aspect and slope angle are approximate and transition zones between dangers exist. No matter what the current avalanche danger there are avalanche-safe areas in the mountains."

All United States Forest Service and National Weather Service forecasts use the United States Avalanche Danger Scale (see table). Skiers should know the meaning of all the terms used in Danger Forecasts. Listen carefully to the reports and take notes. Bring a copy of the report with you. Perhaps the best source of information about skiing conditions in the mountains is people who have just been there, including yourself. Keep in mind that conditions can change rapidly: This morning's powder can turn to mush overnight. Keep a notebook of your tours, including weather and snow conditions and the forecast before the tour.

United States Avalanche Danger Descriptors

Danger Level (& Color)	Avalanche Probability and Avalanche Trigger	Degree and Distribution of Avalanche Danger	Recommended Action in the Backcountry
Low (green)	Natural avalanches very unlikely. Human-triggered avalanches unlikely	Generally stable snow. Isolated areas of instability	Travel is generally safe. Normal caution advised
Moderate (yellow)	Natural avalanches unlikely. Human-triggered avalanches possible	Unstable slabs possible on steep terrain	Use caution in steeper terrain on certain aspects (defined in accompanying statement)
Considerable/ Moderate to High (orange)	Natural avalanches possible. Human-triggered avalanches probable	Unstable slabs probable on steep terrain	Be increasingly cautious in steeper terrain
High (red)	Natural and human-triggered avalanches likely	Unstable slabs likely on a variety of aspects and slope angles	Travel in avalanche terrain is not recommended. Safest travel is on windward ridges of lower angle slopes without steeper terrain above
Extreme (red with black border)	Widespread natural or human-triggered avalanches certain	Extremely unstable slabs certain on most aspects and slope angles. Large destructive avalanches possible	Travel in avalanche terrain should be avoided and travel confined to low-angle terrain and well away from avalanche path run-outs

Snow camping on Mount Saint Helens (Photo by Craig Miller)

MOUNTAIN HAZARDS

Some of the tours described in this guide take place on glaciers and cliffy terrain. You must climb and descend in complete control in these situations. Rope up when ascending active glaciers. Most skiers descend crevassed terrain without roping up, feeling that the rope is more trouble than it is worth. However, failure to carry adequate self-rescue equipment is irresponsible.

During storms that have high winds, crevasses often become bridged. This occurs frequently at higher elevations, but can take place on any glacier. Roping up is cheap insurance. If a tour requires rope, it requires ice axes and crampons as well. (In U.S. national parks, federal law requires roping up to travel on glaciers.) Many spring tours require ice axes and crampons to negotiate short, steep sections safely.

Read *Mountaineering: The Freedom of the Hills* and practice using your equipment in benign environments before an emergency. Obtain competent instruction. It's not the tools that protect you—it's their effective use that increases your security.

Glacier travel is mountaineering and should be approached as such. Those not ready to travel in the glacial environment can still find superb off-glacier tours to very high places, such as the southwest shoulder of Mount Adams.

Mere snowfields and forests conceal hazards, too. Forests with deep snowpacks develop tree wells, voids in the snow underneath the sheltering branches. A skier can fall into a tree well and be trapped upside down and helpless. Death by suffocation can occur in minutes. This need not happen if skiers use the buddy system: always watch your partner ski from a safe position. (Take pictures while you wait!) If there is trouble, you are then in a position to do something about it. Backcountry snowboarders should consider always carrying snowshoes or skis in their packs in the event they are forced into level, deep-snow terrain.

Moats often result when a deep snowpack creeps and melts away from an adjacent cliff. Skiing into a deep moat is similar to skiing off a cliff or into a crevasse. Moats are one reason that steep runs at ski areas are closed in late season. For example, the Trashcan run at Alpental develops large moats; most years, it is closed by late March or early April.

Whiteouts, thick fog or clouds, can make even moderate slopes difficult to ski, and make it impossible to identify hazardous snow or terrain conditions. When confronted by this condition, proceed slowly and stay together until your party has traveled out of the clouds. Taking mental notes of local landmarks on the ascent helps you build a mental map of the route. A GPS receiver programmed with crucial waypoints is a valuable aid to foul-weather or after-dark navigation.

AVOIDING AVALANCHES

The best skiing takes place in avalanche terrain. To ski safely, it is essential to understand avalanche conditions. Factors that affect the likelihood of avalanche include terrain, snowpack strengths and weaknesses, precipitation and wind patterns, cloud cover, temperature and temperature change, and disturbance by travelers.

Keep in mind that most avalanche victims are injured or killed in avalanches

Roman Wall Bergschrund, Mount Baker, in June (Photo by Rainer Burgdorfer)

Slab avalanches sometimes involve large amounts of snow. (Photo by Joe Catellani)

they have triggered themselves. To ski safely, you must be able to determine if a slope can avalanche, and what this would mean to you. To develop this skill, *take an avalanche class!* Check with mountaineering shops and clubs for times and locations. Also see Recommended Reading for books about avalanche safety. Tony Daffern's *Avalanche Safety for Skiers and Climbers* and Ed LaChapelle's *The ABC of Avalanche Safety* are two particularly good resources.

Just in Case

If you are caught in an avalanche, shout "Avalanche!" and discard your skis, pack, and ski poles if possible. Try to "swim" to the top of the moving snow. Work your way to one side of the maelstrom. As you come to a stop, put one arm in front of your face to make an airspace in the snow and thrust the other arm up as high as possible to help your rescuers locate you. If you are buried, remain calm. Do not fight the blackout. Remaining calm and accepting the darkness will help you live longer by conserving oxygen.

If you are a rescuer, be sure it is safe to search! Mark the place where you last saw the victim and begin your search directly downslope from the last known location. Look for a hand, a ski, or bits of clothing. If the victim is not on the surface, use your transceiver to locate the victim, or probe the snow in a systematic fashion using probes of ski poles. If a dog is a member of the party, watch for signs that he or she smells the victim. If not, remove the dog from the site to prevent scent conflicts with potential avalanche rescue dogs. Do not urinate in the avalanche area, again to prevent potential scent conflicts.

Remember that in an avalanche, you are the victim's best hope for survival. Do not leave the scene and go for help, unless help is only a few minutes away. Treat the victim for suffocation and shock, as well as other suspected injuries.

Planning Your Tour

Most tours start with a vision: Someone says, "Hey, let's ski Van Trump Park this weekend!" To ensure a successful tour, *plan* the tour.

Gather weather and avalanche forecasts and topographic maps of the areas. If you've been keeping a record of recent weather reports, you have an added advantage. Call the local ranger station for access information.

Visualize the tour by tracing your path on the map, asking yourself the following questions:

▲ Is the terrain inherently dangerous?

▲ Are there cliff bands or drastic variations in slope inclination above or below the planned route?

▲ Is your path exposed to slopes steep enough to slide (steeper than 25°)?

▲ Are natural avalanches possible?

▲ Are human-triggered avalanches possible?

Consider the snow conditions:

▲ What does the Avalanche Forecast Center say in their "Snowpack Analysis"? Are there reports of avalanche activity? What caused the reported avalanches? Are similar slopes releasing? Are other slopes releasing? (Be aware that several risk factors contribute to an avalanche condition, even if it takes only one to trigger the actual event.)

▲ How deep is the snowpack in the area you plan to tour? (On smooth ground, avalanches can form in as little as 8 inches of snow.)

▲ How much fresh snow has fallen? Warning signs include snowfall rates greater than one inch per hour, or new snow depth greater than six inches (with wind).

▲ Are there weak layers in the snowpack?

▲ On late-spring tours, are temperatures warm or has new snow fallen?

▲ How large are the slopes? Are they wide open? Forested? Gullied? Clear-cut? Crevassed?

▲ What was the wind direction and speed in the period prior to your tour? Could there be cornices, windslabs, or exposed hard glacier ice?

▲ What is the orientation of the slope to the sun? Could direct sun loosen cornices or weaken the snowpack on your route?

▲ How should you time your tour?

▲ If conditions worsen, what will you do?

Research the weather conditions:

▲ Have there been strong winds recently? What direction? Was there high relative humidity during the wind? These conditions will quickly build windslabs.

▲ Have there been (will there be) warm, moist winds? These can turn a stable snowpack into a giant, unstable slush bowl.

▲ Has there been a rapid rise in temperature, say a 10° increase over last week's average, or above freezing temperatures? This can start off a cycle of wet snow avalanching.

▲ Have there been very cold conditions, say below 10° Fahrenheit? This can precipitate faceting and weaken the snowpack, especially when shallow.

▲ Have there been cloudy or hazy days with sun? This condition will sometimes destabilize a slope even if slopes were stable during previous clear days.

▲ Are there weak layers? Is there surface hoar, faceted grains, a weak crust or a poor bond, or water-saturated snow? All of these questions may, with experience, start to occur to you naturally as you ski.

On the Ascent

As you climb, take note of your environment. Perhaps you are leaving old-growth forest to pass through a clear-cut area. Perhaps you are traveling below corniced ridges or an ice cliff and this is a bad place to stop for a break. Ask yourself:

▲ What will this slope be like when we return?

▲ Does the snow seem stable?

▲ Is the fresh snow deep, say, deeper than 1 foot?

▲ Are there signs of sloughing, rolling, or settling of snow?

▲ Is the snow slabby? Are there signs of previous avalanches? Do you feel safe where you are right now?

▲ Are you allowing beautiful weather or group pressure to sway your opinion in this matter?

As you're contemplating a slope, ask yourself:

▲ What will happen to me if the slope releases?

▲ How deep will the sliding layer be?

▲ Is there a cliff, crevasse, or terrain trap below?

▲ Is the slope likely to slide all at once (slab) or grow quickly from a trickle to a torrent (loose snow)? Both can have fatal consequences.

Any more questions? If you have *any* reservations about a slope, stay far away from it! Take an avalanche class and learn how to better utilize terrain

Every backcountry skier should carry an unbreakable avalanche shovel (Photo by Craig Miller)

and judge snow stability. Experienced backcountry travelers all share the sentiment that when the snowpack gets dangerous, the pros go home.

While climbing, evaluate steep test slopes for stability. If in doubt, ask yourself: Would I descend this, knowing it's unstable? When selecting a campsite, ask yourself: Is retreat possible from here if conditions worsen?

On the Descent

Ski using the buddy system. Decide who will ski first and where she will stop. Do not stop in the middle of a slope. Rather, stop only at "safe harbors."

Ridges are safer than bowls, especially bowls that channel into gullies. Enter slopes at the top rather than from the sides. Ski in control, keeping an eye out for escape routes.

Be aware of weak spots in the snow pack. Weak spots sometimes form where the snowpack is relatively thin. When a skier stresses the snowpack, failure tends to occur at the weak spot and propagates to the entire snowpack releasing an avalanche. On suspect slopes, stay to the edge of potential slide paths.

In general, if there is doubt, don't go out. Today's advanced rescue technology should not give you a false sense of security—the fastest victim recovery is of little benefit when a victim has already died of trauma suffered in an avalanche. Backcountry skiers cannot experience the same joyful abandon that lift-served skiers seem to enjoy, at least in the long run. On the other hand, we are able to descend untracked snow for thousands of feet through astounding scenery.

Part II
BACKCOUNTRY TOURS

The Mount Baker Highway climbs to snow country with alpine-style mountain views and winter snow depths usually exceeding 10 feet. While the deep snow accumulations extend the ski season well into summer, they also bring high avalanche danger in the winter and early spring. Some tours are safe only when the snowpack is well frozen, say in cool spring conditions. The weather can be good, especially when a low-pressure system passes to the southeast, under convergence conditions to the south, or when high pressure is building from the northwest. When visibility is good, the views are breathtaking. The grandeur of hanging glaciers, jagged mountains, remote ski runs, and better snow conditions make this region very appealing.

The main watercourse in this area is the Nooksack River, which springs from the mighty glaciers north and east of Mount Shuksan. The Mount Baker Highway follows the river, then climbs to the Mount Baker ski area (8 miles northeast of the volcano). The ski area served as a hatchery for top-class snowboarders and continues as a Mecca for new generations of the faithful. Many of these tours start low in valleys adjacent to the highway and require substantial climbs to get to the skiing. Side roads are generally not maintained in winter and are snow-covered until mid-April. Most of the tours terminate above the treeline and are worthwhile only in good weather.

The town of Glacier is the last population center before the highway climbs to snowline. Food and refreshments are available at local stores and restaurants. The ranger station just east of town sometimes provides useful snow, weather, and road closure information.

▲ ▲ ▲

Tomyhoi Peak

Start Point: Keep Kool Trailhead No. 699, 3,050 feet
High Point: Tomyhoi Glacier, 7,000 feet
Best Time: April to June
Day trip: 11 Miles
Skiing Time: 8 to 12 hours
Skill Level: Alpine
Difficulties: High avalanche potential; some glacier travel; routefinding required; permit/fee area
Maps: USGS Mt. Larrabee, 1:24,000

Tomyhoi Peak is rarely skied, despite its varied terrain and reasonable access (once Twin Lakes Road is clear of snow in late spring). The summit lies less

Skiing on Tomyhoi Peak, with Shuksan in the background (Photo by Jens Kieler)

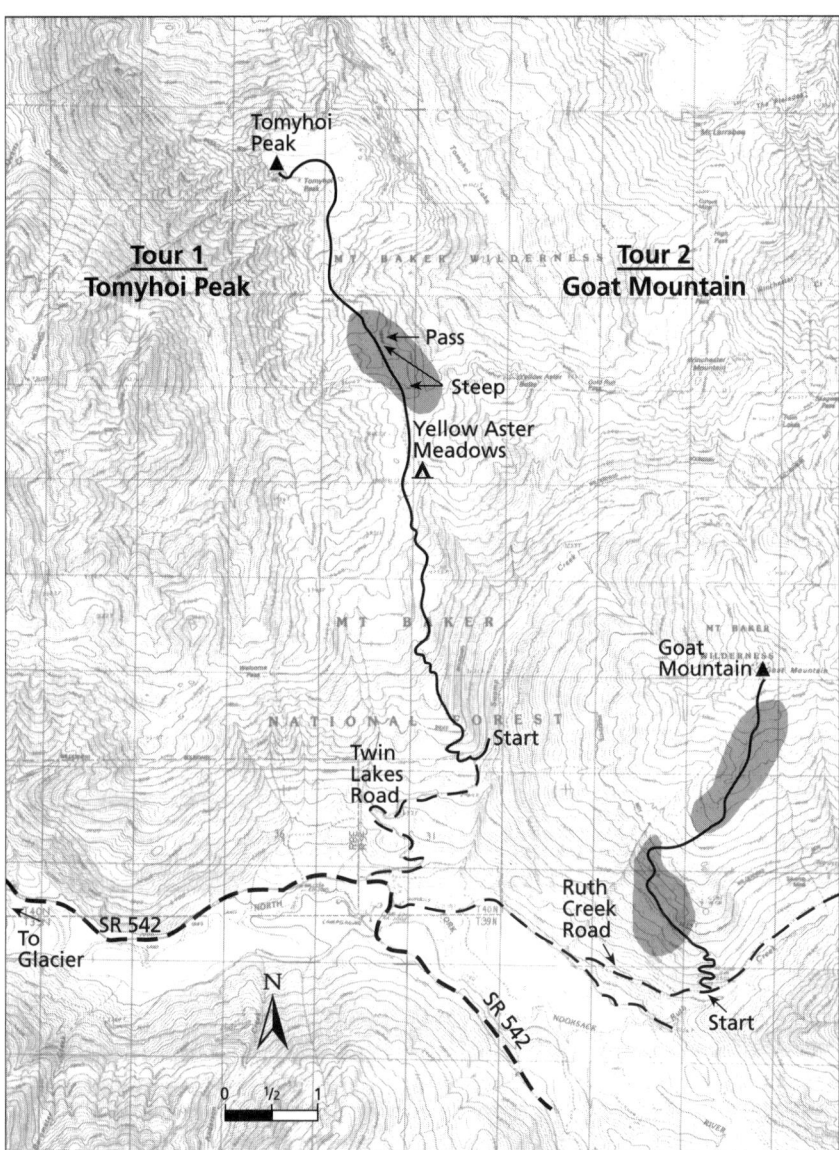

than 2 miles from the Canadian border, and the lights of Chilliwack are visible from here at night.

Take State Route 542 east from Glacier for 12.3 miles and turn left (north) onto Twin Lakes Road. Follow Twin Lakes Road for 2.3 miles to the trailhead on the left (western) side of the road (8.55.257/121.40.699).

The route, a trail in summer, begins in a clear-cut and climbs southwest for about 0.5 mile, with a steep rise looming on the right, before turning back northeast for about 0.2 mile. Now the climb begins in earnest, climbing 1,000 feet in 1 mile with a general heading of north-northwest toward mature forest. In about 3 miles (approximately 5,500 feet), gain Yellow Aster Meadows and head toward a long broad ridge rising to the north-northeast.

Climb over the summit of this ridge (6,500 feet), and then descend northwest for 200 feet to a rounded notch in the ridge. Once through this col, climb the broadening ridge heading due north. There are cliff bands to the east and pinnacles to the west—continue your northerly ascent until you reach the glacier. Runs are possible down the north-facing glacier and, of course, down the route of ascent.

Goat Mountain

Start Point: Trail No. 673, Hannegan Road, 2,470 feet	
High Point: Goat Mountain Glacier, 6,100 feet	
Best Time: March to June	
Day Trip: 8.8 miles	
Skiing Time: 8 hours	
Skill Level: Alpine	
Difficulties: High avalanche potential; permit/fee area	
Maps: USGS Mt. Larrabee, 1:24,000	

Goat Mountain is the handsome peak visible from the Mount Baker ski road, immediately north of the Nooksack River. Although this tour is fairly long, both the northern and southern slopes of this massive mountain offer excellent skiing in good snow conditions. For spring tours, be sure to get an early start.

Drive SR 542 12.8 miles east of Glacier. Just before the road crosses the North Fork Nooksack River, turn left onto Hannegan Road No. 402 (Ruth Creek Road). Drive for 1.5 miles and take the left fork to Ruth Creek Road. Follow Ruth Creek Road for 1.2 more miles to reach the trailhead (No. 637) on the northern side of the road.

The trail climbs steeply for the first mile, heading due north, then reclines a bit and climbs northwest for nearly a mile before steepening and trending north again. If you come to a large stream in a gorge, you've come just a bit too far. Climb the steep rolls immediately above you, heading north-northeast toward the eastern summit. The broad saddle between the eastern and western summits is the high point of the tour. The northern glacier offers delightful thousand-foot runs. Time your descent to avoid new snow or wet snow instability.

Goat Mountain (Photo by Jens Kieler)

Ruth Mountain

Start Point: Hannegan Campground, 3,100 feet
High Point: Ruth Mountain, 7,106 feet, or Icy Peak, 7,070 feet
Best Time: April to July
Day Trip: To Ruth Mountain, 12 miles; to Icy Peak, 15 miles
Skiing Time: Ruth Mountain, 9 to 12 hours; Icy Peak, 11 to 14 hours
Skill Level: Advanced
Difficulties: High avalanche potential; glacier travel; routefinding required; permit/fee area; long hike out for monoboarders
Maps: Green Trails No. 14, Mt. Shuksan

Ruth Mountain is a magnificent touring objective. Of moderate height, its gleaming bulk is visible from much of the approach and its summit overlooks rugged Nooksack Cirque and the spectacular Pickett Range. The peak is reached via Ruth Creek directly, or over Hannegan Pass.

Climbing to Hannegan Pass (Photo by Rainer Burgdorfer)

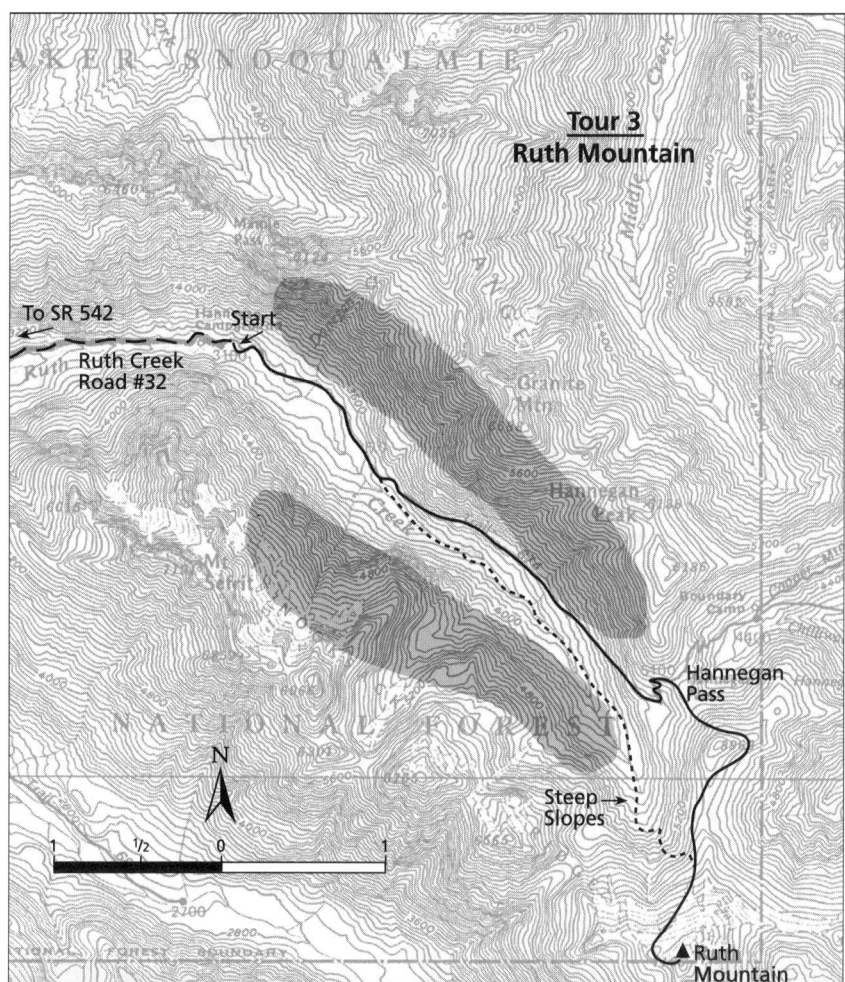

Ruth Creek lies in a deep gorge, headed at the east end by Ruth Mountain. Virtually the entire approach is exposed to large avalanche slopes beginning 3,000 to 4,000 feet above the trail. This tour should be attempted only by very strong parties and only in ideal conditions—when the snowpack is well frozen.

Drive Highway 542 east 12.8 miles past Glacier. Go left on Hannegan Road No. 402. Drive 1.5 miles and take the left fork (Ruth Creek Road) as far as conditions permit. Hannegan Campground (3,100 feet) is at the end of the road, 4.5 miles from the highway. If road conditions prevent driving to the end of the road, park the car and ski along the road to the trailhead. Hike the trail on the north side of Ruth Creek. The trail is usually snow-covered until mid-April.

For the first mile, the trail meanders southeast along the valley floor. Then it climbs, the last mile rising steeply (four or more switchbacks, 1,000 feet) through forest to Hannegan Pass. Looking east from Hannegan Pass, you see the Chilliwack drainage and Copper Peak, another great ski touring objective.

From the pass, your objective is to get around the cliffs on your right (south). Traverse above or below these cliff bands. Once on the ridge, head south for 1 mile to Ruth Glacier. As you climb the glacier, be aware of crevasses that may lurk near the west side of the false summit. Once past this area, the summit becomes apparent and is gained easily.

Alternate Route: A more direct approach to Ruth Mountain crosses Ruth Creek low in the valley, leading over snow and avalanche debris before heading directly for the peak. Climb a steep headwall to gain the saddle between Point 5963 and Ruth Mountain (800 feet). Continue according to the standard route instructions, and retrace your ascent if conditions permit. Make sure that you understand the primary ascent/descent route if you choose this approach.

Icy Peak lies south of Ruth Mountain. To reach Icy Peak, begin at the first notch northwest of Ruth Mountain's summit (approximately 600 feet from the summit) and traverse south along a west-facing snowfield until you come to a gully just before a south-facing ridge. Find the gully that descends to the Ruth-Icy saddle. Then climb the gently sloping glacier that leads to the summit. The view is worth the extra 3 hours, but plan your trip accordingly. This glacier is considerably more crevassed than the Ruth Glacier.

An ice ax and crampons are recommended for this tour.

Hannegan Pass is also the entry point for a ski traverse of the Pickett Range and other high routes. The Pickett Range's rugged scenery and isolation are unsurpassed in the lower 48 states.

4
Mount Ann

Start Point: Mount Baker Ski Area, 4,200 feet

High Point: Mount Ann, 5,688 feet

Best Time: December to April

Day Trip/Overnight: 9 miles

Skiing Time: 6 to 8 hours

Skill Level: Advanced

Difficulties: High avalanche potential; permit/fee area; snowboarders must climb up to get out

Maps: Green Trails No. 14, Mt. Shuksan

This tour offers easy access to unusual winter views of Mounts Shuksan and Baker, and opportunities for skiing on slopes of nearly all aspects. While Mount Ann is a reasonable day trip, it may be more rewarding as an overnighter because of all the nearby slopes begging for tracks. If you decide to make this an overnight trip, be sure to make overnight parking arrangements with the ski-area management. Mount Ann is not identified on many maps.

From the Mount Baker ski area, follow Austin Pass Road past the Austin run. Skiing the road is faster than riding the lift. Just past the run, climb steeply uphill to rejoin the road 400 feet above. Follow the road to Austin Pass (4,700 feet, 48.51.066/121.40.993) and drop over to the southeast side of the pass to upper Swift Creek Valley, 400 feet below. Shuksan Arm now looms immediately to the northeast and large avalanche paths fringe the valley.

Ski southeast for 0.8 mile along the valley bottom. Inviting glades rise on either side. On your way to Lake Ann Butte, it is best to stay to the left (east) of Swift Creek to avoid problems in crossing it lower down.

Soon, the valley bottom begins to steepen. Enter the forest on the left, traversing southeast and descending slightly to avoid steeper slopes above. In 1 mile you'll break out of the forest after climbing through an unavoidable avalanche path, and soon you'll arrive at a saddle northwest of Lake Ann (4,835 feet). The lake is 0.2 mile southeast from the saddle.

Lake Ann Butte lies 0.2 mile west of Lake Ann. The easiest (still quite steep) path to the top lies along the northern ridge. Head 0.25 mile northwest from the north end of Lake Ann to gain this ramp. Once on the ridge, stay on the crest and avoid the cornices that sometimes form on both sides. When stopped by steeper terrain, drop slightly southeast and regain the ridge beyond the

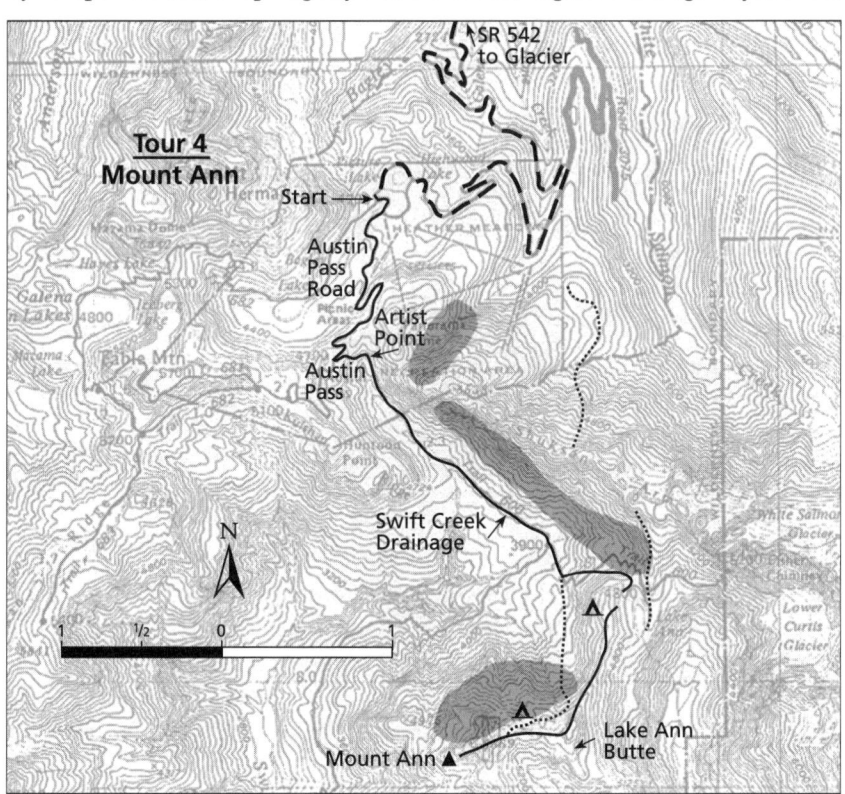

Crash landing (Photo by Rainer Burgdorfer)

peak by heading north. The high point, Mount Ann, lies about 0.9 mile from the start of the ridge.

Reverse the approach to return to the car.

5
Coleman Pinnacle

Start Point: Coleman Pinnacle Trailhead, 5,068 feet; or Mount Baker Ski Area, 4,200 feet
High Point: Coleman Pinnacle, 6,414 feet
Best Time: October to June
Day Trip: 9 miles
Skiing Time: 6 to 10 hours
Skill Level: Intermediate
Difficulties: High avalanche potential; routefinding required; permit/fee area; snowboarders must climb up to get out
Maps: Green Trails No. 14, Mt. Shuksan

Coleman Pinnacle is distinguished for the grandeur of its setting, its occasional views of nearby Mount Baker, and the miles of untracked powder it may offer

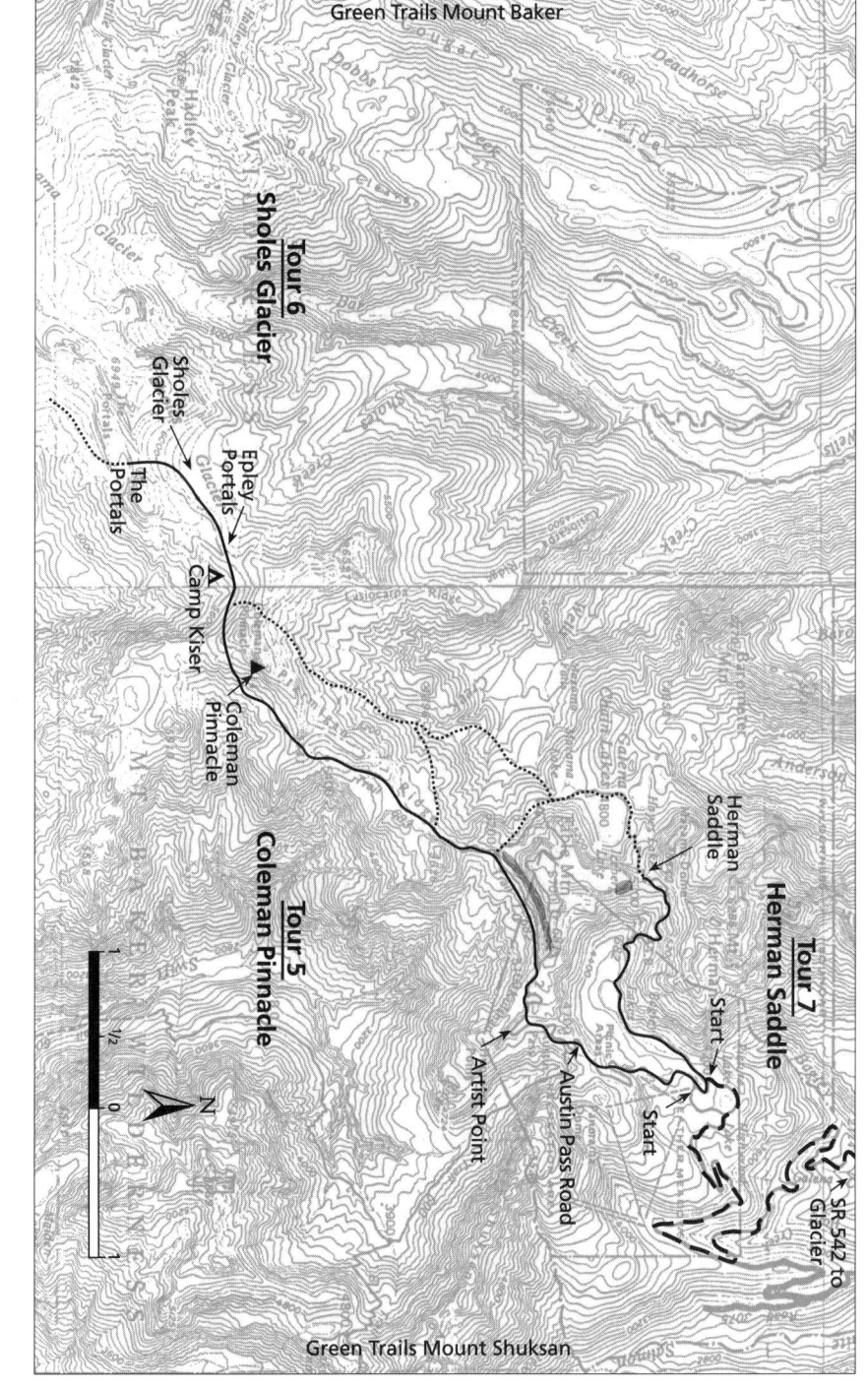

to early season visitors. Because of its complexity and the possibility of sudden whiteouts, navigation skills are useful on this tour. Attempt this tour only in low avalanche hazard conditions with no warming trends in the forecast. Be sure to choose your route with an eye to the safest reasonable path. This tour is unsuitable for snowboarders.

Drive to the Mount Baker ski area. From the ski area parking lot, follow Austin Pass Road past the Austin run. Just beyond the top of the run, climb steeply uphill to rejoin the road 400 feet above. Follow the road until it begins to head southeast toward Artist Point. Here, take a shortcut by climbing southwest to rejoin the road 200 feet above. Continuing west for 0.15 mile brings you to a large, nearly level area, the summer-season parking lot. Table Mountain looms to the west. (In early season, it may be possible to drive the highway all the way to the summer-season parking lot. If so, park your car and start your tour here, keeping in mind that a large snow dump could trap your car.)

From the western edge of the parking lot, descend slightly and traverse west for 1.25 miles beneath the steep south face of Table Mountain. Your objective is the saddle due south of the summit. Maintain a constant elevation of 5,100 feet.

From the pass, Ptarmigan Ridge, the long ridge connecting to Coleman Pinnacle, becomes obvious. Drop a few hundred feet to the west and climb gradually to the southwest, heading for the pinnacle. It is easiest to contour on

Sulphide Glacier; Mount Baker with Coleman Pinnacle and Hadley Peak is visible to the right. (Photo by Rainer Burgdorfer)

either side of Ptarmigan Ridge between 5,000 and 5,200 feet. This volcanic plug can also be approached via Herman Saddle and the Chain Lakes. (This alternative route has more up-and-down travel, but is less prone to snow slides than the sun-warmed southern side of Table Mountain.) Whether or not you decide to reach Coleman Pinnacle, there are abundant possibilities for runs over 1,500 feet in length. Retrace your tracks to return to your car. If a warming trend develops, and the south face of Table Mountain becomes unstable, return to your car via Herman Saddle (Tour No. 7).

6
Sholes Glacier

Start Point: Coleman Pinnacle Trailhead, 5,068 feet;
or Mount Baker Ski Area, 4,200 feet

High Point: The Portals, 6,161 feet

Best Time: April to July

Day Trip: 9 miles

Skiing Time: 6 to 10 hours

Skill Level: Intermediate

Difficulties: High avalanche potential; glacier travel (optional); routefinding required; permit/fee area; snowboarders must climb up to get out

Maps: Green Trails No. 14, Mt. Shuksan; No. 13, Mt. Baker

In late season good weather, Sholes Glacier offers the quintessential summer tour: warm temperatures, green heather benches, sprays of alpine flowers, mountain goats, and great corn-snow skiing. This adventure carries you to a seldom-visited side of Mount Baker.

Sholes Glacier can be considered a logical extension of the Coleman Pinnacle tour (No. 5), but is included here as a distinct tour because of its different objective, range, and season.

Hike or ski southwest from the Coleman Pinnacle trailhead to the pinnacle. The last portion of the trail, often snow-covered until mid-August, lies on the south side of Ptarmigan Ridge. Just west of the pinnacle (0.3 mile) is a broad saddle (Camp Kiser, 5 miles, 6,144 feet) where you can make camp. Ski west from Camp Kiser to Epley Portals (about 6,000 feet), a shallow saddle opening west to the gently sloping Sholes Glacier. Once over the saddle, ski left (southwest) for about 1 mile to The Portals (6,200 feet), a broad saddle defined by two peaks at coordinates 48.48.566/121.46.116. Camp here.

From camp, you can take runs to the north on the Sholes Glacier or to the south on the Rainbow Glacier. Both glaciers have some crevasses—take the requisite gear. Return via Herman Saddle, or retrace your route to go home.

Descending a glacier (Photo by Ron Proper)

Sholes Glacier is also the beginning of two possible traverses: over the summit via Boulder Glacier, or a lower-level traverse of Hadley Peak and Chowder Ridge (see Tour No. 8).

7
Herman Saddle

Start Point: Mount Baker Ski Area, 4,200 feet
High Point: Herman Saddle, 5,300 feet
Best Time: October to June
Day Trip: 9 miles
Skiing Time: 6 to 10 hours
Skill Level: Intermediate
Difficulties: High avalanche potential (especially on Table Mountain loop); routefinding required on Table Mountain loop; permit/fee area
Maps: Green Trails No. 14, Mt. Shuksan

Herman Saddle is the broad pass between Mazama Dome and the northern face of Table Mountain. This short and popular tour offers west- and east-facing runs, an overview of the ski area, and fabulous views of the two dominant peaks in the region.

Drive to the Mount Baker ski area. From the lodge, climb south, using the Blueberry cat track, for 0.3 mile. Descend to Bagley Lakes, and then head due west, climbing the steepening slopes for about 0.5 mile. Stay north of the obvious deep gully. Climb north to 4,700 feet, and then head west to Herman Saddle. Wind sculpting will change the snow surface from season to season—simply choose the path that affords the safest, easiest route.

From the saddle, you can yo-yo ski to the west or return via the approach.

Alternate Route: Explorers may opt to return via the Table Mountain loop (3 additional miles). If you descend the approach route from Herman Saddle, retrace your tracks north for the first 0.3 mile before skiing down to avoid the cliff bands below Table Mountain.

Chowder Ridge

Start Point: Wells Creek Road, 4,700 feet
High Point: Hadley Peak, 7,515 feet
Best Time: July to November (late-season tours are dependent on fresh snowfall)
Day Trip/Overnight: 10 miles
Skiing Time: 8 to 12 hours
Skill Level: Intermediate
Difficulties: Moderate avalanche potential; some glacier travel; routefinding required
Maps: Green Trails No. 13, Mt. Baker

Chowder Ridge offers a wild, scenic approach and excellent early and late-season skiing over moderate terrain. In good weather, spectacular views of Mounts Baker and Shuksan and the American Border Peaks heighten the experience. A United States Forest Service–imposed "migratory goat closure" and deep snow packs turn this day tour into an overnight tour. Before July, those with more time can bicycle or hike the long approach road. USFS plans to permanently close Wells Creek Road near the 6-mile mark. Skiers who love this area are encouraged to protest this decision.

Drive Mount Baker Highway (State Route 542) east from Glacier for 8 miles. Just past the Nooksack Power Plant, turn right onto Wells Creek Road. After crossing the Nooksack River, drive 1.5 miles and turn right at the first fork.

Wells Creek Road follows the creek for about 2 miles past the fork (4 miles past the Nooksack crossing). Five miles from the bridge, the road crosses Wells Creek and follows Bar Creek for 1 mile, then winds uphill toward the crest of

Hadley Peak on the north side of Mount Baker (Photo by Rainer Burgdorfer)

Cougar Divide. Continue driving as far as conditions permit, possibly parking in a clear-cut near the ridge crest (4,700 feet). Near the end of the road, you will encounter a fork; take the left road. This road is rough.

Climb south, first through a clear-cut area, then through a narrow band of old-growth forest. The subalpine zone soon appears, along with a stunning head-on view of Mount Baker's northern ridge. The lights of Bellingham are visible from this vantage. The route snakes over undulating terrain, forested in some spots and gladed in others. Continue your south-southwest course through the undulating forest until you break out onto heather benches (5,800 feet and higher). Ski on the eastern side of the crest to avoid cliffs. Another fabulous tour, Skyline Divide, is visible to the west.

Chowder Ridge (about 7,000 feet) lies 3 miles to the southwest. If you decide to turn around, you can take a few good runs right here, but you must retrace your approach. Direct descents to lower parts of the road are untested.

If you decide to continue, a good objective is Hadley Peak, the eastern end and high point of Chowder Ridge. Scramble Hadley from the south side. (Small cliffs on the north side prevent a direct descent from the summit, so leave your skis near Hadley's east ridge, where an easy descent can be made to the north-side glacier.

From the summit, you have an unobstructed view across the west face of Mount Baker, the Coleman and Roosevelt glaciers, Heliotrope Ridge, and the San Juan Islands in shimmering Puget Sound.

Runs are possible on both the northern and southern slopes. The Hadley Glacier is crevassed but may be skied with care if the snowpack is deep.

One-way traverses are possible by skiing over Chowder Ridge and exiting over Ptarmigan Ridge, or vice-versa.

To return to the car from Hadley Peak, traverse west along the Hadley Glacier until you can gain Cougar Divide, then retrace your tracks to the car.

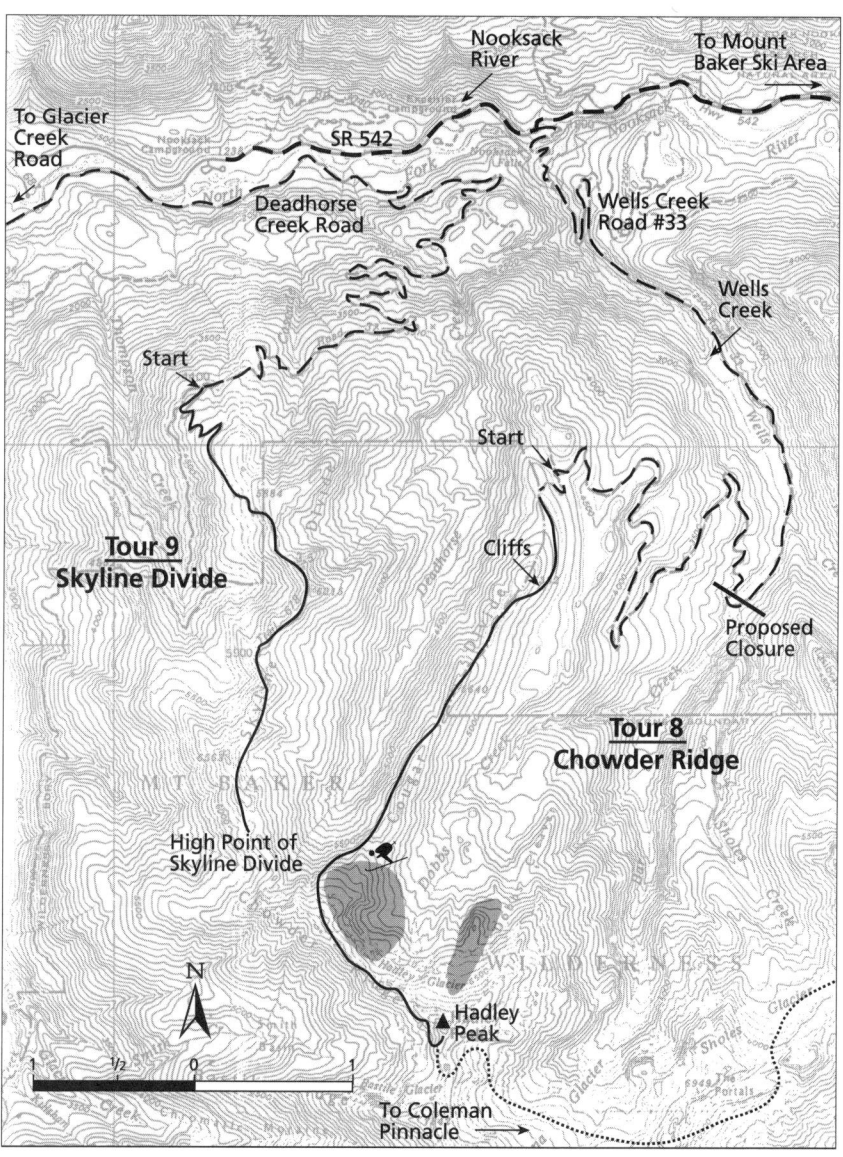

Skyline Divide

Start Point: Skyline Divide Trailhead, No. 678, 4,300 feet
High Point: Point 6565; 6,565 feet
Best Time: October to November/May to July
Day Trip/Overnight: 9.5 miles
Skiing Time: 8 to 10 hours
Skill Level: Intermediate
Difficulties: High avalanche potential; permit/fee area
Maps: Green Trails No. 13, Mt. Baker

The primary obstacle to this tour is finding the road snow-free with adequate snow cover for the tour. When this occurs, count yourself lucky. All the superlatives attached to Chowder Ridge apply here as well.

Drive State Route 542 for 1 mile beyond Glacier. Turn right onto Glacier Creek Road No. 39, and in 100 yards turn left onto Deadhorse Creek Road No. 37. Drive the road for 13 miles, or as far as snow conditions permit. Ignore side roads and spurs. The trailhead lies at the upper end of the parking lot at 4,300 feet.

The trail climbs through gladed forest, trending south. In 2 miles, you break out of the forest (5,800 feet) onto an expansive snowfield. Continue climbing south to the high point of the tour. Ski where you will.

Alternative Route: It seems feasible to connect Skyline Divide with Chowder Ridge on skis, but this route is untested.

Coleman Glacier

Start Point: Heliotrope Ridge (Mount Baker Trail) Trailhead No. 677; 3,650 feet
High Point: Coleman Glacier, 7,500 feet
Best Time: October to November; April to June
Day trip/Overnight: 9 miles
Skiing Time: 7 to 10 hours
Skill Level: Advanced
Difficulties: High avalanche potential; glacier travel; permit/fee area
Maps: Green Trails No. 13, Mt. Baker

This tour contrasts a remote, if popular, alpine environment with sunset views of the San Juan Islands and the Strait of Juan de Fuca. The tour, which follows

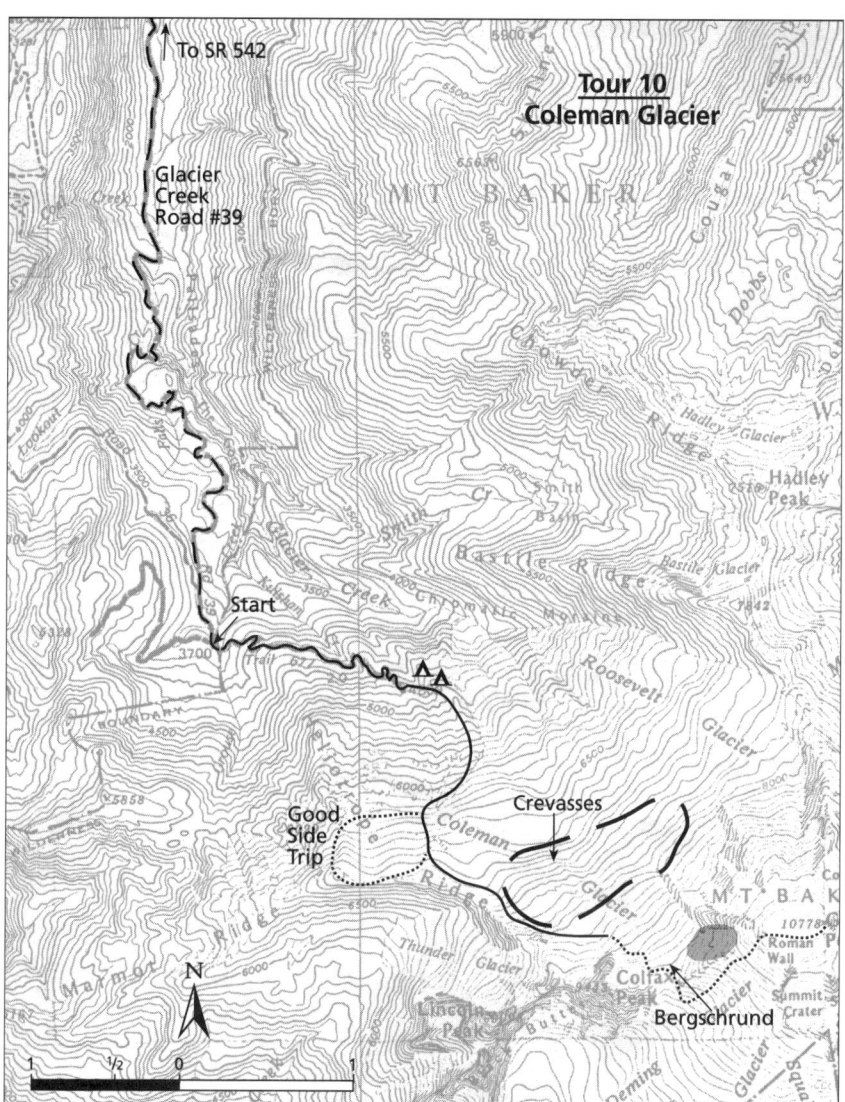

the first part of the classic summit route, offers glacier skiing on the northwest side of our northernmost volcano.

Drive State Route 542 past Glacier and turn right onto Glacier Creek Road No. 39. Turn right and drive 8.5 miles to the Heliotrope Ridge trailhead.

The trail dips into the forest at the eastern edge of the parking lot and is evident even when covered with snow. Metal markers on trees help show the way to the site of former Kulshan Cabin (2 miles, 4,700 feet). The trail climbs through forest, crossing several small streams. Continue climbing east-southeast

On Mount Baker's Coleman Glacier with the San Juan Islands and Puget Sound in the background (Photo by Rainer Burgdorfer)

from the cabin site, breaking out of the trees near 5,200 feet. If you decide to make this an overnight tour, this is a good place to camp. Early in the season, the best skiing is found on Heliotrope Ridge, just above this area, but below 6,200 feet. To reach the ridge, climb the slope south of camp, bearing slightly east, and ascend a steep, narrow moraine until you reach a broad bench. (Good skiing may be found along this bench.) Turn southeast to climb higher, until you approach the crest of Heliotrope Ridge. Maintain elevation to stay clear of crevasses on the lower Coleman Glacier. The crest is a scenic place to camp.

Alternative Route: The junction of Heliotrope and Marmot Ridges (approximately 7,000 feet) is a good spring touring destination. Scenic camp and bivouac sites abound, and excellent views of the Black Buttes, the Coleman Headwall, and the San Juan Islands can be had in good weather.

NORTH CASCADES HIGHWAY, STATE ROUTE 20

The North Cascades Highway (State Route 20) provides year-round access to much of the terrain along its corridor. In most years, the highway is closed by late November. Nevertheless, on the west side, it is driveable to Diablo Lake year-round. On the east side, the highway often is plowed to within 8 miles of Washington Pass.

Many tours in this area take place within national park and national recreation areas. Backcountry permits, which may be obtained from the National Park Service, are required for overnight tours, and many areas are designated "limited entry." Pets are unwelcome within national park boundaries. Information is sometimes available from district ranger offices at Marblemount and Winthrop. There is fierce competition for berths in high-use areas, so it is best to make alternative plans in case you cannot obtain a permit for your area of choice. Some outstanding skiing objectives in the region, not described in this guide, lie to the east: Fawn Peak and Robinson Peak provide fine, long runs with overnight access. Other touring possibilities include Buck Mountain, Oval Peak, Reynolds Peak, Abernathy Peak, and Big Craggy.

Slate Peak

Start Point: Harts Pass, 6,200 feet
High Point: Slate Peak, 7,440 feet
Best Time: May to July
Day Trip: 4 miles or more, at your discretion
Skiing Time: 7 hours
Skill Level: Intermediate
Difficulties: High avalanche potential; permit/fee area
Maps: USGS Slate Peak, 1:24,000

This tour inserts the skier into the rolling mountains of the Pasayten Wilderness, which can provide insulation from storms that may be dumping on more

West of Harts Pass (Photo by Rainer Burgdorfer)

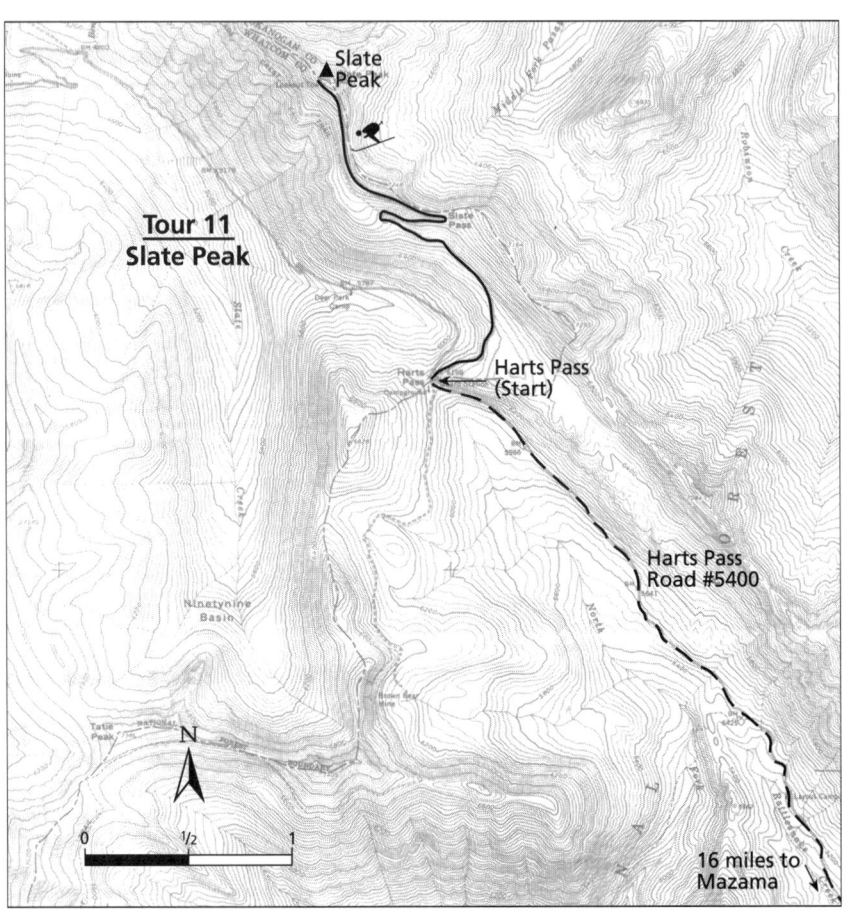

westerly areas. Slate Peak sports the highest unpaved road in Washington State. When road conditions permit, you can drive to the Slate Peak parking lot, step out of your car, step into your bindings, and carve 1,000 feet of north-facing turns, just for starters.

Drive State Route 20 to the hamlet of Mazama (east of Washington Pass, west of Winthrop). The road in front of the post office is Harts Pass Road No. 5400. Drive this steep and exposed road for 19 miles to Harts Pass at 6,200 feet. If snow blocks the road, park and ski the road to the pass. Once at Harts Pass, continue through and turn right onto Slate Peak Road. The summit and its lookout are just 1,200 feet above you. Climb the road until you reach a crest (in summer, this is a small parking area). From here, it is possible to ski the northeast bowl of Slate Peak, cornices permitting. The summit plateau lies a few hundred feet to the north.

Silver Star Mountain

Start Point: Silver Star Creek, 3,400 feet
High Point: Saddle between east and west summits, 8,600 feet
Best Time: January to May
Day Trip: 8 miles
Skiing Time: 12 hours
Skill Level: Advanced
Difficulties: High avalanche potential; glacier travel; routefinding required; permit/fee area
Maps: USGS Silver Star Mtn., 1:24,000

The skiing doesn't get any better than this. Relatively easy access and a long run among huge granite towers and larches—often in powder—make Silver Star a worthy objective. The Washington State Department of Transportation plows State Route 20 past Silver Star Creek, making this area generally accessible in winter. Helicopter skiers frequently invade Silver Star, reducing the wilderness aspect of this tour.

From the parking lot, climb into the forest on the east side of Silver Star

Silver Star from Harts Pass (Photo by Rainer Burgdorfer)

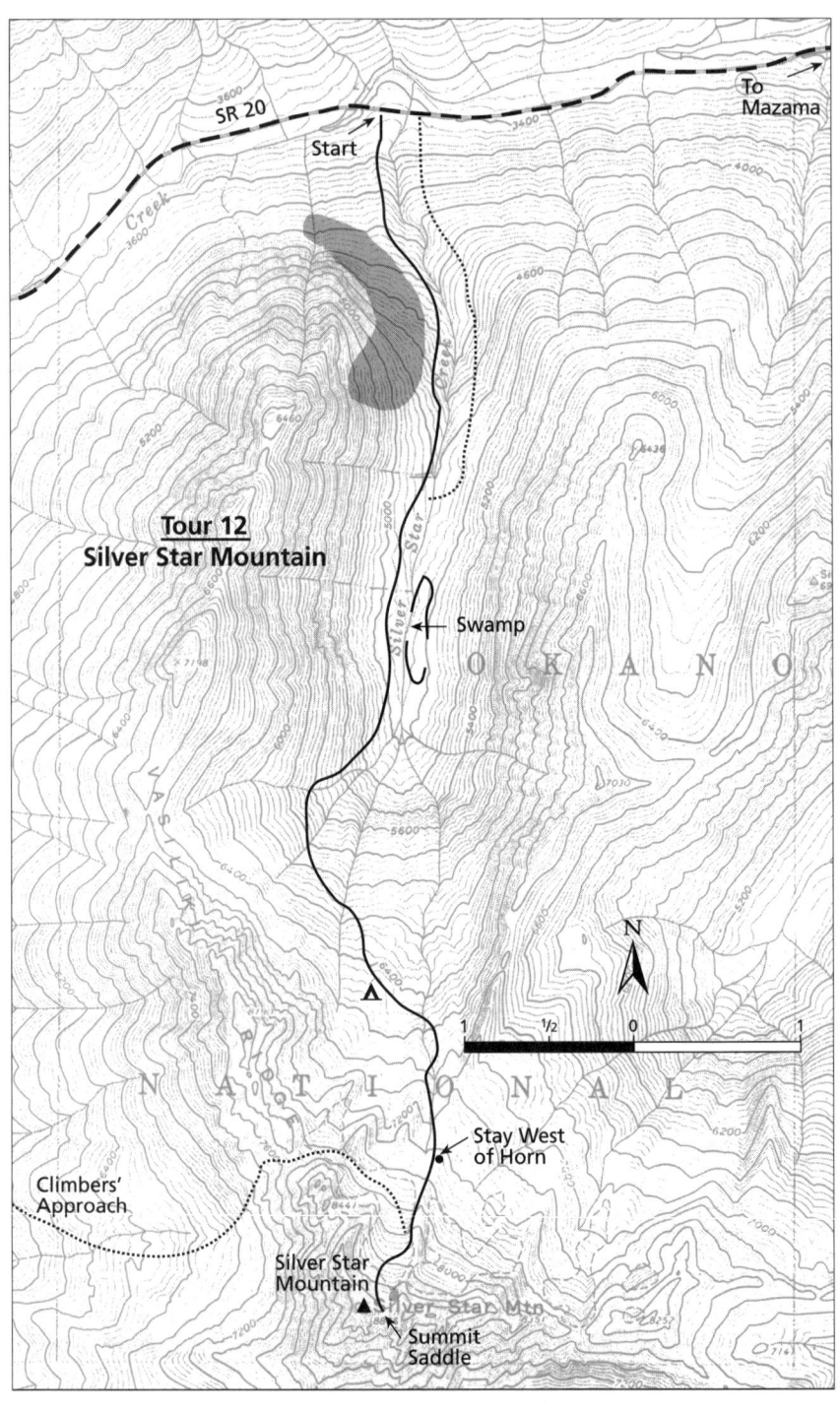

Creek. Stay well above the streambed. The valley flattens out in 1.1 miles (4,700 feet). Continue climbing to the head of the valley, crossing the stream as required. Near 5,600 feet, bear right to avoid a steep section, then continue climbing south. The headwall is divided into three sections by granite ribs. The left (eastern) glacial trough is the gentlest of the three. Even so, it is often windloaded. As you approach the steep slopes below the saddle, climb right to gain the pass (8,600 feet). The true summit lies just east of the pass, but can be a technical challenge in winter conditions.

Return via the approach. In season, you can ski all the way back to your car, a run of over 5,000 vertical feet.

Delancey Ridge

Start Point: North Cascades Highway, Silver Star Creek
High Point: 6,000 feet
Best Time: January to March
Day Trip: 2 miles
Skiing Time: 4 hours
Skill Level: Alpine
Difficulties: High avalanche potential; permit/fee area
Maps: USGS Silver Star Mtn., 1:24,000

Delancey Ridge lies north of State Route 20, just across the valley from Silver Star Mountain. Aspen glades and avalanche chutes form south-facing powder

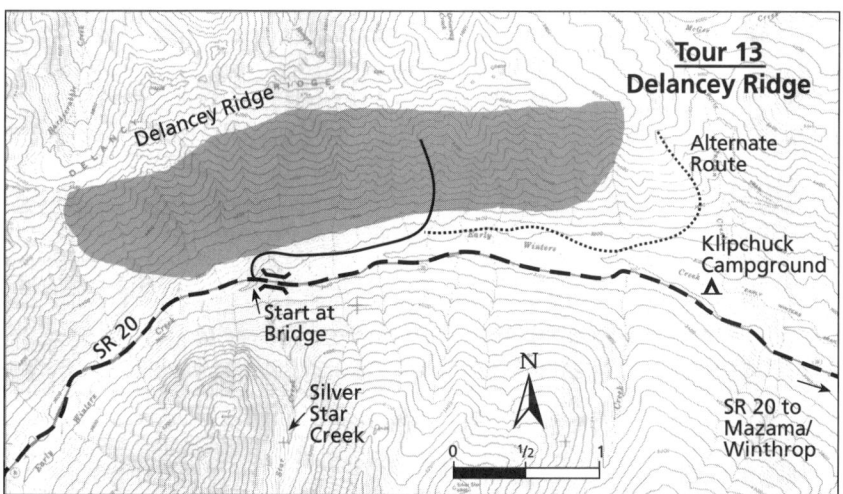

Footprints in the snow (Photo by Rainer Burgdorfer)

caches that, in stable conditions, permit a full day of yo-yo skiing within a few hours of the road. There are many choices here, but only two are described.

Option 1. Drive State Route 20 to its plowed end at Silver Star Creek. Head west across Silver Star Creek Bridge, then ski down Klipchuck Campground Trail No. 522 on to the north side of Early Winters Creek. From here, head east, looking for likely runs. When you see one, climb it and go! Careful scrutiny as you drive State Route 20 will suggest further runs. This adventure requires a Low Avalanche Hazard Forecast. Climb ridges, then descend the gullies after ensuring slope stability.

Option 2. Cross Early Winters Creek near Klipchuck Campground and climb ribs to the northwest to gain Delancey Ridge.

Early Winters

Start Point: Blue Lake Trailhead, 5,280 feet
High Point: Early Winters Spire–Blue Peak Notch, 7,600 feet
Best Time: As day trip, April to June, immediately after the highway opens; as an overnight, from January to June
Day Trip/Overnight: 4 miles; Sally Portman's Birthday Tour, 10 miles
Skiing Time: 4 hours; Sally Portman's Birthday Tour, 7 hours
Skill Level: Intermediate; Sally Portman's Birthday Tour, Advanced
Difficulties: High avalanche potential; Sally Portman's Birthday Tour requires routefinding
Maps: USGS Silver Star Mtn., 1:24,000

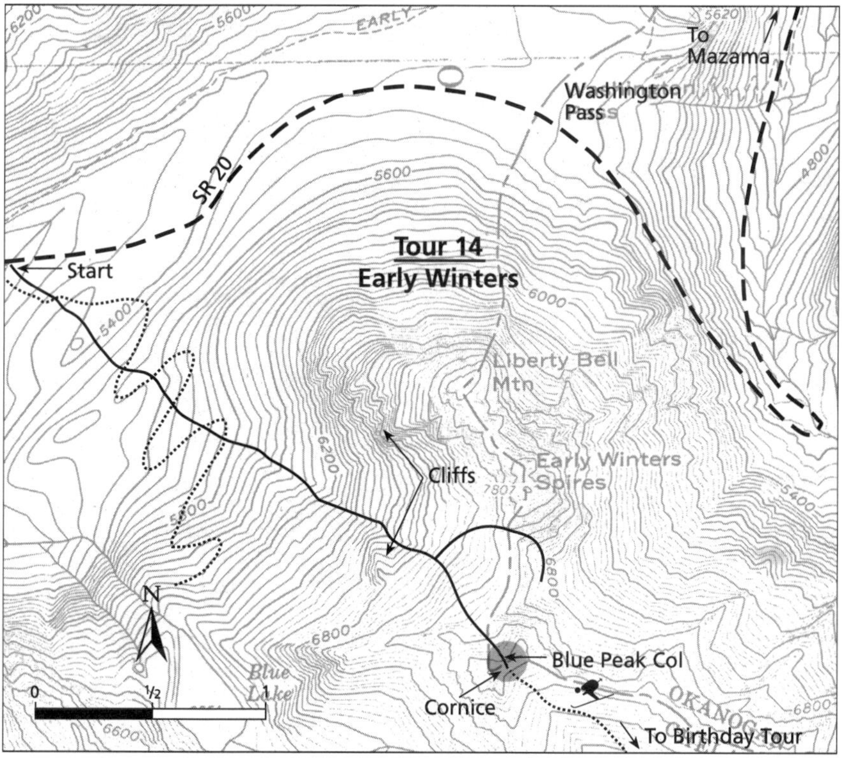

This tour offers the potential to ski huge slopes among larches and to enjoy unusual views of Liberty Bell. The good weather associated with the eastern

slope of the Cascades doesn't hurt, either. Sally Portman's Birthday Tour is an intricate, interesting circle around the Liberty Bell massif with skiing on all aspects, which does not require two cars.

Drive State Route 20 to Washington Pass. Park either at Washington Pass, or at Blue Lake Trailhead, 1.2 miles west of the pass on the south side of the road. In early season, you must ski or snowmobile the 9 miles from Silver Star Creek to Washington Pass. In this case, this tour becomes an overnight trip.

From the Blue Lake trailhead, climb uphill through forest, trending

Saddle behind Early Winter's spire (Photo by Ken Ritland)

southeast-east. In 0.3 mile, you'll enter a large avalanche deposition zone. Climb through snow blocks and debris to a steep headwall near 6,200 feet; to overcome this obstacle, pass through a gully on the right side. Continue climbing on open slopes and benches, then top out at the saddle (7,400 feet), 0.3 mile south of South Early Winter Spire. Intermediate skiers are advised to end their tour here and make runs back to the car.

Alternative Route: To do Sally Portman's Birthday Tour, head south from the broad saddle, climbing 250 feet (0.3 mile) to reach Blue Peak Col (7,600+ feet). (An ice ax is handy for this.) From the col, descend to the southeast, starting your eastward traverse at approximately 6,000 feet. Continue due east, heading up the valley below Copper Pass. Once you reach the head of the valley, explore to find a notch that will drop you down over the north side. It is easiest towards Kangaroo Pass to the southeast. From near the pass, descend to the valley bottom at 5,800 feet, then ski straight down the valley to rejoin the highway at the first hairpin turn.

Heather and Maple Passes

Start Point: Rainy Pass, 4,855 feet

High Point: Maple Pass , 6,600 feet

Best Time: April to July; November

Day Trip: 7 miles

Skiing Length: 6 hours

Skill Level: Intermediate

Difficulties: High avalanche potential

Maps: USGS Mount Arriva, Washington Pass, 1:24,000

Rainy Pass is the entry point for a number of tours accessible from the North Cascades Highway. This area is far enough east to offer an alternative to west-side tours made risky due to bad weather. Weak weather systems sometimes fail to penetrate as far east as Rainy Pass; often, skiers can make successful tours here while the Cascade Pass area is receiving rain.

Park your car at Rainy Pass on the southwestern side of the highway.

The trail begins on the southwestern side of the highway and continues southwest, switchbacking to gain 500 feet in 0.5 mile in subalpine forest. Trail No. 740 continues climbing to the west, and in 1.3 miles enters Lake Ann cirque. Pass Lake Ann on its northern shore, climbing 1 steep mile west to Heather Pass, a good place for a break. From Heather Pass you can see the way to Wing Lake, beneath the southern face of Black Peak. Consider the possibilities here.

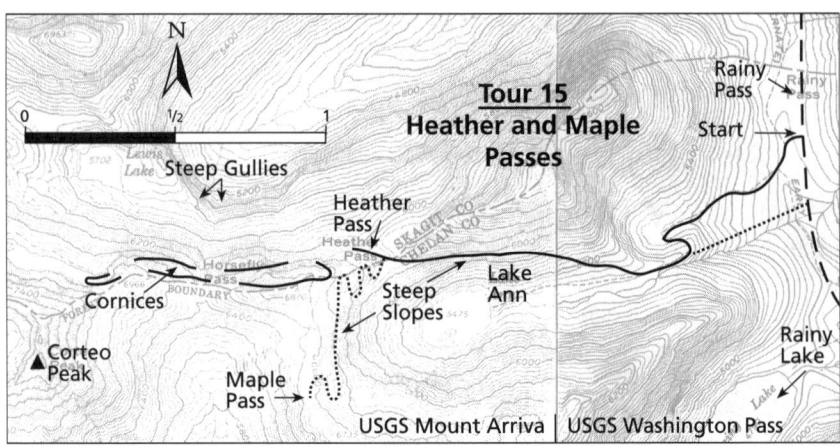

Our tour, however, heads south to Maple Pass. Maple Pass is one of the high divides in the North Cascades. Waters draining toward Lake Ann ultimately flow into Puget Sound. Precipitation falling on the west side of Maple Pass ultimately flows into the Columbia River via Lake Chelan.

From Heather Pass, climb 250 feet toward Corteo Peak. Where the terrain permits, head south over steep benches to Maple Pass and climb 250 feet to gain the saddle. Short runs can be made from Maple Pass toward Maple Creek, especially near the south ramp of Corteo Peak. Retrace your approach from Maple Pass to return to your car.

Cutthroat Pass

Start Point: Rainy Pass, 4,855 feet
High Point: Cutthroat Pass, 6,830 feet
Best Time: May to June
Day Trip: 10 miles
Skiing Time: 8 hours
Skill Level: Intermediate
Difficulties: Moderate avalanche potential; routefinding required
Maps: USGS Washington Pass, 1:24,000

Cutthroat Pass offers medium-scale skiing on moderate slopes accentuated by jagged peaks. A fairly easy approach and a delightful roller-coaster descent double its appeal. The actual pass lies 1.7 miles north of Cutthroat Peak.

Skiing on Mount Logan, with Buckner in the background (Photo by Jens Kieler)

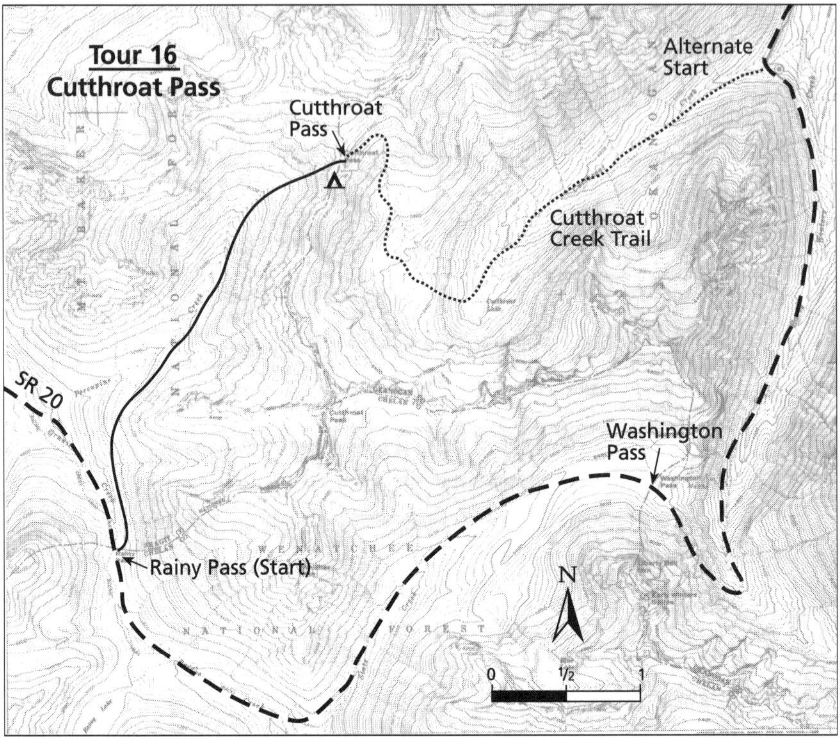

Tour 16
Cutthroat Pass

Cutthroat Pass

Cutthroat Creek Trail

Alternate Start

Washington Pass

Rainy Pass (Start)

SR 20

N

0   1/2   1

Drive State Route 20 to Rainy Pass. The route (in summer, Pacific Crest Trail No. 2,000) leaves the east side of the highway, heading due north for 0.8 mile. Near 5,200 feet, start climbing northeast up the right side of the Porcupine Creek drainage and maintain this heading until you reach the Pass. The trail passes through dense forest and subalpine forest onto alpine slopes. Runs

Cutthroat Pass, looking north (Photo by Rainer Burgdorfer)

are possible on both sides of the pass and to the Cutthroat Lake Trailhead. Do a traverse when the highway is open! A more adventurous tour involves a ridge traverse north to Granite Pass.

To return to the car, retrace your approach.

Alternative Route: Park at Cutthroat Creek Campground 4.7 miles west of Washington Pass and climb along Cutthroat Creek to Cutthroat Lake. The basin above the lake offers good skiing. Head southwest to climb to Rainy Pass.

17
Névé Glacier

Start Point: Pyramid Lake Trailhead, 1,150 feet
High Point: Colonial-Névé Col, 6,840 feet
Best Time: January to June
Overnight: 11 miles
Skiing Time: 9 hours
Skill Level: Alpine
Difficulties: High avalanche potential; routefinding required; glacier travel; permit/fee area
Maps: Green Trails No. 48, Diablo Dam

This tour is a heroic objective and grants the tenacious skier access to unusual views and skiing on ice-cap glaciers. It is accessible year-round since State Route 20 is always open to the trailhead, and beyond. Low avalanche hazard conditions are essential for this tour.

An alternative approach (or escape) can be made via the abandoned Colonial Creek Trail, which follows its namesake, but the brush on this route is known to have made grown men weep.

Drive State Route 20 east from Newhalem. The Pyramid Lake trailhead is 0.5 mile beyond Gorge Lake. The trail leaves the road from the south side and climbs to Pyramid Lake in 2.1 miles.

Pyramid Peak (the name is descriptive) lies southwest of the lake. To get there, climb south to the ridge that descends from the peak. Ascend the ridge to 5,400 feet, 3.8 miles from the car, and make camp, or if time and energy permit, press on.

Ski to the highest level of the bench (5,800 feet), where the north face converges with the northeast ridge, and peek south over the edge to the Colonial Creek Basin. Descend a steep gully, with cliffs to your right, and then climb south for 0.8 mile. You will contour at first. Then, when the terrain permits, climb steadily, up very steep snow, onto the northern edge of the Colonial Glacier.

As you gain the glacier, the lay of the land becomes more apparent. You'll see that Pyramid Peak is really the northern terminus of the ridge crowned by Paul Bunyans Stump and Pinnacle Peak. Rope up for the climb: the Colonial Glacier is crevassed.

Continue climbing until you are on line between Paul Bunyans Stump and Colonial Peak (about 6,100 feet). Then ski due south for 0.5 mile to the gentle Colonial-Névé Glacier col (6,860 feet).

There is magic in reaching a pass in the high mountains. The gradual revealment of new peaks and sudden panoramas is deeply thrilling. In this regard, this pass, Snowfield Peak, and the Névé Glacier are exceptional.

Yo-yo descents of all aspects are possible. Keep in mind that the Ladder Creek and Névé Glaciers are crevassed.

Return by retracing the approach.

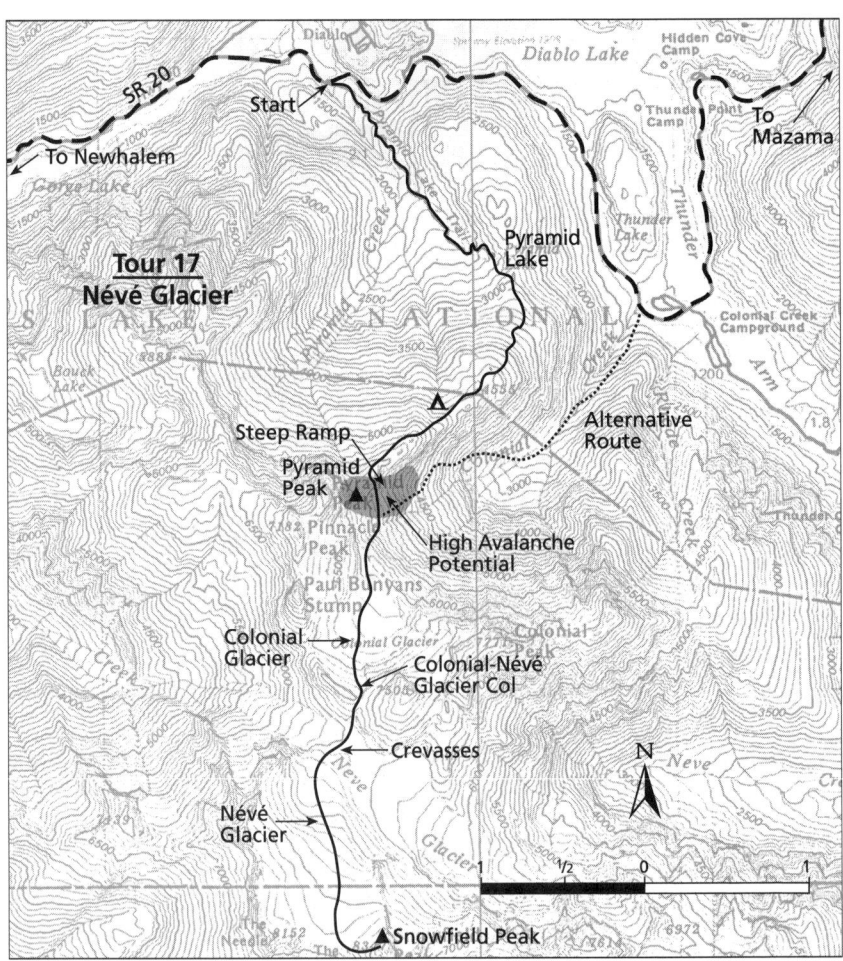

The Névé Glacier is remote, high, and only moderately crevassed. (Photo by Harry Hendon)

Teebone Ridge

Start Point: Cascade River Road, 1,200 feet
High Point: Little Devil Peak, 6,985 feet
Best Time: December to May
Overnight: 10 miles
Skiing Time: 14 hours
Skill Level: Alpine
Difficulties: High avalanche potential; routefinding required; permit/fee area
Maps: Green Trails No. 47, Marblemount

This tour has year-round access because Cascade River Road is below the snow line. However, this makes for a punishing approach, in terms of elevation gain.

Once in high country, the long runs and west-slope views of the North Cascades make the climb worthwhile. Small snowshoes can make the steep approach easier.

Drive State Route 20 to Marblemount. Cross the Cascade River and continue east 7.5 miles on Cascade River Road to the Lookout Mountain–Monogram Lake Trailhead No. 743. The trail climbs a rib on the steep hill north of the road through old-growth forest. If snow obscures the trail, stay on the rib, or just right of it, for 2.3 miles (3,400 feet). The lack of brush makes routefinding easy for the first part of the trip.

At this elevation, the terrain begins to ease back and the prominent rib blends into the overall slope. The route starts to trend northwest, crossing the east branch of Lookout Creek in 0.7 mile (3,950 feet). Continue another 0.3 mile to a trail junction (4,200 feet, 48.33.302/121.18.541) and take the right fork. If snow covers the trail and sign, climb northeast through open forest of large fir and hemlock. This is steep terrain and routefinding becomes more difficult.

Continue climbing northeast for 1 mile, staying west of a large avalanche path. The forest ceases abruptly and a large basin, with a steep crest on its right side, appears. This slope is the western end of Teebone Ridge.

Be sure to note where you leave the woods so that you can find your way back to the trail. Climb east across the alpine slope and ascend one of several gullies toward a slight pass on the eastern crest (5,400 feet).

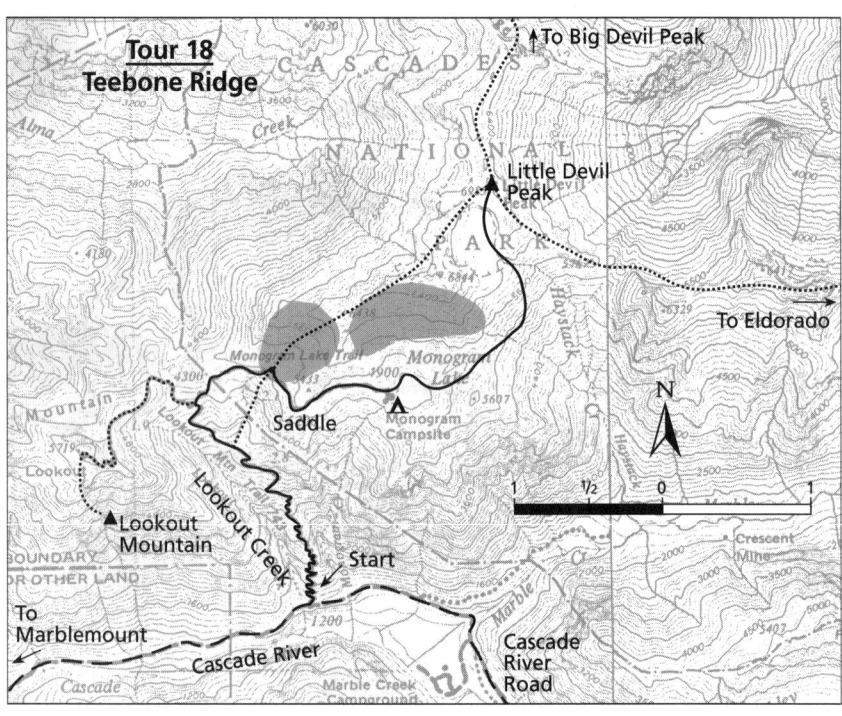

Once at the crest, take a moment to view snow-covered Monogram Lake and the surrounding peaks. The peak behind and to the left of the lake is a subsidiary summit (6,840 feet) of Little Devil Peak (6,985 feet). Little Devil is barely visible from this vantage, but the summits are 0.8 mile apart.

Descend to the southwestern shore of Monogram Lake, connecting a series of benches to make the descent. The area near the southern shore of Monogram Lake offers good, reasonably level campsites.

To continue the ascent from the lake, cross to the northeastern shore, and then climb a series of gullies to a pass north of a small knob (approx. 5,650 feet). From the pass, descend northeast for 200 feet, then climb north to Little Devil (about 1.6 miles) and make the final descent via the southwestern ridge.

Runs can be taken to the northwest, to the southeast, or back to Monogram Lake. To return to the car, simply reverse the approach, or ski to the southwestern end of Teebone, and then head southwest toward the approach trail where you first left the woods.

Eldorado

Start Point: Cascade River Road, 2,100 feet
High Point: Eldorado Peak, 8,868 feet
Best Time: April to June
Overnight: 12 miles
Skiing Time: 12 hours
Skill Level: Advanced
Difficulties: Moderate avalanche potential; glacier travel; routefinding required; permit/fee area
Maps: USGS Eldorado Peak, Forbidden Peak, Sonny Boy Lakes, Cascade Pass, 1:24,000

This tour provides rapid access to a remote area with many days of skiing potential. The approach via Eldorado Creek is straightforward. In early season, much of the brush and talus is covered with snow, making travel relatively pleasant.

Drive Cascade River Road east from Marblemount for nearly 20 miles. Park at the gravel pit on the right side of the road near the 20-mile marker and head north from the road. Cross the Cascade River on logs, noting their location, and find a path that climbs north through open timber. Stay 100 to 200 feet left (west) of Eldorado Creek, which joins the Cascade River just upstream of your crossing. Be sure you are in the Eldorado rather than the Roush Creek drainage. Careful odometer reading on the drive in should keep you from going astray.

Climb for 1.5 miles, to about 3,600 feet. Continue right, around a huge

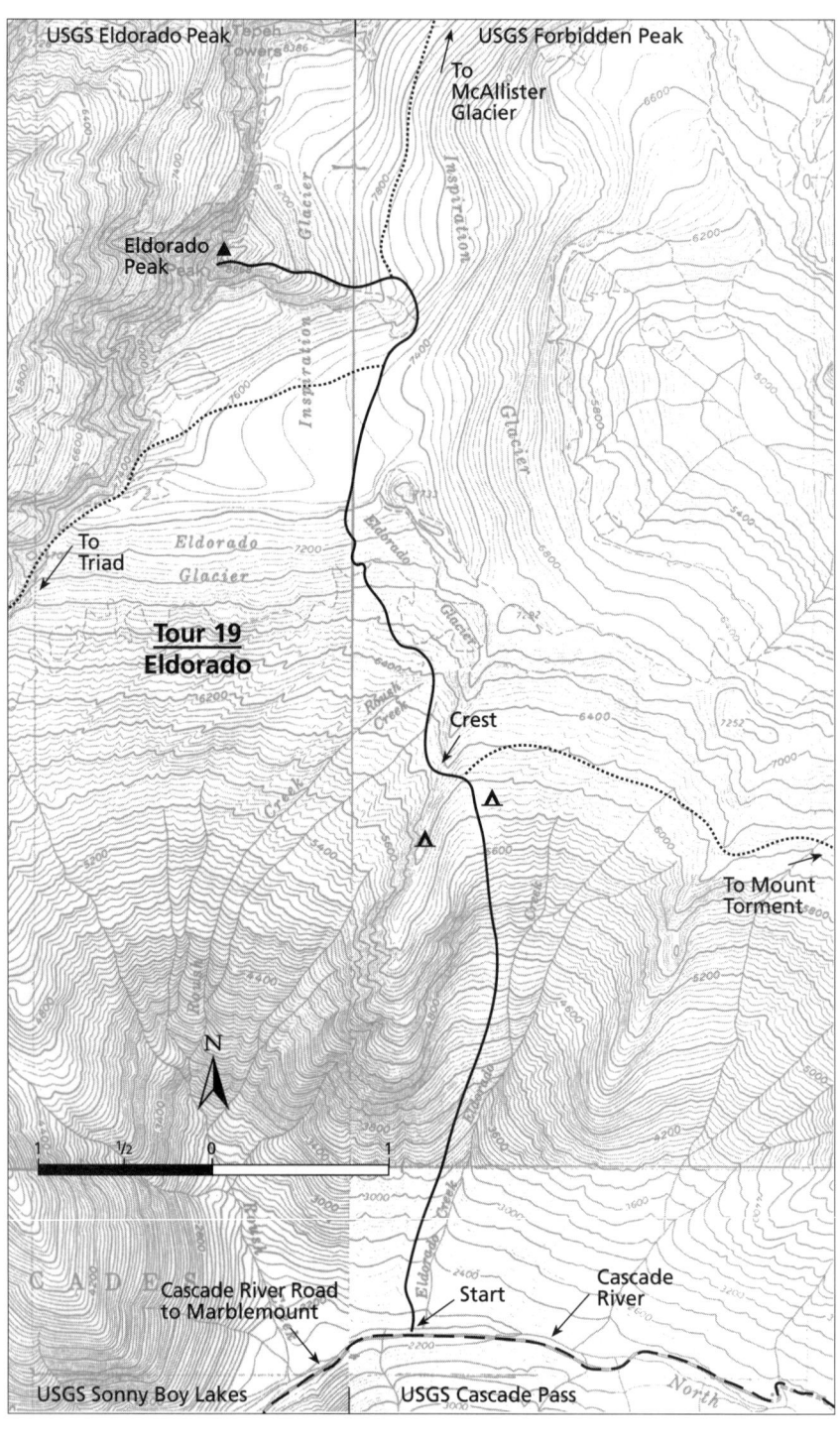

USGS Eldorado Peak

USGS Forbidden Peak

To
McAllister
Glacier

Inspiration

Glacier

Eldorado
Peak

Glacier

To
Triad

Eldorado
Glacier

Tour 19
Eldorado

Crest

To Mount
Torment

N

Cascade River Road
to Marblemount

Start

Cascade
River

USGS Sonny Boy Lakes

USGS Cascade Pass

buttress (4,000 feet) to a talus field of house-sized blocks. Find a path along the right edge of the boulder field. Continue north for another 1.5 miles.

Just beyond the talus field (about 5,000 feet), the angle eases off, except for a few small cliff bands. Keep heading north (in late season, this section is an alder patch) until you reach gentler open slopes.

Looking west, you can see both your next obstacle and a good place to camp. The crest dividing Eldorado and Roush Creeks lies about 0.3 mile due west.

Head for the crest, intersecting it near 6,000 feet, about 500 feet below the looming cliffs. This is a good place to camp. Find an easy place to cross the rib and descend 100 feet to the west, into the Roush Creek drainage. Head north-northwest onto the Eldorado Glacier, staying clear of cliffs above your right.

Bivouac on Eldorado; Eldorado Glacier is on the left. (Photo by Rainer Burgdorfer)

In 1 mile you should be abreast of Point 7733 and on the Inspiration Glacier "flats." Rope up on the glacier and mark any dubious crossings.

The route turns slightly east here, to make an end run around the east end of the south face of Eldorado (0.6 mile).

Once you reach the terminus of the south face, turn sharply left (west) and climb the east ridge 0.8 mile (1,400 feet) to the summit area. In most years the actual summit is a knife-edged snow ridge, precipitous on either side. Mortals may require an ice ax and rope to climb to the true summit. While you're looking around from the summit of Eldorado, notice the glacier northeast of you and consider the touring possibilities. Descend by retracing the approach.

Boston Basin

Start Point: Cascade River Road, 3,200 feet
High Point: Boston-Sahale Saddle, 8,589 feet
Best Time: April to June
Day Trip: 8 miles
Skiing Time: 6 hours
Skill Level: Intermediate
Difficulties: High avalanche potential; glacier travel; permit/fee area
Maps: USGS Forbidden Peak, Cascade Pass, 1:24,000

As spring turns to summer, Cascade River Road melts out and grants access to the farther reaches of this mountain fastness. Boston Basin provides fine spring skiing and exciting views of Johannesburg's calving glaciers. This trip requires stable snow conditions: huge slides from the surrounding peaks frequently fill the entire basin.

Drive Cascade River Road as far as conditions allow. Five miles past Mineral Park Campground there is a spur road (3,200 feet). Park here. Hike the road northeast to the Diamond Mine site and up the brushy hill beyond.

The trail is muddy, brushy, and steep, and it leaves the mine site near its left (northeast) corner. Continue climbing through forest, sometimes following streambeds. The route continues east past timberline (5,500 feet) and the terrain becomes less steep. Midas Creek should be on your left as you leave the woods (48.29.167/121.03.976). Note the place where you leave the woods. It is important to locate the trail for your return home.

Climb the large moraine ahead (6,300 feet). Descend the uphill side and climb northeast toward Sharkfin Tower and Boston Peak on its right. The Quien Sabe Glacier is crevassed and a bergschrund may block passage near 8,300 feet. When convenient, head directly toward the broad saddle (8,589 feet).

For a sense of what the Alaska Range looks like, look east over the pass

An aerial view of Forbidden Peak with Boston Basin and Colonial Mountain in the background (Photo by Rainer Burgdorfer)

toward the massive Boston Glacier. Glacier conditions permitting, you can take runs to the northeast. Otherwise, be content with a view that road-bound people will never see, and then ski the west-facing slopes of Boston Basin. Retrace your approach to return to the car.

 Sahale Arm

Start Point: Cascade River Road, 3,523 feet
High Point: Sahale Mountain, 8,715 feet
Best Time: April to June
Day Trip: 6 miles
Skiing Time: 7 hours
Skill Level: Advanced
Difficulties: High avalanche potential; glacier travel for summit climb; permit/fee area
Maps: USGS Forbidden Peak, Cascade Pass, 1:24,000

Cascade Pass is one of the most spectacular, easily accessible viewpoints in the North Cascades. It is also the entry point for three spectacular high routes: the Ptarmigan Traverse, the Bullsnake Traverse, and the Teebone Ridge–Cascade Pass

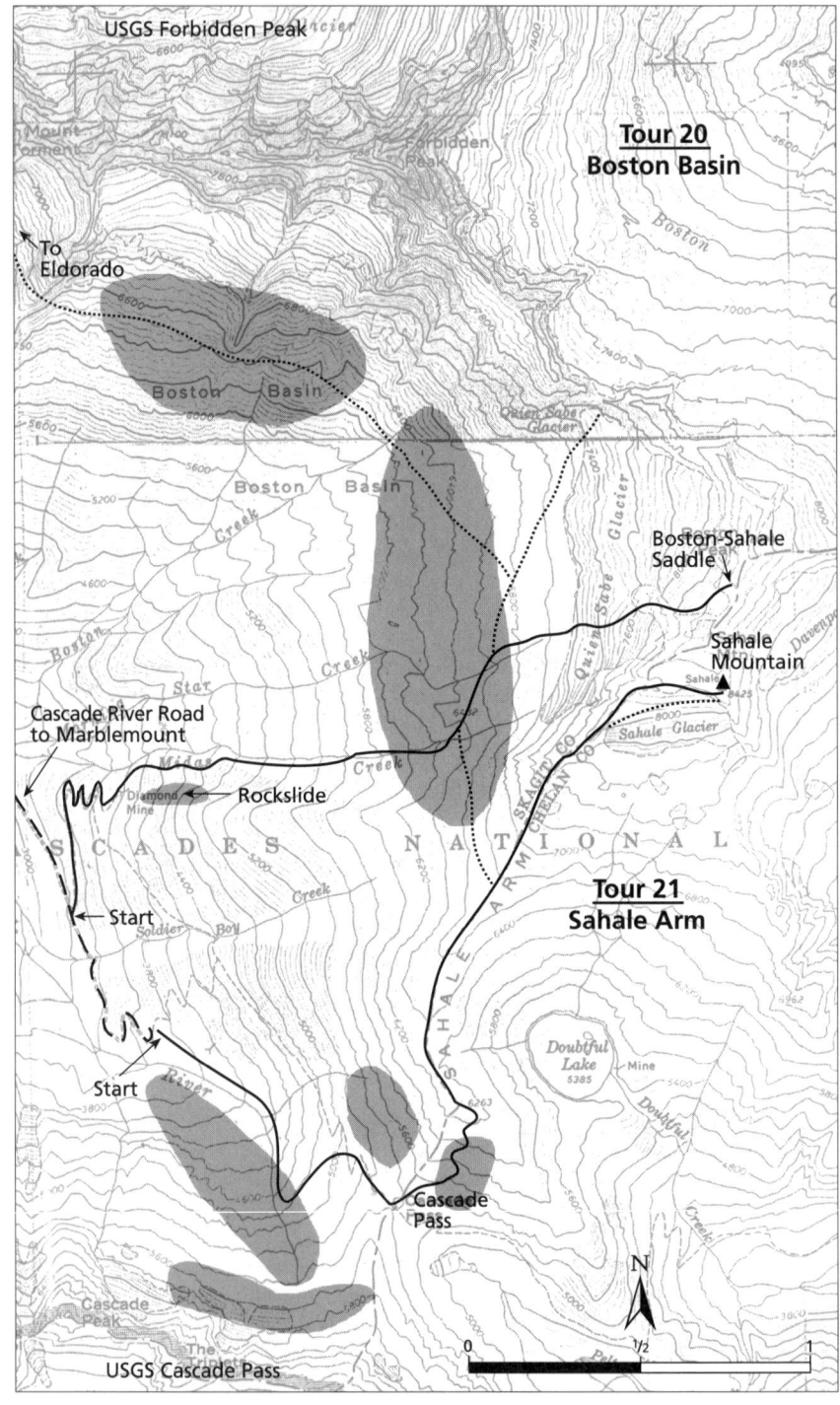

USGS Forbidden Peak

Tour 20
Boston Basin

To Eldorado

Boston Basin

Boston Basin

Boston-Sahale Saddle

Sahale Mountain

Cascade River Road to Marblemount

Rockslide

CASCADES NATIONAL

Tour 21
Sahale Arm

Start

Start

Doubtful Lake

Cascade Pass

N

0   ½   1

USGS Cascade Pass

Traverse. The skiing in the immediate vicinity of the pass is pretty good, too.

Drive Cascade River Road as far as conditions permit. The road ends in 25 long miles (3,600 feet). Leave the road from the second switchback just below the parking loop and head straight up (southeast) the drainage toward Cascade Pass. Some routefinding is necessary to penetrate the short cliff bands

Sahale Arm (Photo by Rainer Burgdorfer)

that break up the snow slope. In early season, this direct ascent is desirable because it is short (1.5 miles) and it avoids avalanche slopes below Sahale Arm.

From Cascade Pass, climb east of the narrow crest leading to Sahale Arm. This slope is steep; in 0.5 mile and 800 feet, you will reach the eastern shoulder of the arm. Enjoy the view of Doubtful Lake to the east. Follow the ridge northwest past Point 6263, then continue north to Sahale itself. Follow the western margin of the glacier to the summit apron, then scramble to the summit (class 4-5).

Descend by retracing the approach down to Cascade Pass, or for easier skiing, cross north into Boston Basin near 6,700 feet. Then simply reverse the Boston Basin approach. To return via Cascade Pass, descend 0.2 mile to the northwest to 5,000 feet. Head southwest for 0.1 mile, dropping 200 feet. Descend a very steep section for another 200 feet, avoiding cliffs to the west, and then ski the fall line to your car.

22
Snowking Mountain

Start Point: South Side Cascade River Road, 2,480 feet
High Point: Snowking Mountain, 7,433 feet
Best Time: March to June
Overnight/Weekend: 12 miles
Skiing Time: 10 hours
Skill Level: Advanced
Difficulties: High avalanche potential; routefinding required
Maps: USGS Snowking Mtn., Sonny Boy Lakes, 1:24,000

Snowking Mountain and its southeastern neighbor, Mount Buckindy, are not usually noticed by roadbound travelers. The area is unknown to many mountain skiers—even though it offers astounding descents from January to May.

Drive Cascade River Road for 16.5 miles from the Skagit River Bridge. Turn right at the South Side Cascade River Road 1570 (high ground-clearance vehicles only), crossing the Cascade River on a concrete bridge in 1.6 miles. Continue, coming to a fork in 0.4 mile. Take the right fork and continue uphill, making a right hairpin turn to the northwest-west. In 0.7 mile, take a left fork and drive the winding road as far as road conditions permit. A washout stops all vehicular traffic at 2,483 feet (48.27.608/121.13.851).

From your car, climb up the road until you reach the stream bisecting the road. Head uphill, crossing the stream where possible. Within 0.1 mile west of the stream, head south-southwest, climbing through old-growth forest to 3,500 feet. Now head due south for 0.8 mile, bypassing steeper sections on your right, until you find yourself on a shoulder with a knoll to your right and

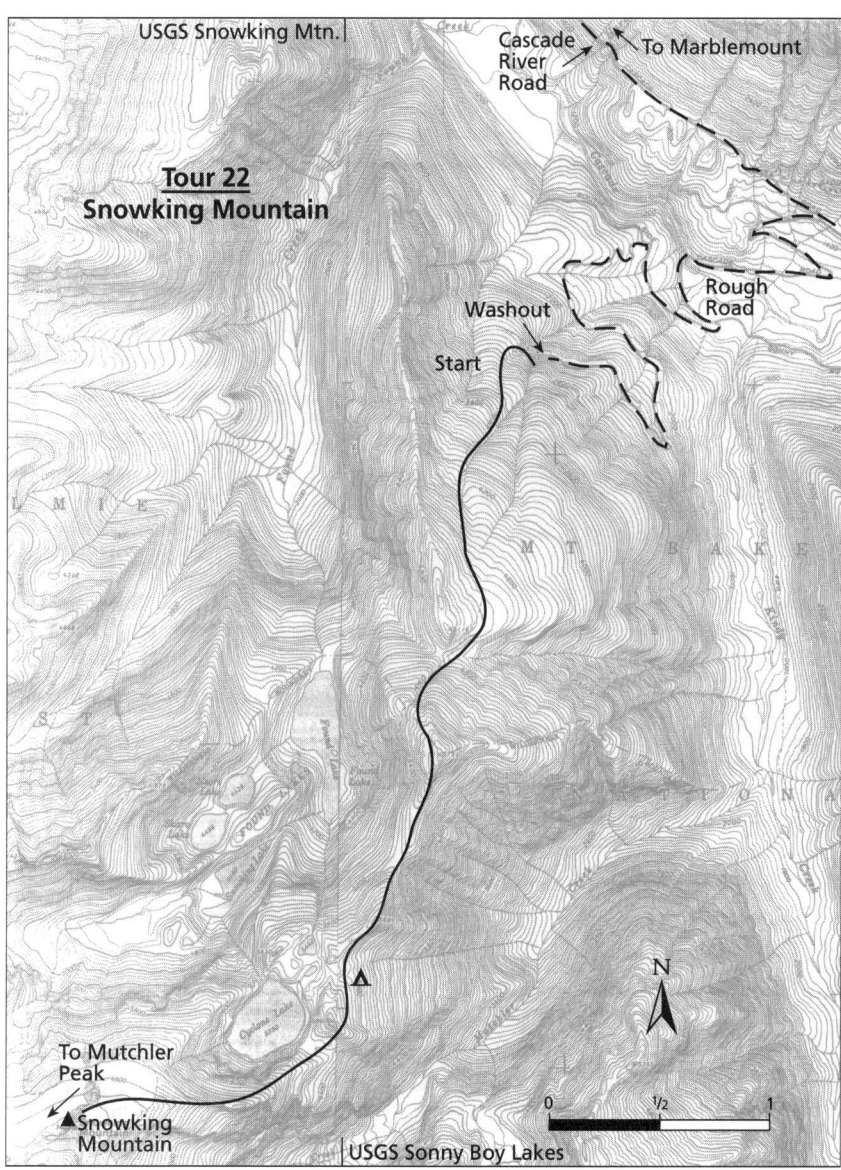

drainages to your left (4,800 feet). Climb south-southwest for 0.4 mile, gaining the ridge east of Found Lake (5,300 feet).

Stay on this ridge, heading southeast to 5,700 feet, and then head south for 1.3 miles, keeping to the ridge crest. Camp on the rolling ground east of Cyclone Lake. From this vantage, you can see the northeast ramp to Snowking, and the long couloirs plunging to Cyclone Lake from Snowking Mountain. An

Snowking as seen from Cyclone Lake. Note the gully systems descending to the lake. (Photo by Sue Harris)

easy ridge romp takes you clockwise around Cyclone Lake to the summit. In season, it is possible to descend directly to Cyclone Lake via a steep gully on its southwestern side. Excellent runs are possible on Mutchler Peak and its north-facing glacier, 2.3 miles to the southeast.

To return to the car, retrace your approach. It's all downhill!

23 Sauk Mountain

Start Point: Sauk Mountain Trailhead No. 613, 4,500 feet

High Point: Sauk Mountain, 5,541 feet

Best Time: May to June

Day Trip: 5 miles

Skiing Time: 6 hours

Skill Level: Advanced

Difficulties: High avalanche potential; permit/fee area

Maps: USGS Sauk Mtn., 1:24,000

Sauk Mountain, an elongated cockscomb just north of the Skagit River Valley, is visible from the city of Mount Vernon. This little tour offers a short hike, a steep 1,300-foot east-facing run down to Sauk Lake, and a climb up and over to return to the car, all with nonstop views of the western North Cascades. This is an outstanding snowboard tour.

Drive State Route 20 toward Rockport (6.9 miles east of Concrete). Rockport State Park lies 1.7 miles east of Rockport. Just west of the park, Sauk Mountain Road heads north from the highway. Drive this logging road for 7.7 miles. Turn right at a fork here, and park at the trailhead 0.2 mile ahead. If avalanche debris blocks the road, and conditions are stable, simply climb the debris cone directly up Sauk's west face. This is steep and requires snow- or ice-climbing tools and expertise. Ski descents of this slope are extreme and not recommended. Late-season tours avoid this difficulty.

From the parking lot you can see the trail stitching up the west face of Sauk Mountain. This generally melts out by early June, while the east face maintains a deep snowpack as late as July. Take the trail, coming to the south ridge in 1.5 miles. Once on the ridge, climb north along its east shoulder until you reach the summit block; to gain the summit, climb the west side. Snow

Aerial view of Sauk Mountain, in the left foreground (Photo by Rainer Burgdorfer)

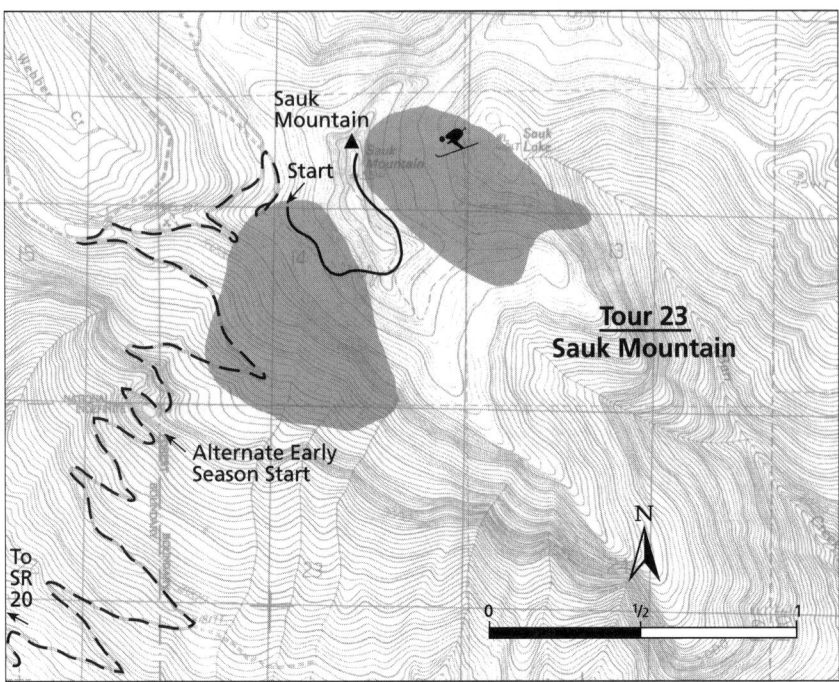

accumulations or cornices may prevent a safe summit ascent.

The cirque walls that face to the east above Sauk Lake provide excellent skiing. These slopes are complex and steep enough to fill up an entire afternoon. To go home, retrace the approach.

 Mount Watson

Start Point: Anderson–Watson Lakes Trail No. 611, 4,156 feet
High Point: Mount Watson, 6,200 feet
Best Time: May to June
Day Trip: 10 miles
Skiing Time: 8 hours
Skill Level: Intermediate
Difficulties: Moderate avalanche potential; routefinding required; permit/fee area
Maps: Green Trails No. 46, Lake Shannon; No. 47, Marblemount

Mount Watson is a scenic tour east of Baker Lake with a panoramic view of the Bacon Peak massif. Although it only offers yo-yo skiing and requires a hiking approach, its position and character make it a worthwhile spring tour in good weather.

Drive State Route 20 to Birdsview, 21 miles east of Interstate 5. Turn north on Baker Lake Road (No. 25), and drive 14 miles to Koma Kulshan Campground Road. Turn right and drive 1.5 miles to upper Baker Dam. Cross the dam and drive to the trailhead (10 miles, 4,156 feet).

The trail climbs steeply to the north for 200 feet (0.2 mile), then heads east for 0.7 mile. Near 4,750 feet, there is a left fork to Anderson Butte. Save this for another day. Continue southeast for 0.3 mile, passing between a low hump on your right and the cliffy mountainside on your left. Descend two hundred feet, trending east, and gain the pass at 4,800 feet. Watson Lakes lie in the basin 0.3 miles to the east.

Descend to lower Watson Lake. The easiest route to Mount Watson involves skiing northeast-east for 1.5 miles along the northern shore of Watson Lakes to their eastern end, then climbing due south to the summit area of Mount Watson (1.0 mile). The summit crags are class 3-4 climbs.

To return to the car, retrace your approach.

Bacon Peak

Start Point: Anderson–Watson Lakes Trail No. 611, 4,156 feet
High Point: Bacon Peak, 7,070 feet
Best Time: May to July
Extended Trip: 17 miles
Skiing Time: 24 hours
Skill Level: Alpine
Difficulties: High avalanche potential; glacier travel; routefinding required; permit/fee area
Maps: Green Trails No. 46, Lake Shannon; No. 47, Marblemount

Bacon Peak, high point of a massive plateau east of Baker Lake, is unknown to many mountaineers: it is invisible from State Route 20 and hard to approach from any side. Nevertheless, its large glaciers and snowfields and its remote situation offer the possibility of a real adventure within hours of the Puget Sound region.

Drive State Route 20 to Birdsview, and then drive Baker Lake Road to upper Baker Lake Dam. Cross the dam and follow the road to the Anderson Lakes trailhead. Hike the Anderson Lakes Trail to the Watson Lakes–Anderson Lakes fork (1.8 miles), and then take the left fork to Watson Lakes. From the eastern end of the lakes, ski south-southeast, traversing below the northern slopes of Mount Watson for nearly 2 miles, to the saddle dividing Diobsud and Noisy Creek drainages (5,400 feet, 48.39.117/121.32.464).

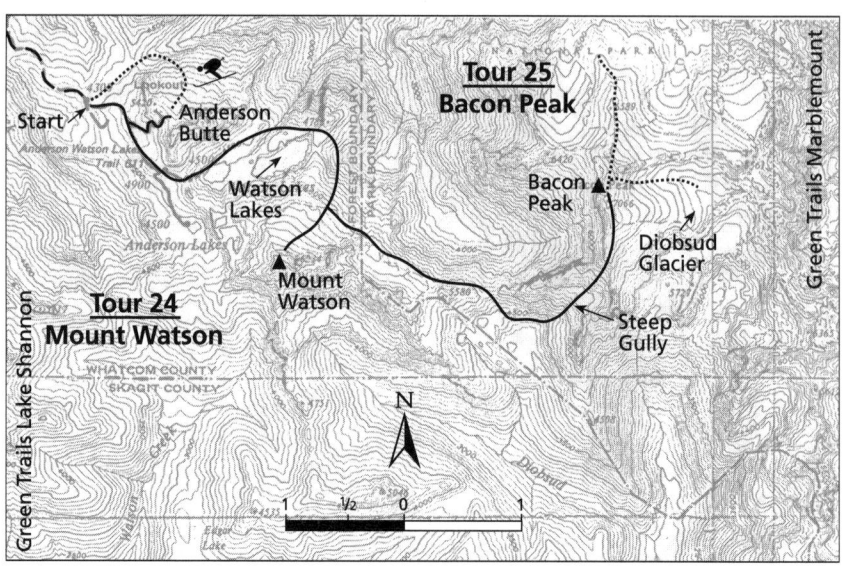

From the saddle, descend southeast into a basin. As you descend, look for the ramp leading northeast to Diobsud Glacier. Take this and a steep gully to the summit plateau. The way to the summit of Bacon Peak is self-evident from here. Skiing possibilities abound on the plateau. Remember that these are crevassed glaciers.

Return via the approach.

Mount Shuksan

Start Point: Shannon Creek Road, 2,400 feet

High Point: Mount Shuksan, 9,127 feet

Best Time: February to June

Day Trip/Overnight: 12 miles

Skiing Time: 9 hours

Skill Level: Advanced

Difficulties: High avalanche potential; glacier travel; permit/fee area

Maps: USGS Mt. Shuksan, 1:24,000

The Mount Shuksan tour has, for some skiers, an aspect of pilgrimage. Barely visible from most lowland vantages (it can be seen from high places in Seattle), the mountain only reveals itself as you approach it more closely. Once on its icy south flank, you'll wonder how you ever got there, and how you'll ever get back. The mountain lies within the North Cascades National Park. No pets are allowed. This is a popular tour.

Drive Baker Lake Road past the Koma Kulshan guard station, continuing on for 9.8 miles. Turn left onto Road 1152 and drive it for 0.2 mile, then turn right at the first fork.

Drive 3 miles to Road 14 and drive as far as conditions permit (approximately 2,400 feet).

The trail follows an abandoned logging road, rounding two buttresses and entering an overgrown clear-cut. Climb this heading north into the forest-covered ridge above you. Once in the woods, continue climbing north for 1 mile until you break out of the timber near 4,800 feet. A small notch lies to the northeast, your gateway to the Sulphide Glacier.

Climb the steep slopes to the notch (about 5,400 feet) and pause to examine the route ahead. Just north of your perch is Point 6466. From the notch, climb northeast on 35-degree slopes around a corner. These slopes are frequently wind-loaded. Proceed slowly, and with caution, as you pass the cliff bands above and below. Once around the corner, the terrain eases off. Take a moment to memorize the route for the descent.

Once you gain the small crest at the eastern end of the traverse, begin heading north to the snout of the Sulphide Glacier. Stay left, fairly close (but not too close) to the cliffs above your left to avoid crevasses. Consider wanding the route (or entering GPS coordinates) from here on, because a whiteout would make the descent problematic. The lower part of the glacier is quite flat; it

Mounts Hagan and Bacon in the middle distance, looking south (Photo by Brian Sullivan)

steepens above 6,500 feet. Avoid the broken-up eastern edge of the glacier.

Continue climbing to the summit pyramid, which may be climbed either by gullies on its southwest face or the southeast ridge. The views from the summit are well worth the climb.

The adventurous can cross the southeast ridge of the summit pyramid near 8,100 feet and ski 1.3 miles north across the Crystal Glacier, past the northern shoulder of Mount Shuksan. This side trip yields unusual views of Nooksack Tower and Icy Peak.

Back on the Sulphide Glacier, the descent looks improbable. Although the route reverses your ascent of the Sulphide, the glacier seems to plunge to unseen canyons on all sides. Begin by following your tracks. Stay reasonably close to the western edge of the Sulphide Glacier. Do not ski the fall line (southeast) toward Sulphide Lake, because the eastern edge of the Sulphide and the snout

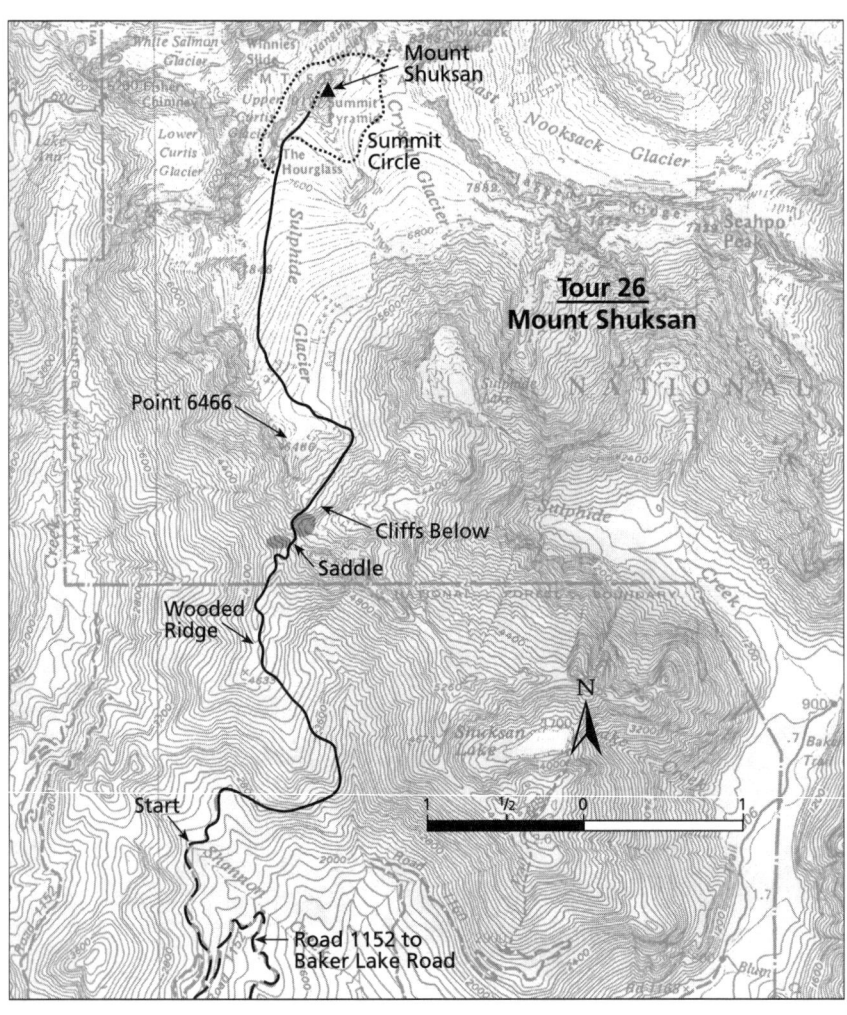

Sulphide Glacier with the summit of Mount Shuksan in the background (Photo by Sue Steindorf)

of the Crystal Glacier are steep and extremely broken. Also, do not descend through the notch at 6,380 feet, just above the first pinnacle visible from the pass at 5,400 feet. This way looks feasible but leads to cliffs below. The notch at 5,400 feet is the only reasonable return route.

Before descending to the notch, re-evaluate snow conditions. It is better to wait until the slopes stabilize, even if it means a bivouac, than to risk a ride over the cliffs below. Once at the pass, pick your line of descent and once you're in the woods, you're "out of the woods." This tour is better done early, rather than later in the season.

Mount Baker: Boulder Glacier

Start Point: Boulder Ridge Trailhead, 2,700 feet
High Point: Mount Baker Summit, 10,778 feet
Best Time: April to July
Overnight: 8 miles
Skiing Time: 14 hours round trip to summit
Skill Level: Advanced
Difficulties: High avalanche potential; glacier travel; lahar area; permit/fee area
Maps: USGS Lake Shannon, Hamilton, Mt. Baker, Mt. Shuksan, 1:24,000

I *like* this tour. Boulder Glacier is not only an excellent climbing route, but also an excellent mid- to late-season ski tour because of its challenging approach, good spring skiing, and feeling of remoteness. People who don't enjoy diversity won't like this tour. Geothermal activity near Sherman Crater can result in lahar (snow and earth slide) warnings for this route. Heed these warnings. USFS-mandated road closures sometimes occur here. Be sure to call ahead.

Below Park and Boulder Glaciers (Photo by Brian Sullivan)

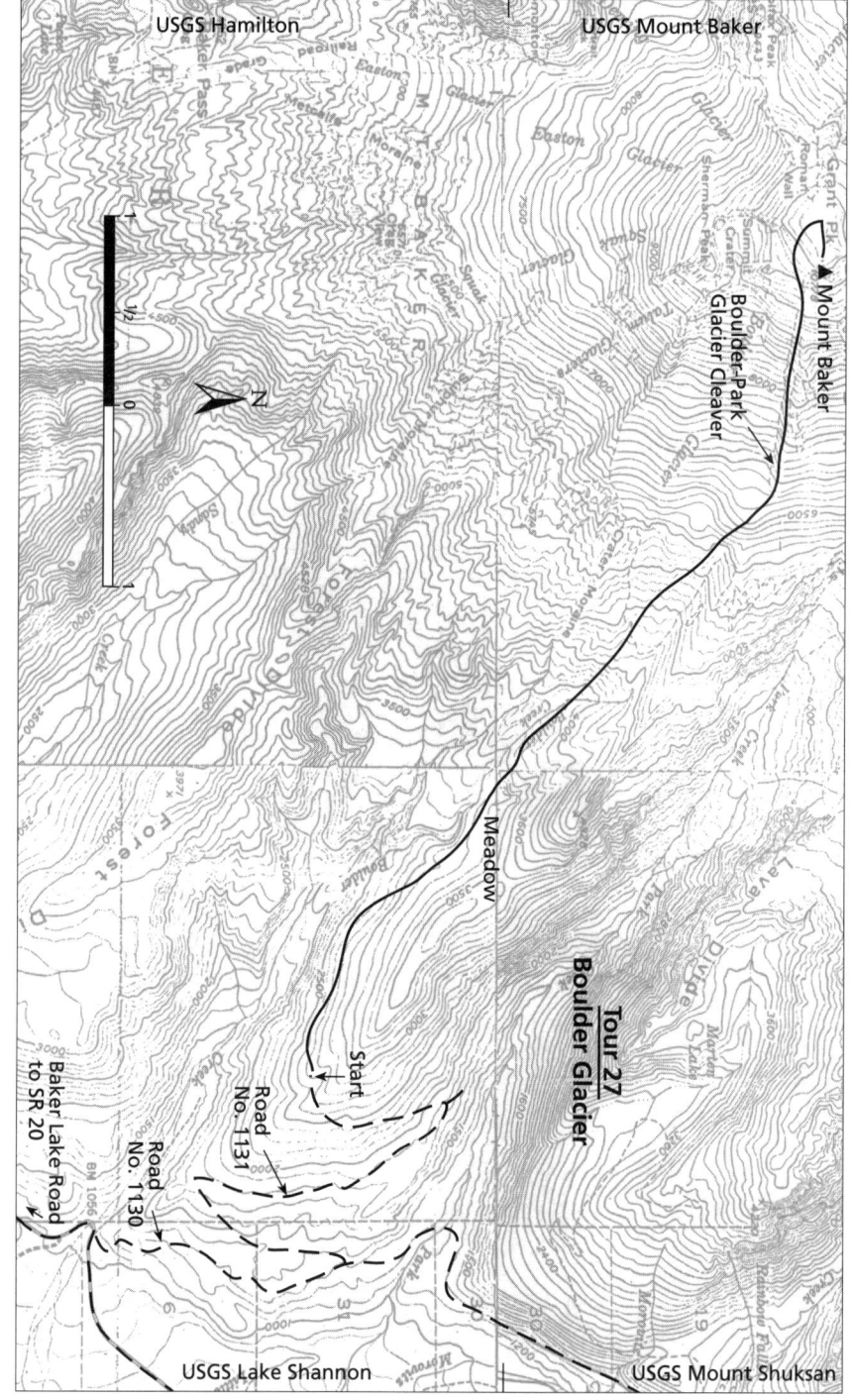

USGS Hamilton

USGS Mount Baker

▲ Mount Baker

Grant Pk

Boulder-Park
Glacier Cleaver

Meadow

Start

Road
No. 1131

Road
No. 1130

Baker Lake Road
to SR 20

Tour 27
Boulder Glacier

USGS Lake Shannon

USGS Mount Shuksan

Drive State Route 20 to Birdsview and turn north onto Baker Lake Road. Drive for 18.4 miles (4.4 miles past Koma Kulshan ranger station) over Boulder Creek Bridge and turn left onto Boulder Ridge Trail Road. Take the left fork at 4.2 miles to the end of the road.

Hike or ski a road remnant northwest through an old clear-cut. In 0.2 mile, you'll reach old-growth forest and swampy, primitive trail. (This is where your love of diversity will help out.) Continue northwest through the woods, passing a small meadow (3,400 feet, 2.1 miles) and making an exposed traverse near Boulder Creek higher up. In 0.5 mile you'll come to a shallow gully. Climb this groove until the terrain levels somewhat, and continue uphill via the easiest route. The flat tops of knolls provide campsites with good views, even if they are somewhat exposed to downslope winds.

Once on the glacier, rope up. The Boulder Glacier sometimes exhibits unpredictable crevasse patterns—unroped skiers are at risk, especially on the ascent. To gain the summit plateau, most climbers make a clockwise (analog) traverse near the 10,000-foot level to avoid cliffs, and then climb to the summit area. Do not attempt the steep summit climb unless your party is equipped for icy conditions.

Retrace your route of ascent. In most seasons, the skiing is best below 9,000 feet. The glacier seems to be less crevassed on its western edge. In broken-up conditions, the east side of the Boulder-Park Glacier Cleaver is often crevasse free.

Mount Baker: Easton Glacier

Start Point: Schreibers Meadow Trailhead, 3,320 feet
High Point: Mount Baker Summit, 10,778 feet
Best Time: April to July
Long Day/Overnight: 11 miles
Skiing Time: 12 hours
Skill Level: Advanced
Difficulties: Moderate avalanche potential (high above 9,000 feet); glacier travel; permit/fee area
Maps: USGS Mt. Shuksan, Hamilton, Mt. Baker, Lake Shannon, 1:24,000

In good weather, ever-expanding vistas, with the spectacular Black Buttes as nearby companions, distinguish this tour. While most mortals will require a two-day trip to reach the summit, even skiing to 7,000 or 8,000 feet will give skiers a long run with grand views and varied terrain.

Drive east on State Route 20 from Sedro Wooley for 14.4 miles and turn left on Baker Lake Road. Drive for 12.5 miles and turn left onto Loomis-Nooksack

Road No. 12 (the sign reads "Mt. Baker/Schreibers Meadow Road"). Drive Road 12 for 3.5 miles and turn right onto Schreibers Meadow Road 13. Drive to road end (7 miles) or as far as conditions permit. This is a mixed use (snowmobile) area in winter and early spring.

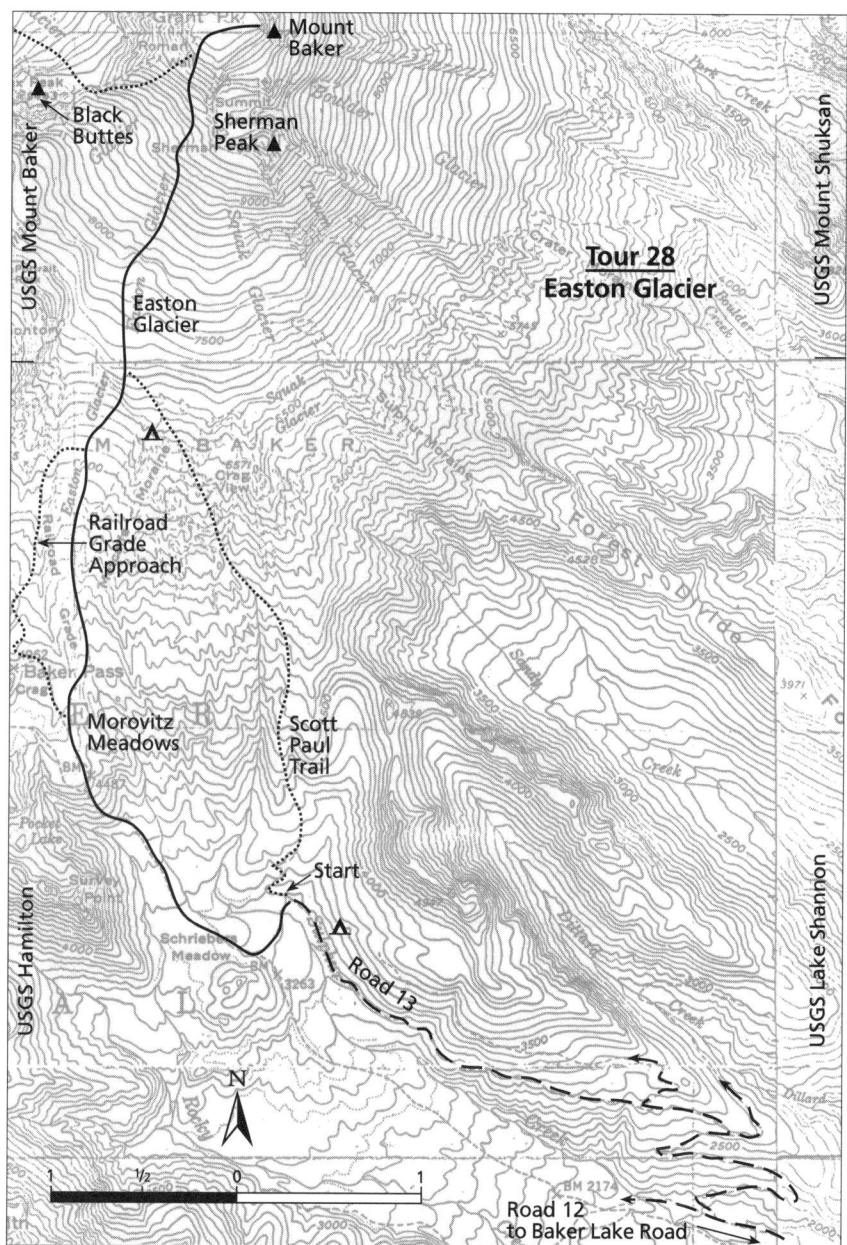

Easton Glacier (Photo by Rainer Burgdorfer)

Signs indicate the trailhead to Schreibers Meadow. Head northwest, immediately crossing a branch of Sulphur Creek. The trail then turns southwest, signed by trail markers to Schreibers Meadow (0.5 mile). The trail turns uphill (north) at the streambed. This route is the direct approach to the snout of the Easton Glacier. Once you climb out of the streambed, you are skiing on the glacier itself—ropes and prusik slings are advised. Continue up as time and energy allow, passing west of Sherman Peak and its crater. The crater notch is at 9,700 feet. To continue to the summit, go left (west) of the cliffs above the crater notch.

Be sure to allow enough time for the descent. In early season, the lower slopes freeze hard as soon as they fall into the shadow of the Railroad Grade moraine. The resulting skiing can only be called gruesome.

Alternative Route: Another approach to the Easton Glacier heads north from the end of the road, climbing through clear-cuts and timber. A summer trail called the Scott Paul Trail Loop echoes this approach. In early season, this approach avoids some of the snowmobile traffic. (This is a popular place.) In late season, it is easier simply to take the Scott Paul Trail, or, for variety, to hike the Railroad Grade Moraine Trail until it approaches the Easton Glacier.

Park Butte

Start Point: Schreibers Meadow Trailhead, 3,320 feet
High Point: Park Butte, 5,450 feet
Best Time: March to June
Day trip: 8 miles
Skiing Time: 7 hours
Skill Level: Intermediate
Difficulties: Moderate avalanche potential; permit/fee area
Maps: USGS Hamilton

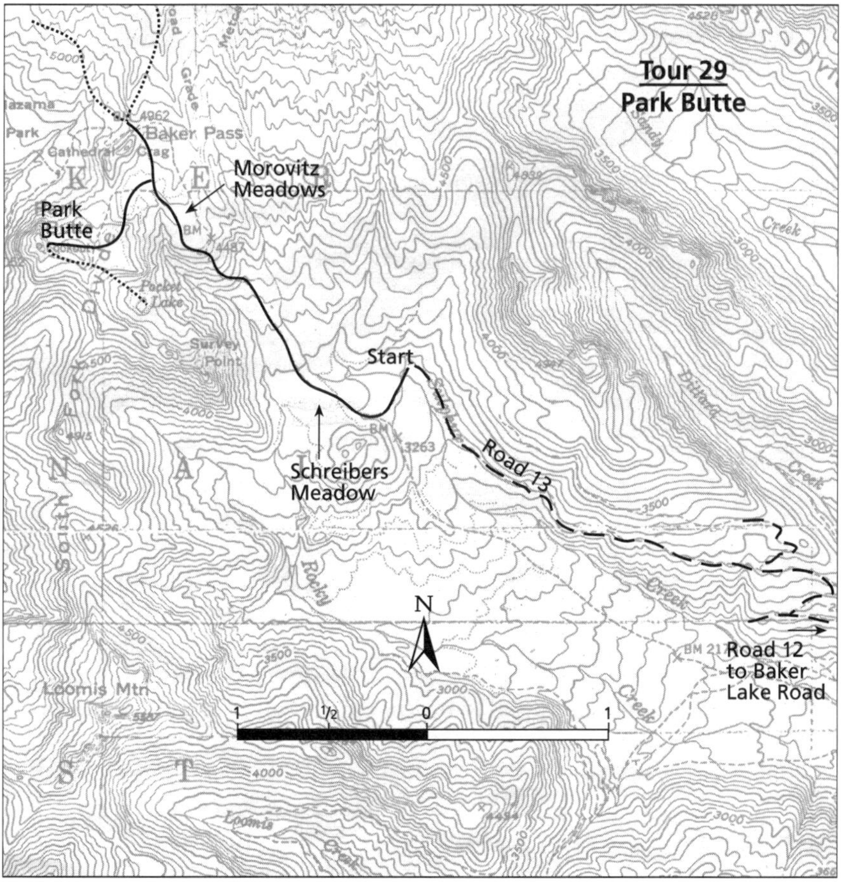

Park Butte offers excellent runs on slopes of many aspects and a spectacular vantage for viewing Mount Baker Twin Sisters. Late in spring, as the snowpack

diminishes, snowmobiles are excluded from Schreibers Meadow and the approach becomes more manageable. The result is a pleasant ski tour in spring conditions.

Drive to the Schreibers Meadow trailhead (See Tour 28). Cross Sulphur Creek and ski trending northwest to Schreibers Meadow (3,263 feet, 0.5 mile). Continue northwest for another mile, crossing the stream descending from the Easton Glacier. Continue heading northwest into the woods, climbing the steep summer trail to lower Morovitz Meadows (1 mile, 4,100 feet). An alternate approach climbs the gentle toe on the western moraine of the long-receded Easton Glacier to the meadows. Either way, climb to upper Morovitz Meadows (4,500 feet) and head west to Park Butte (1.0 mile, 5,450 feet).

Climb the eastern slope of the peak to reach the summit. This is also the best side for skiing. Adventurous skiers may head southeast to Survey Point, and then to Pocket Lake. Descending from Pocket Lake to Rocky Creek is steep, with cliff bands in places. It is more straightforward, if less adventurous, to simply retrace your approach to get to your car.

The final mile is made more pleasant if you have wax instead of climbing skins (or nonwaxing skis).

Twin Sisters

Start Point: Dailey Prairie Road, 3,200 feet
High Point: Twin Sisters Saddle, 5,850 feet
Best Time: April to June
Day Trip: 7 miles
Skiing Time: 6 hours, possibly longer depending on road status
Skill Level: Intermediate
Difficulties: High avalanche potential; glacier travel; gate
Maps: USGS Hamilton; USGS 15-minute series, Wickersham

You can't get there from here, at least on weekends. At the time of writing, the access road for this tour is open only during the week. On weekends, the road is gated at Mosquito Lake Road. This may change if a Nature Conservancy land purchase goes through. Until then, mountain bikes or motorcycles offer the only hope for weekend skiers who long to ski the 2,000-foot north side of Twin Sisters while looking Mount Baker in the eye. Skiers should be advised that logging roads, which may be closed at any given time, crisscross the area west of Twin Sisters. Be prepared to ferret out an alternate approach to this charming area.

From the south, head north from State Route 20 on State Route 9. As you

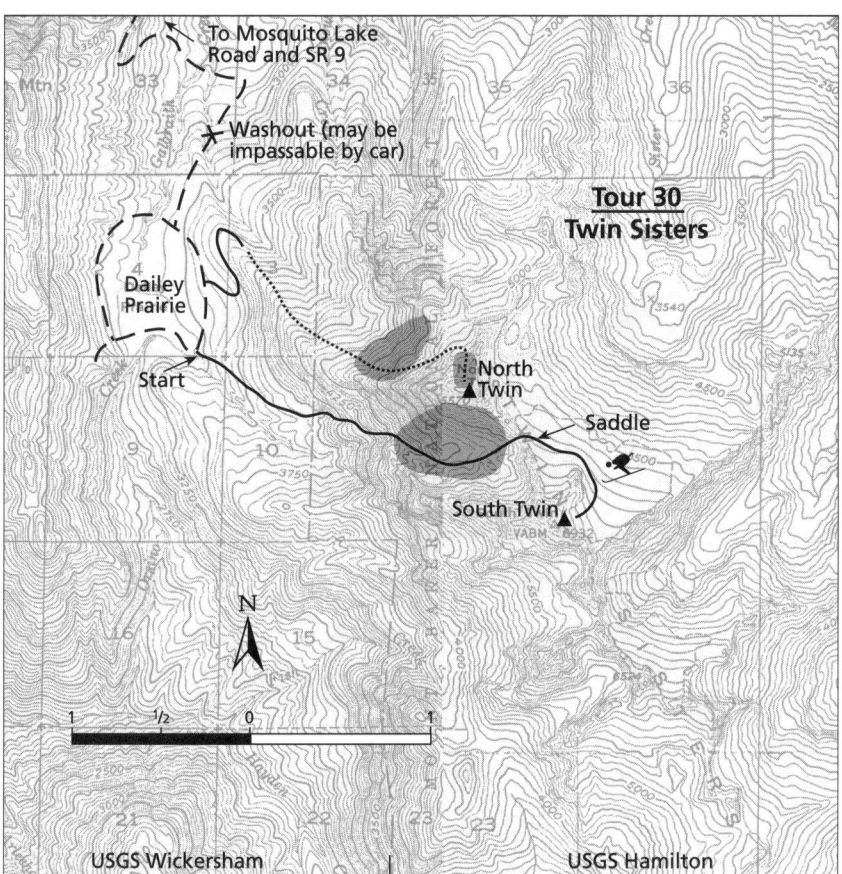

approach the hamlet of Acme, the Twin Sisters Range can be seen to the east. Drive through Acme. Just past the Nooksack River Bridge, turn right on Mosquito Lake Road. Drive 4.1 miles through alternating forest and clear-cuts, then turn right onto a gravel logging road guarded by a substantial gate. Continue through the gate. (If the gate is closed, park your car and continue on bicycle.) Follow the road for 1.7 miles to a junction at Musto Marsh (a "swamp," really). Take the left fork and drive it for 7.1 miles to the northern end of Dailey Prairie, a swamp just east of Bowman Mountain. Keep right at 0.5 mile and left at 6.3 miles. From there drive either left or right around Dailey Prairie to get to its southeastern side (1.5 miles). Then look for a spur road heading southeast (48.43.244/122.01.930). Road conditions may force you to walk from Dailey Prairie.

Climb this road southeast for 0.4 mile and take the left fork. Continue southeast for another 0.6 mile to 3,640 feet. The road remnant makes a left turn here. Leave the road and climb the steep headwall heading due east along

East side of Twin Sisters (Photo by Rainer Burgdorfer)

the stream. In 0.8 mile, you'll be well in the valley between the Twins (4,900 feet). Climb directly to the col.

Numerous descents are possible to the east. The direct line to the east is obvious. Less obvious but more glorious are the northeastern and eastern lobes of the Twin Sisters Glacier. From the saddle, traverse to the right, around the graceful northern ridge of South Twin and explore this complex, if diminutive range. (Note that the Sisters glacier is crevassed and that there are cliff bands near 4,500 feet.) Return to the car by retracing your approach.

Alternative Route: A spectacular route climbs the west ridge of North Sister (exposed class 2), then drops into the steep north bowls of North Twin Sister. Take a spur road slightly north of those previously mentioned for an easier approach and return. This descent is visible from Mosquito Lake Road north of Twin Sisters.

MOUNTAIN LOOP HIGHWAY AND STATE ROUTE 530

The tours in this region carry with them a wild flavor. The western tours are wild despite their popularity because of their gloomy and precipitous approaches, and the eastern tours seem so because of their remoteness.

The primary rivers in this area are the Sauk, the Suiattle, and the White Chuck. Most roads follow these drainages, enabling mountain travelers to reach areas ranging from Mount Pilchuck in the west to Dome Peak in the east. The tours in this area are good in early or late season. Midwinter access is usually difficult, except to Whitehorse Mountain.

Useful information can sometimes be obtained from the USFS ranger stations on Darrington-Rockport Road and the Mountain Loop Highway at Verlot.

Glacier Peak

Start Point:	White Chuck River Trailhead, 2,300 feet
High Point:	Glacier Peak, 10,541 feet
Best Time:	May to June
Overnight:	24 miles
Skiing Time:	16 hours
Skill Level:	Advanced
Difficulties:	High avalanche potential; glacier travel; permit/fee area
Maps:	Green Trails No. 111, Sloan Peak; No. 112, Glacier Peak

A spring ski ascent of Glacier Peak, although properly in a wilderness area, can hardly be thought of as a "wilderness experience." The number of people entering this area increases every year. One recent Fourth of July saw over 50 skiers and climbers on the summit of the volcano. Such crowds may make it difficult to find campsites in Boulder Basin. Come early, or avoid high-use periods such as weekends and holidays. Be sure to bring a rope, ice axes, and crampons.

Drive State Route 530 to Darrington. Head south from Darrington on the Mountain Loop Highway (Forest Road 20) for 9.5 miles. Cross the Sauk River,

Glacier Peak, as seen from Johnson Ridge (Photo by Rainer Burgdorfer)

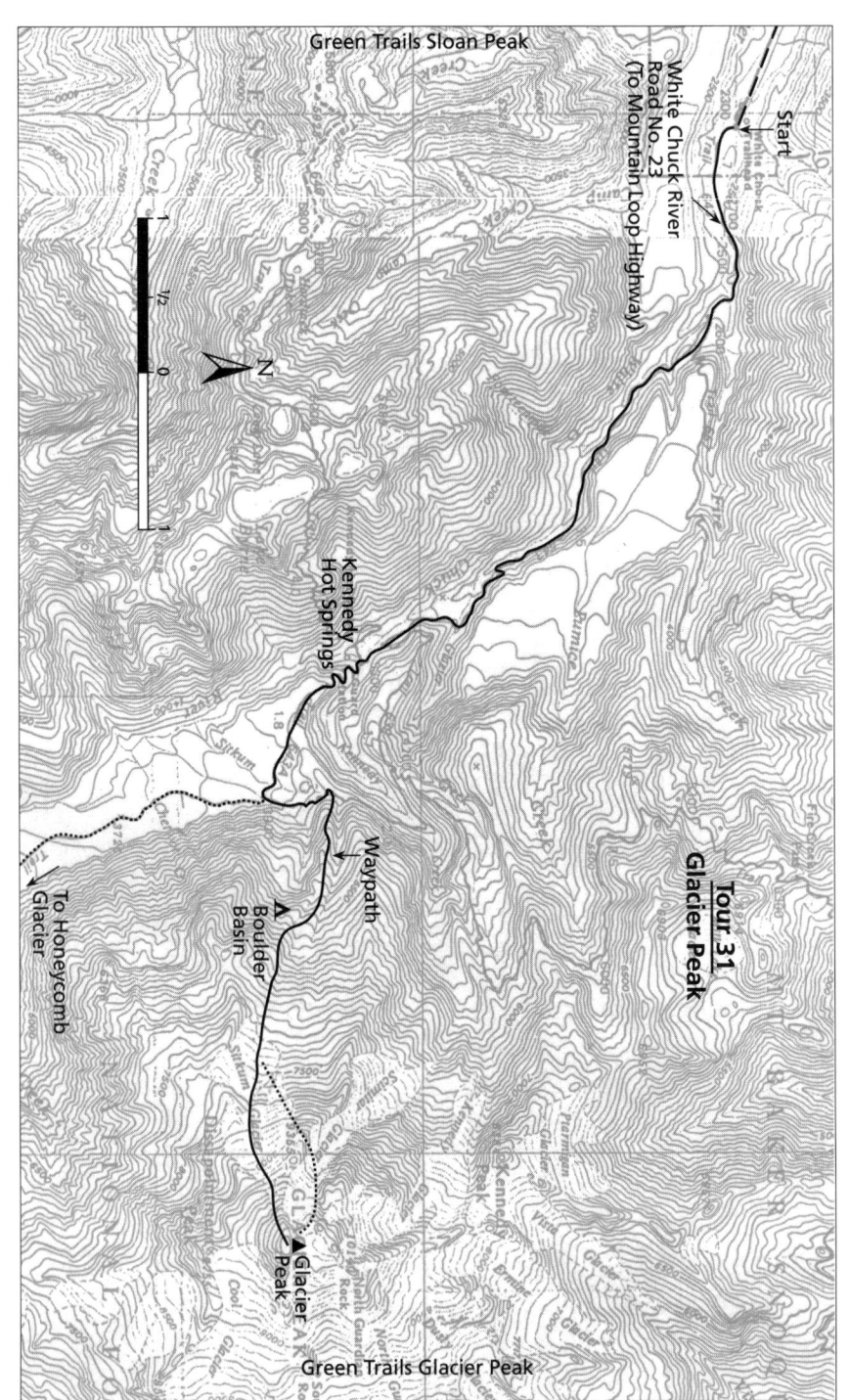

Green Trails Sloan Peak

White Chuck River
Road No. 23
(To Mountain Loop Highway)

Start

Tour 31
Glacier Peak

Kennedy
Hot Springs

Waypath

Boulder
Basin

To Honeycomb
Glacier

Glacier
Peak

N

Green Trails Glacier Peak

turn left on White Chuck River Road No. 23, and drive 10.5 miles to the end of the road. Park here.

Hike the undulating White Chuck River Trail past Kennedy Hot Springs (5.3 miles, 3,300 feet) to its junction with the Pacific Crest Trail 2,000 (7.1 miles, 3,900 feet, 48.07.173/121.11.548). Turn left at the junction and follow the trail north for 0.5 mile. Look for a waypath descending from the steep hill on your right. Climb this for 2,000 feet.

The route follows this wooded ridge near its crest. In early season, the path may be obscured by snow. In that case, simply climb the ridge for 1.5 miles to timberline (5,600 feet). Head east until you clear the trees, then turn south to gain Boulder Basin. This is a good place to camp.

Continue to climb southeast toward the crest above the basin, keeping right of the headwall above and to your left (north). It is possible to climb the Sitkum Glacier directly to the summit. An interesting variation involves crossing north to the Scimitar Glacier via a small saddle at 9,300 feet, then heading directly to the summit, gaining it from the north.

To descend, ski the southwest headwall, then drop west to the Sitkum Glacier to rejoin your ascent route at Boulder Basin.

One of the highlights of this tour is the opportunity to soak in Kennedy Hot Springs on the way out. Please don't use soap in the hot springs or near the river.

32
Johnson Ridge

Start Point: Sloan Creek Road (Johnson Ridge Road), 3,040 feet
High Point: Johnson Mountain, 6,721 feet
Best Time: May to June
Length: 11 miles
Skiing Time: 8 hours
Skill Level: Intermediate
Difficulties: High avalanche potential; not recommended for snowboarders; permit/fee area
Maps: USGS Glacier Peak West, Benchmark Mtn., 1:24,000

Johnson Ridge is an undulating steep-sided ridge that culminates in 6,700-foot Johnson Mountain. A trip up the ridge rewards the climber with panoramic views of the North-Central Cascades. It is not necessary to reach Johnson Mountain to benefit from this tour—travel as far as you like, take a few runs, then ride the roller coaster back to the jump-off point.

From the south, drive the Mountain Loop Highway east from Granite Falls to Barlow Pass. Turn left (north) and drive 7.2 miles to just past Bedal Campground, where there is a logging road (Road 49) on the right. Take this up the

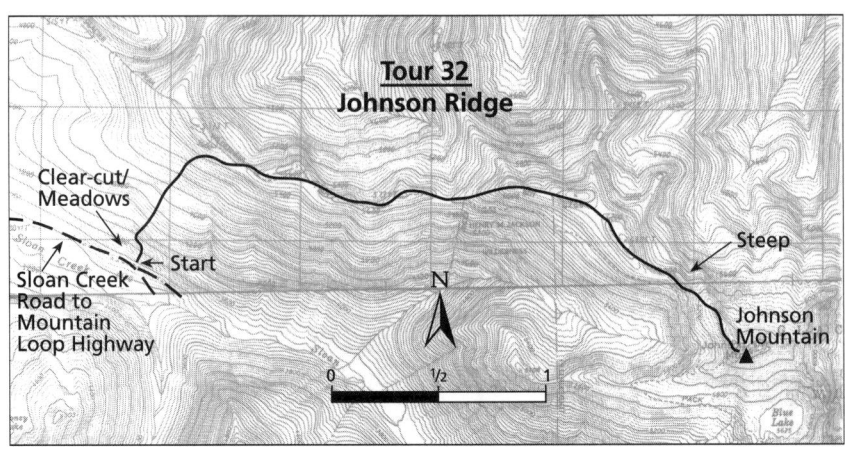

north fork of the Sauk River for 6.8 miles to the turnoff for Sloan Creek camp-ground. Keep right and drive for 2.4 miles along Sloan Creek. At the fork, keep left and drive to road's end (approximately 2.6 miles).

From the car, climb a steep hill northeast through clear-cuts, then mead-ows, to its crest (1 mile, 1,700 feet). At the crest the views improve markedly. Climb the ridge to your southeast, navigating around cornices and over hummocks and peaks for 3.8 miles to Point 6265. From here, continue south-east for 1.3 miles and climb the summit dome of Johnson Mountain. Runs tend to be short on Johnson Ridge because of its steep flanks. Nevertheless, there are numerous short-run possibilities. The big prize is the ridge-run back.

Keep your eyes open for the herds of mountain goats that live here.

Three friends on Johnson Ridge (Photo by Rainer Burgdorfer)

33
Vesper Peak

Start Point: Vesper Creek Trail, 2,300 feet (Sunshine Mine Road end)
High Point: Vesper Peak Summit, 6,214 feet
Best Time: April to June
Day Trip: 7 miles
Skiing Time: 8 hours
Skill Level: Alpine
Difficulties: High avalanche potential; glacier travel (optional); permit/fee area
Maps: USGS Silverton, Bedal, 1:24,000

Seen from Seattle, Vesper Peak is the broad pyramid at the front of the range, just north of Glacier Peak. The southern slopes may be seen from US 2 south of Monroe. This tour has an engaging "up and over" approach that is augmented by a speedy return to the trailhead, snowpack permitting.

From Granite Falls, drive east on Mountain Loop Highway. Follow the road for 29.6 miles and turn right on Sunrise Mine Road, No. 4065. Drive 2.3

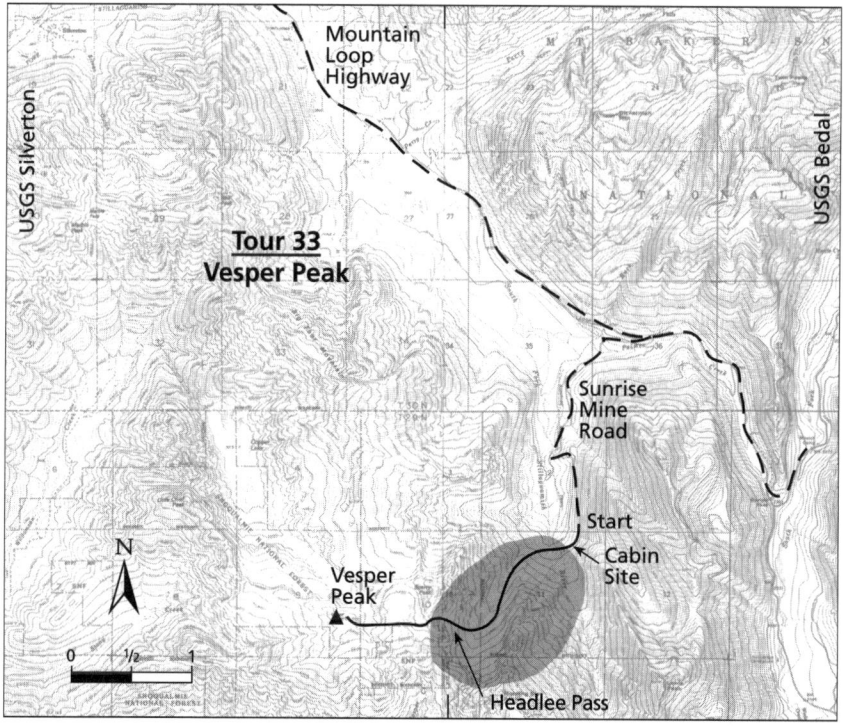

miles to the end of the road. Trail No. 707 heads south from here.

Reach the remains of Manleys Cabin in 0.4 mile, then cross a small but swift branch of the Stillaguamish River and start climbing southwest. Switchbacks start near 2,800 feet and climb to 3,200 feet, where you round the toe of the north ridge of Morning Star Peak. Drop west into Wirtz Basin and climb southwest, keeping to its east side. Headlee Pass is gained near 4,600 feet (1.6 miles from Cabin site) at the western side of the valley. An ice ax is handy here.

Ski west for 0.3 mile to a level snow patch, and continue west for 0.7 mile up an easy ramp to gain the summit. From the summit you can ski west- to south-facing slopes. If bergschrunds, cornices, or crevasses don't prohibit entry to the glaciers lying to the northwest and north of Vesper Peak, the saddle north of the lake is a possible entry route to a fine, steep run to Copper Lake.

Return via the approach.

34
Green Mountain

Start Point: Green Mountain Trailhead, 3,500 feet
High Point: Green Mountain, 6,500 feet
Best Time: November–December, May–June
Day Trip: 8 miles
Skiing Time: 7 hours
Skill Level: Advanced
Difficulties: High avalanche potential; permit/fee area
Maps: USGS Huckleberry Mtn., Downey Mtn., 1:24,000

This tour brings the skier to perfect early season skiing terrain: large, smooth, open heather and grass slopes that require only a few feet of snow for adequate cover. On the negative side, this terrain provides little anchoring power for the snowpack; avalanche potential is high. From Green Mountain, the views of the Buckindy Massif, Glacier and Dome Peaks, and Mount Formidable are stunning. The trick to this tour is to do it when there is enough snow to ski, but not so much that the road is blocked. If you don't ski Green Mountain, at least hike it in summer.

Drive State Route 530 north for 7.2 miles from the Darrington Ranger Station, or drive State Route 530 south from Rockport for 11.2 miles. Turn east on Suiattle River Road 26. Drive 19.4 miles to Green Mountain Road No. 2680, and turn left. Drive the road to its end (5.6 miles) or as far as possible. (If the road is blocked, park your car and hike or ski to the trailhead.)

The trail starts on the uphill side of the road, a short distance from the road end. Follow the trail climbing steeply north. If it's snow-covered, the safest route is to climb right (north) toward an open shoulder. Climb this to 5,300 feet, then traverse to a small basin southwest of Green Mountain. From here, it

Descending Vesper Peak (Photo by Rainer Burgdorfer)

is 1.0 mile to the summit, which lies just north-northeast of you. Approach the mountain directly, moving to the southeastern rib when it becomes convenient (near 6,000 feet). Climb the rib to the summit.

Descents are possible on the eastern and southern slopes of Green Mountain. To go home, retrace your approach.

35
Dome Glacier

Start Point: Downey Creek Trailhead, 1,400 feet
High Point: Spire Col, 7,760 feet
Best Time: April to July
Overnight: (3 to 5 days), 36 miles
Skiing Time: 24 hours
Skill Level: Alpine
Difficulties: High avalanche potential; glacier travel; routefinding required; permit/fee area
Maps: Green Trails No. 80, Cascade Pass; USGS 7.5 minute series, Dome Peak and Downey Mountain

Rarely seen Dome Peak is the monarch of the Cascade Crest north of Glacier Peak. The Dana and the Dome, two large glaciers north and west of the peak,

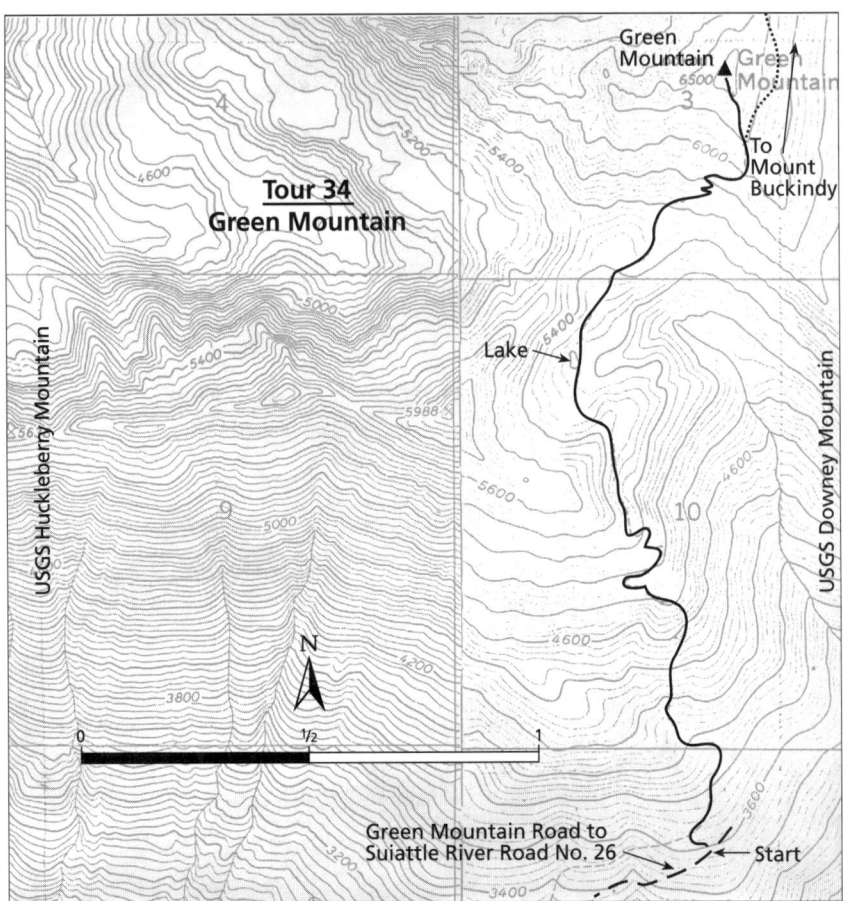

Tour 34
Green Mountain

Green Mountain Road to
Suiattle River Road No. 26 ← Start

offer excellent spring skiing amid spectacular scenery. The glaciers are crevassed, but easily negotiable. The approach to Dome Peak is long—18 miles to the glacier—but its variety alleviates some of the misery of the hike and, in early season, snow cover makes for rapid downhill travel. Downey Creek Trail had 100 tree blowdowns across it in June 1998.

Drive Suiattle River Road to Downey Creek campground (20.5 miles from the Sauk River bridge, 1,400 feet). The trail heads north from the campground along the east side of Downey Creek. This trail climbs a deep glacial trough, which heads in several large cirques. These cirques frequently release avalanches that reach all the way across the bottom of the valley.

The trail gains elevation rapidly, then levels out for the last 5 miles to Sixmile Camp. To get to camp, use foot logs to cross Bachelor Creek. Sixmile Camp is a good spot to prepare for the morning hike.

East of Sixmile Camp is a waterfall stream, Bachelor Creek. The trail ascends

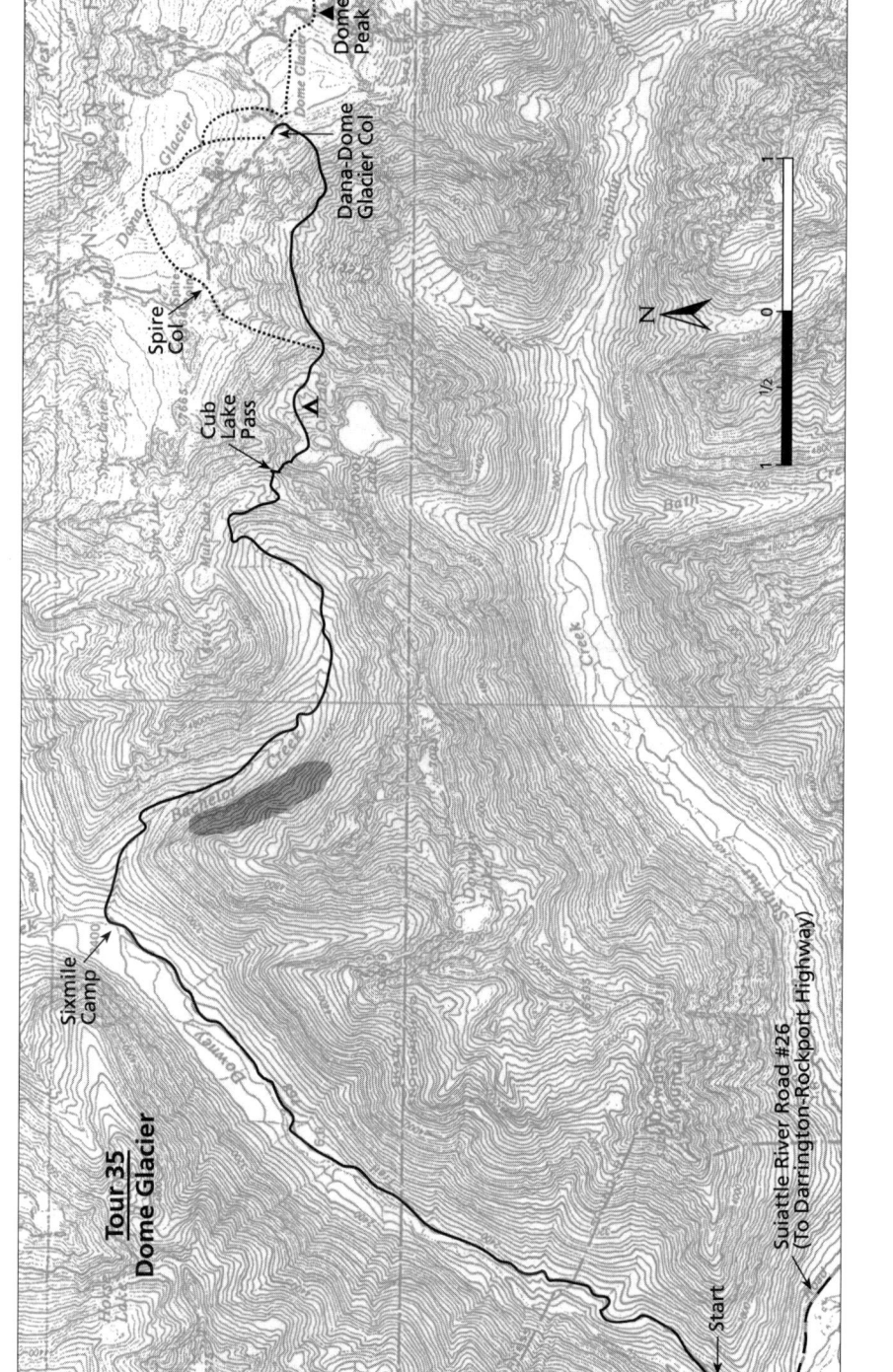

Tour 35
Dome Glacier

this drainage, keeping generally north of the stream. Hike this trail for 7 miles, crossing a 6,000-foot pass and dropping 700 feet to reach Cub Lake.

Itswoot Lake lies 500 feet lower and 0.2 mile south of Cub Lake. Descend to Cub Lake, traverse east to a bench just below Itswoot Ridge and camp. Itswoot is the rib descending southeast from Spire Point.

Climb to a saddle (6,200 feet) on this rib. From here, your view encompasses Spire Point to the north and Dome Glacier and Dome Peak to the east. To ski the western lobe of the Dana Glacier, climb the left (west) side of Itswoot Ridge to Spire Col (1 mile, 7,760 feet, 48.18.925/121.03.991). Some sections are steep—an ice ax is recommended. From the col, simply cross over to the Dana Glacier. Ski the glacier, heading northeast. The terrain is moderately steep and only lightly crevassed. When the skiing becomes hazardous below, retrace your path, or, if glacier conditions permit, head east near 6,500 feet to reach the eastern lobe of the Dana Glacier. Once you're there, climb south to Dana-Dome Glacier Col (0.8 mile, 7,520 feet, 48.18.541/121.02.699). From the col, head east to make one run on the Dome Glacier, then descend back to Itswoot Ridge and camp.

To return to the car, simply retrace the approach.

Alternative Route: Downey Creek is also the exit for the Ptarmigan Traverse, a high route starting at Cascade Pass. In good conditions, this advanced tour can be done in 4 days. It involves routefinding, steep glacier skiing, exquisite scenery, and high avalanche potential.

Whitehorse Mountain
36

Start Point: Whitehorse Trail No. 653
High Point: Whitehorse Mountain, 6,852 feet
Best Time: February to May
Day Trip: 7 miles
Skiing Time: 10 hours
Skill Level: Alpine
Difficulties: Glacier travel; routefinding required; high avalanche potential; permit/fee area
Maps: USGS Whitehorse Mtn., 1:24,000

Whitehorse Mountain is one of the most spectacular outposts of the Cascade Range. This tour is unique because a good portion of it, the climb to and descent from High Pass, is visible from Interstate 5 near Lynnwood. The summit portion is, of course, visible from the Darrington Highway. For this tour, a reasonable snowpack down to 3,000 feet is necessary. You will need ice axes, crampons, and a rope.

Looking down the summit of Whitehorse over a snow arête (Photo by Rainer Burgdorfer)

Drive State Route 530 towards Darrington. Turn right (south) at the Whitehorse Store, 5 miles west of Darrington and drive 1.9 miles to Whitehorse Trail No. 653 (918 feet). The end of the road, and the beginning of the trail to the northern wall of Whitehorse, lie 0.7 mile southeast.

The trail climbs due south, switchbacking through forest for 1.2 miles (2,500 feet). The trail then turns west and continues to climb steeply, emerging from timber near 3,200 feet. Near 3,400 feet, climb left (southeast) around a buttress to an avalanche runout near 3,800 feet. Climb directly up this avalanche deposition area for a few hundred feet, weaving around several gullies, then traverse

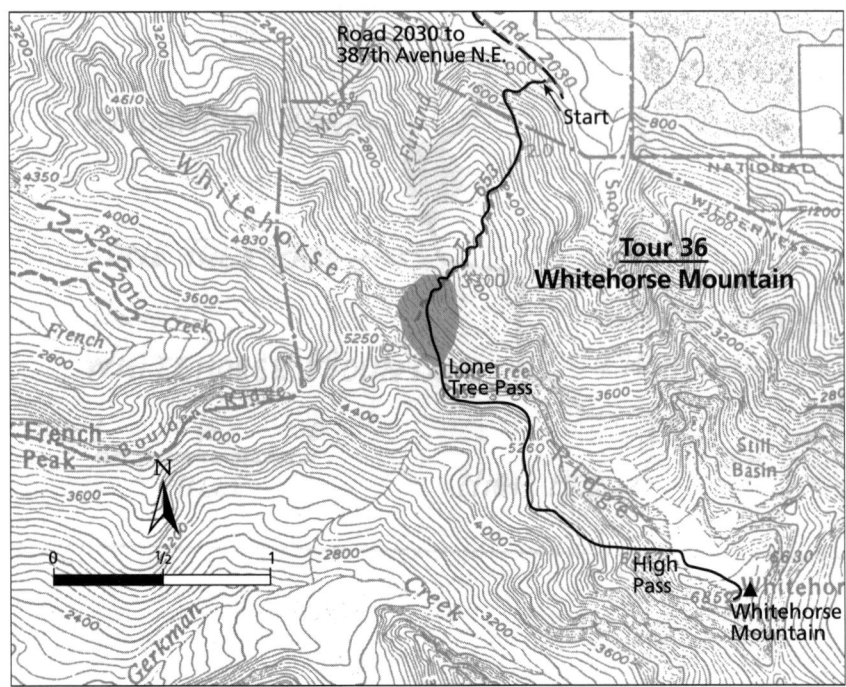

southeast toward Lone Tree Pass (4,800 feet). Pick a safe way through the cornices at the pass and cross to the southern side of Whitehorse Ridge. Head east for 0.5 mile, climbing through forest along the way. A large rock tower seemingly blocks progress. Descend a gully for 400 feet to reach the base of these ramparts. Make a climbing traverse to the southeast, turning a corner through a steep patch of timber. (Now you know why you brought the ice ax.) On leaving the trees, descend a few feet to a bench near 4,600 feet that runs southeast, parallel to the ridge above. Watch for falling ice from cliffs above the gully. Follow this bench for 0.3 mile until you come to a steep snow gully. Climb the gully directly to High Pass (6,000 feet).

High Pass is the entrance to the So-Bahli-Ali Glacier. Ski through a wind-sculpted corridor, then make a southeast climbing traverse to approach the summit. Keep well to the east to avoid several steep wind rolls on the glacier. You can ski to within 100 feet of the summit. The final section is steep and exposed; it requires an ice ax and possibly crampons. (Now you'll learn why you brought the rope.)

As your head pops over the summit, the view of Three Fingers will make the approach seem worthwhile. The ski descent is the icing on the cake. Ski the fall line to 6,000 feet, then traverse back to High Pass. (Be sure not to descend too far in the woods below High Pass and Lone Tree Pass or you'll miss your trail.)

Alternative Route: The So-Bahli-Ali Glacier is sometimes climbed and skied in midwinter; however, the glacier and its surrounding snowfields are active creepers, and the last leg of the tour requires a steep and brushy traverse above Snow Gulch. The glacier should be climbed only under well-consolidated conditions, and it is necessary to return to the car before dusk.

37
Three Fingers

Start Point: Canyon Creek Road, 3,000 feet
High Point: Saddle between South and Middle Finger, 6,130 feet
Best Time: April to June
Day Trip/Overnight: 13 miles
Skiing Time: 10 hours
Skill Level: Advanced, Alpine beyond Goat Flat
Difficulties: Glacier travel; high avalanche potential; routefinding required; permit/fee area
Maps: USGS Meadow Mtn., Whitehorse Mtn., 1:24,000

Three Fingers and its companion, Whitehorse, are an unmistakable sight to the east from the flatlands near Everett. The gleaming Queest Alb Glacier leads

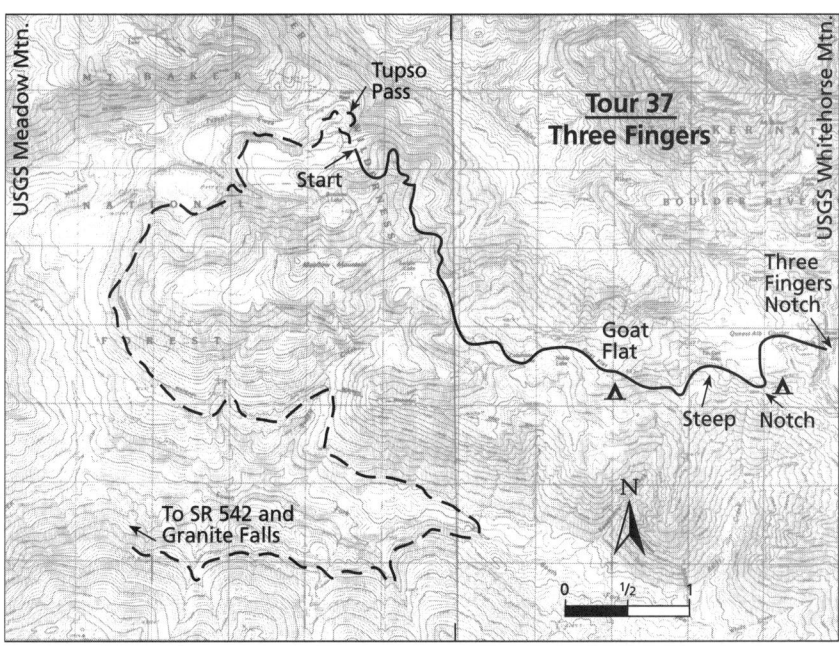

From the summit of Whitehorse, looking toward Three Fingers (Photo by Rainer Burgdorfer)

to the saddle between South and Middle Finger, the high point of this tour. This tour is more suited to skiers than to snowboarders. It is best done when the road has just melted out (unless you have a snowmobile).

Drive the Mountain Loop Highway for 7.5 miles east from Granite Falls. Turn left onto Canyon Creek Road and drive for 1 mile. Stay right at the fork and drive to the next fork (1.7 miles) and keep left. At the 6-mile fork, take the left branch and drive to the 7.8-mile fork. Take the left road, driving to the 13.2-mile branch and turn right. The trailhead lies 17.4 miles up the road (48.11.620/121.46.215) (3,000 feet).

The trail heads southeast from the road for 0.3 mile. Then it veers left to climb a steep rib, making an end run in 0.4 mile (3,400 feet). Once around the rib, the trail trends south, switchbacking as necessary and arriving at Saddle Lake (3,780 feet) in 1.3 miles. From Saddle Lake, continue south-southeast for 0.6 mile, arriving at a fairly level area near 4,100 feet. Head east, climbing to Goat Flat (4,950 feet) in 1.2 miles. This terrain is open and fairly gentle.

The summer trail heads east from Goat Flat and makes a climbing traverse on the steep southern flank of the ridge just east of the flat to top out at Camp Pass (1.5 miles, 5,900 feet). Tin Can Gap (5,750 feet) lies 0.2 mile to the west (no trail). In winter conditions it may be simpler to follow the ridge crest and then drop into Tin Can Gap, or into another pass just west of Tin Can.

Cross the gap, then descend 400 feet down-glacier in an easterly traverse. Once past the west ridge of the South Finger, climb directly up the Queest Alb Glacier to the high point of the tour, a saddle overshadowed by the Three Fingers. The longest ski descents on this tour take place on the two lobes of the glacier. Shorter, less challenging runs are possible on the ridges above Goat Flat. Mount Pilchuck looks spectacular from here.

Retrace your approach to go home.

Mount Pilchuck

Start Point: Mount Pilchuck State Park Road, 3,000 feet
High Point: Mount Pilchuck, 5,324 feet
Best Time: January to March
Day Trip: 4 miles
Skiing Time: 3 to 5 hours
Skill Level: Advanced
Difficulties: High avalanche potential; permit/fee area
Maps: Green Trails No. 109, Granite Falls

Mount Pilchuck is the western outpost of the Cascades between Mount Baker and Snoqualmie Pass. Its forested southwestern slopes and summit are clearly visible from Everett and, to a lesser degree, Seattle. This tour offers panoramic views of the western scarp of the Cascades and steep fall-line runs from the summit area to the road 2,200 feet below.

Drive State Route 92 east from Granite Falls. One mile past the Verlot ranger station, just over the Stillaguamish River bridge, turn right on Mount Pilchuck State Park Road No. 42. Drive until road's end (6.9 miles, 3,129 feet) or until road conditions force a halt.

Depending on where the driving stopped, either ski along the state park road (2 to 4 miles) or ski uphill (south or southwest) to the site of the former Mount Pilchuck ski area parking lot (3,200 feet). The trail heads south from the parking lot about 0.1 mile west of the end of the road; it switchbacks to the northwestern ridge of Mount Pilchuck near 4,600 feet.

Conservative skiers may now head southeast to slopes topping out at 5,000 feet below the summit crags. Avoid lingering beneath the huge cornices that lurk there—instead, ski north-northwest in the fall line to return to the car. More adventurous souls can follow the trail to the summit. Cross to the southwestern shoulder near 4,600 feet and climb east, up steep alpine forest to the summit ridge. Stay well away from the corniced northern edge. Southeast summit gullies offer another descent alternative.

To descend, climb back down to the meadows on the north side, and then ski north-northwest back to the parking lot.

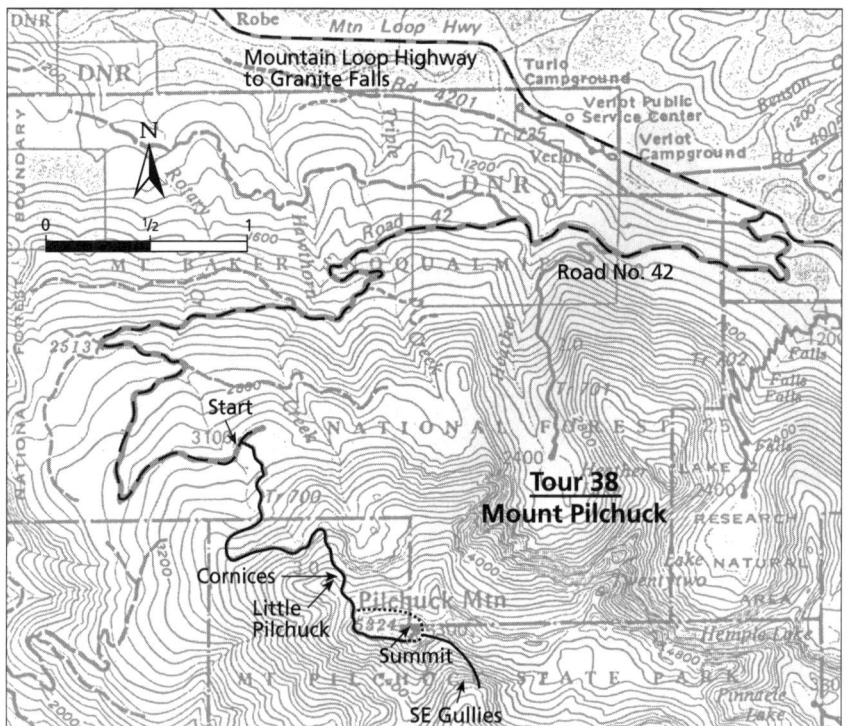

Alternative Route: In deep-snowpack conditions, it is possible to descend directly from the parking lot to rejoin the Park road near 2,200 feet. This route often requires some bushwhacking.

STEVENS PASS HIGHWAY, US 2

The Stevens Pass Highway provides a fast approach to year-round skiing in the North-Central Cascades. Most of the tours in this area are concentrated east of the Cascade Crest, where the weather tends to be slightly drier than it is to the west. Primary roads in this area are open in all seasons, and tours that lead from them are accessible year-round. Those tours reached via secondary or back roads may be accessible only in early or late season. Included in this section are tours in adjacent subranges, namely the Chiwaukum, Entiat, and Stuart ranges, all of which can be conveniently reached from US 2 or US 97.

This area is of great interest to skiers, topographically speaking. Slopes tend to be slightly gentler than those to the north, and elevations tend to be

Southeast gully on Mount Pilchuck (Photo by William C. Shigley)

higher than those to the south. The result is snow and terrain that are well suited to backcountry skiing.

Big Snow Mountain

Start Point: Lake Dorothy Trailhead, 2,280 feet or North Fork Snoqualmie River Road, 2,926 feet
High Point: Big Snow Summit, 6,680 feet
Best Time: March to June
Day Trip: 15 miles (Lake Dorothy approach); 7 miles (Taylor River approach)
Skiing Time: 14 hours
Skill Level: Advanced
Difficulties: High avalanche potential; routefinding required; permit/fee area
Maps: USGS Snoqualmie Lake, Big Snow Mtn., 1:24,000

Big Snow Mountain lies just north of the Middle Fork of the Snoqualmie River. Its domed summit provides large-scale ski descents well into June, while its central position provides a spectacular vantage for viewing the North-Central Cascades. There are two approaches: from the north and from the south. The northern approach, described here, is longer, but provides a better ski tour than the southern route. The southern approach may require fords and serious bush-whacking, or a mountain bike, depending on the condition of Middle Fork Road.

Drive US 2 east from Monroe for 31 miles. Turn right at Money Creek Campground and drive Old Cascade Road for 1 mile. At the junction turn right onto Miller River Road No. 6410. Drive this road for 3.6 miles to West Fork Campground. Take the left fork and drive 2.4 miles up the East Fork Drainage to a junction. Take the right branch and drive 3.2 miles to road's end at the Lake Dorothy Trailhead. This trail is very popular in the spring, so come early to ensure a parking spot.

The trail switchbacks east for the first 0.2 mile, then heads south-southeast for 0.6 mile where it crosses Camp Robber Creek. Lake Dorothy lies 0.4 mile southwest of the creek crossing. Pass the lake by a trail on its eastern shore (1.8 miles), then climb Camp Robber Creek drainage on the southeastern head of the lake for 1.2 miles to 3,600 feet. Continue southeast for 1 mile, entering a steep-sided canyon. Near 4,200 feet, climb due west along a stream sluicing from Gold Lake. Climb to the lake and to the stream that enters on its southern shore (4,838 feet, 0.7 mile).

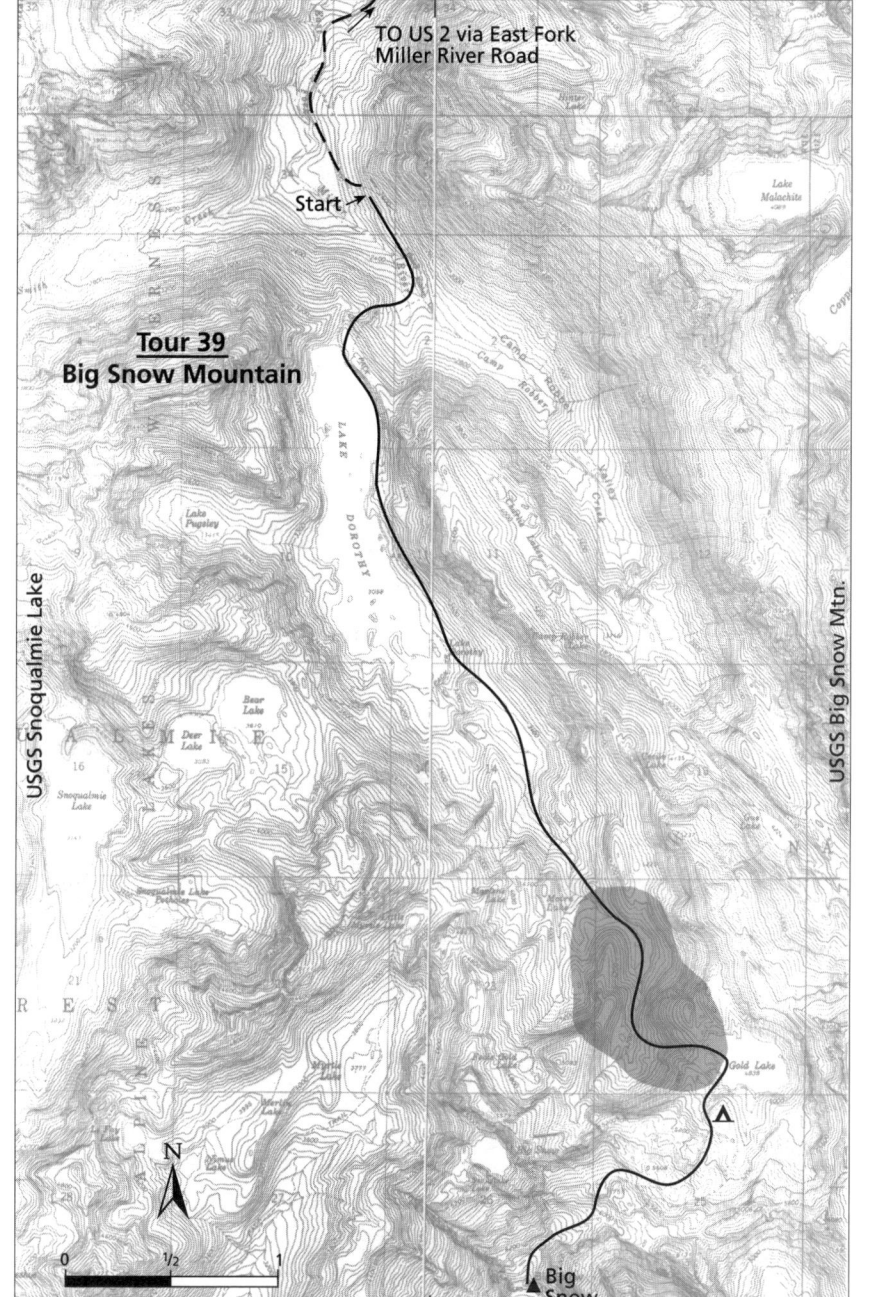

TO US 2 via East Fork
Miller River Road

Start

**Tour 39
Big Snow Mountain**

USGS Snoqualmie Lake

USGS Big Snow Mtn.

N

0   ½   1

Big
Snow

From the lake, climb southwest to the summit area of Big Snow Mountain. Short runs are possible on the northern and southern shoulders, but the longest runs are found on the northeastern shoulder toward Gold Lake.

Cowboy Mountain

Start Point: Top of Seventh Heaven Chair
High Point: Cowboy Mountain, 5,700 feet
Best Time: December to April
Day Trip: 1.5 miles
Skiing Time: 1 hour to ski area
Skill Level: Intermediate
Difficulties: Moderate avalanche potential; chair ride to top
Maps: USGS Stevens Pass, 1:24,000

This tour is accessible for snowboarders and anybody with alpine ski equipment: simply ride the lifts to the top of the Seventh Heaven chair, and ski the "backside" of Cowboy Mountain. While navigation is not a problem on this tour, avalanche potential is—parties must be equipped to effect self-rescue. Check at the Stevens Pass avalanche control center for snow and avalanche conditions, and follow their recommendations. This tour is only worthwhile with a good snowpack. Extremely dense timber, exposed stumps and brush can make the route a horror show in low-snowpack years.

From the top of the Seventh Heaven chair lift, make a climbing traverse southwest around the right side of the summit of Cowboy Mountain (0.3 mile).

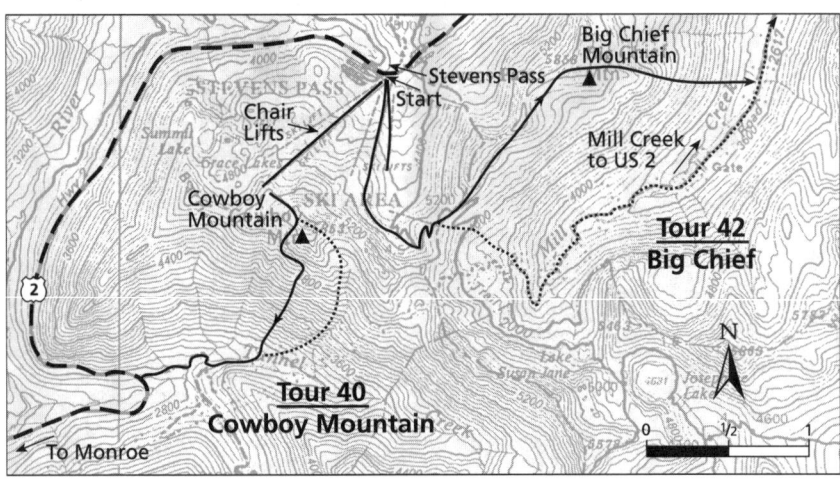

Back side of Cowboy Mountain (Photo by Brian Povolny)

Just past the summit, ski due south for 0.1 mile and 400 vertical feet, then head slightly east and down to a drainage. Avoid several small cliffs and deep ravines in this section. Follow the stream south, staying out of gully bottoms, then head west to the highway (hairpin turn) to meet your ride back to the pass.

Snowboarders should bring along small snowshoes or skis in addition to their regular backcountry kit.

41
Heather Ridge (Skyline Ridge)

Start Point: Stevens Pass Summit Parking Lot, 4,060 feet
High Point: Heather Ridge, 5,400 feet
Best Time: November to March
Day Trip: 3+ miles
Skiing Time: 4 hours or more, depending on your inclination
Skill Level: Intermediate
Difficulties: Moderate avalanche potential; parking (get an early start)
Maps: USGS Labyrinth Mtn., Stevens Pass, 1:24,000

Heather Ridge is the mountain directly across US 2 from the Stevens Pass ski area. It is unmarked on Green Trails maps. Heather Ridge is sometimes called

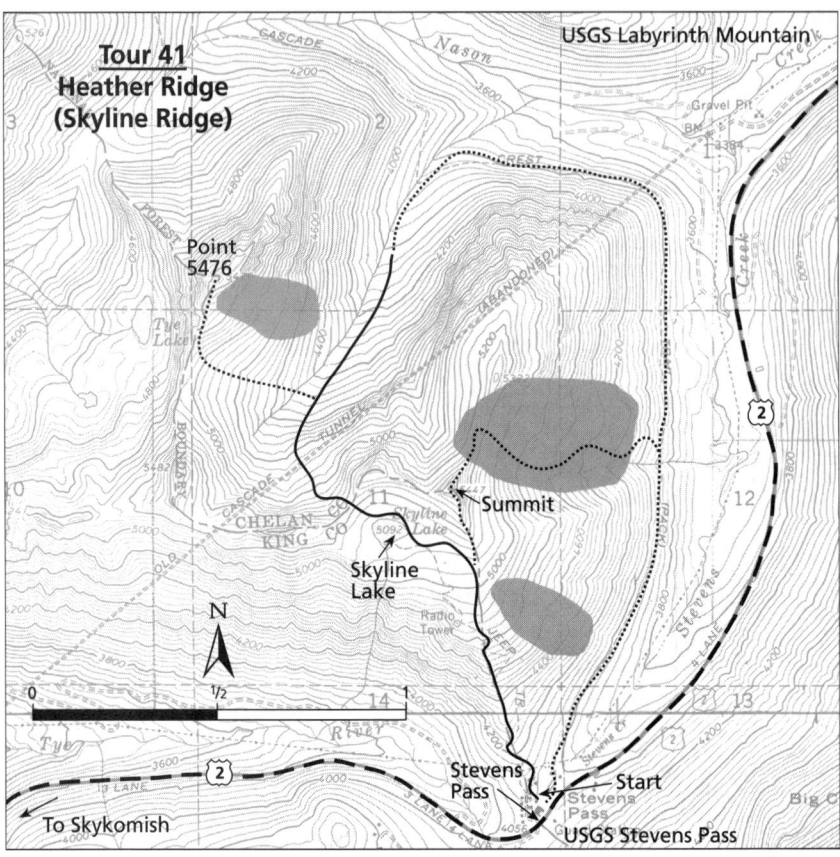

Skyline Ridge, perhaps after Skyline Lake, a small body of water near the summit. This short tour is a pleasant alternative to riding the lifts at the Stevens Pass ski area. Ski runs range in difficulty from intermediate to advanced, with slopes facing every point of the compass. This tour offers at least three possibilities, each with a distinct character.

The tour departs from the parking lot north of US 2 at Stevens Pass. Start climbing behind and to the left of the electric substation at the northeastern corner of the parking lot. The trail (actually a maintenance road) winds up the hill, heading north until it breaks out into clearings. From here, you have three options.

To ski the eastern flank of the northern branch of Heather Ridge (a good route when snow deposits are high and wind velocity is low), climb directly north until you've gained the crest, then continue north until you find the glade of your choosing. Then ski, climb, and ski for effect. Descend to an old railroad grade (you'll encounter some brush along the way), and hike back to the parking lot.

To ski the powder bowls north of Skyline Lake, continue to the top of the ridge, then head west to Skyline Lake (1.5 miles, 5,092 feet). Continue northwest from the lake to the crest. Find your way through cliff bands (steep at the top), drop into the bowls, and enjoy up to 1,000 vertical feet of skiing through gladed old-growth forest. The slopes immediately around Skyline Lake offer good intermediate skiing.

The third option is to ski the bowls north of Heather Ridge, then climb basins farther north, exploring connecting valleys and ridges until the sun tells you to go home.

From your ultimate point, either ski out Nason Creek, or regain Heather Ridge and descend to the parking lot.

Southeast slope (Moonlight Bowl) on Heather Ridge (Photo by Donal O'Sullivan)

Big Chief Mountain

Start Point: Stevens Pass Summit Parking Lot, 4,060 feet
High Point: Big Chief Mountain, 5,858 feet
Best Time: November to April
Day Trip: 7 miles
Skiing Time: 6 hours
Skill Level: Advanced
Difficulties: High avalanche potential; snowboarders need snowshoes
Maps: USGS Labyrinth Mtn., Stevens Pass, 1:24,000

Big Chief Mountain is the high point of the ridge radiating northeast from Tyee–Mill Creek saddle at Stevens Pass ski area. A brief passage through the ski area elevates the backcountry skier above the din onto open slopes and gladed forest to brief solitude and lofty views of Jim Hill Mountain.

From the south side of the Stevens Pass parking lot, either climb just left of the Big Chief chair lift, then continue east and battle your way to the ridge crest, or ski east for 0.6 mile, then climb southeast to the ridge crest (0.4 mile,

Big Chief Mountain (Photo by Rainer Burgdorfer)

5,600 feet). (The latter route is slightly less steep than the former.)

Alternatives include riding the Big Chief–Double Diamond chair lifts to the ridge, or climbing alongside the ski runs to the Tyee–Mill Creek saddle, then continuing northeast along the ridge crest to Big Chief summit (2.6 miles). This last route is easiest, but requires the climber to avoid downhill ski traffic, especially along the ridge above Tyee–Mill Creek saddle.

Once on the ridge crest, continue northeast to the summit, or stop at some convenient place along the way. Descents are possible directly to the east and north from the summit. If you choose the eastern descent, ski down for 800 feet, then head north for 0.1 mile in a gradual descent, and finally ski the fall line to the brush and creek crossing below (0.9 mile). The Stevens Pass Nordic Center lies 2.7 miles down the well-groomed ski trail.

The northern descent route climbs over the summit and descends north for 0.8 mile along the ridge (4,800 feet), then follows the fall line, heading due east to 4,200 feet. The route jogs northeast for 0.2 mile to 3,800 feet before descending to the bottom of the valley through evergreen thickets and brush, and across a river to reach the groomed trail (1.8 miles to the Nordic Center). It is 6.2 miles from the Nordic Center to Stevens Pass ski area and your car.

Yodelin

Start Point: Stevens Pass Highway, 3,200 feet

High Point: Big Chief's north shoulder, 5,000 feet

Best Time: January to March

Day Trip: 4 miles

Skiing Time: 4 hours

Skill Level: Intermediate

Difficulties: Moderate avalanche potential

Maps: USGS Labyrinth Mtn., 1:24,000

Yodelin was once a residential development and ski area just east of Stevens Pass. The homes remain, and are located north of US 2, while the ski area, now defunct, lies just across the road. This short tour climbs the ridge just east of the former ski area and offers fine, short north-facing runs with little time commitment. It is basically an uphill road trip followed by downhill runs through old-growth forests and clear-cut areas; an aerobic, but not exhausting little tour. Despite the diminutive aspect of this tour, the usual avalanche precautions must be observed.

Drive US 2 east from Stevens Pass for 6.2 miles to the Nordic Center, take the U-turn route and head west about 2 miles, parking at Smith Brook Snowpark.

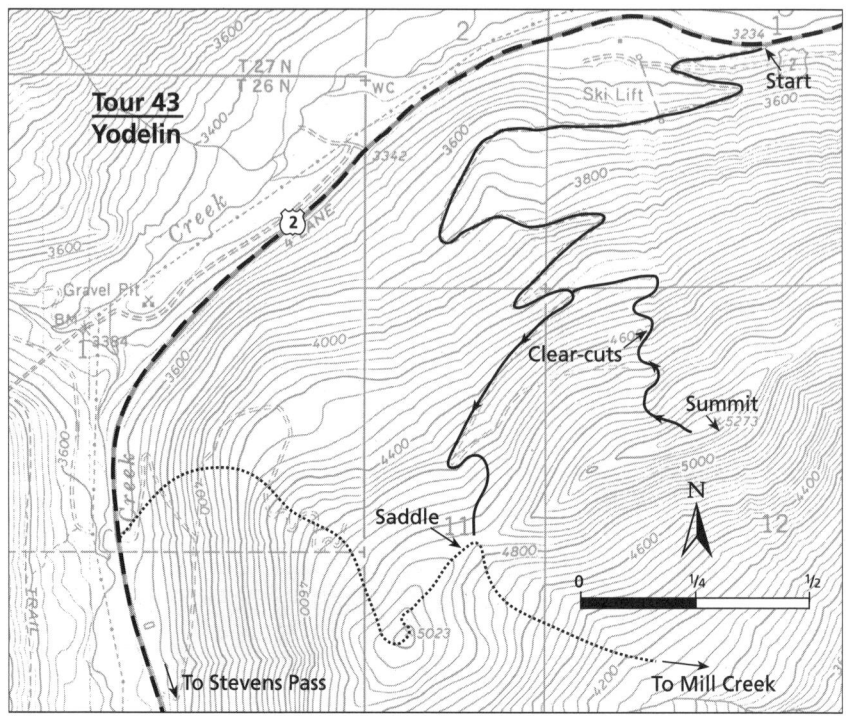

Walk or ski 0.5 mile west to an unplowed road on the south side of US 2. (Be careful.) Follow this road southwest, taking the first left fork available. Continue skiing the road past another switchback and through a large clear-cut area. Follow the road around another switchback, which leads east into a remnant of mature forest. Continue heading east for 0.5 mile to a junction.

Here you have a choice of routes. Those inclined toward gentler touring may follow a switchback to the right (west) through a clear-cut area, toward a broad saddle near 4,800 feet, and then along the ridge toward Big Chief summit, until steep slopes suggest a halt. The saddle near 4,800 feet lies due south of the trailhead and is the perfect place to start a direct descent to the car.

Alternative Route: For a more challenging circle tour, continue west from the saddle toward Big Chief, keeping near the ridge crest. In 0.6 mile, descend northwesterly through the abandoned Yodelin ski area toward US 2, and then return along the highway. (Another option is to drop into the Mill Creek Valley instead, and then ski out the trail to the Nordic Center.)

Steep and deep fall-line skiing lies on the north face of the eastern end of the Yodelin ridge. Head northeast-east from the broad saddle, skiing the ridge crest for 0.8 miles to 5,100 feet. From the crest, descend north through alternating bands of forest, blown-down trees, and clear-cut areas. Head northeast as you approach 3,600 feet, and ski the road back to your car. This diversion requires an ample snowpack.

Union Peak

Start Point: Stevens Pass Highway (Smith Brook Road, 3,100 feet)
High Point: Union Peak, 5,696 feet
Best Time: December to April
Day Trip: 11 miles
Skiing Time: 8 hours
Skill Level: Advanced
Difficulties: High avalanche potential; routefinding required; permit/fee area; snowmobile traffic near Rainy Pass
Maps: USGS Labyrinth Mtn., 1:24,000

Union and Jove Peaks lie less than 1 mile apart and can be combined into a single tour. However, each peak has unique characteristics and skiers may enjoy exploring them separately. This tour offers outstanding views and wonderfully complex runs in old-growth forests. Jove Peak offers astonishing, steep fall-line descents from a pointed summit down large avalanche paths.

Drive US 2 to the Smith Brook Road turnoff, 4.2 miles east of Stevens Pass Summit. Eastbound travelers must drive 4.8 miles past Smith Brook Road to the Mill Creek U-turn road, then drive west on US 2 to Smith Brook Road parking area. Park well off the highway in the plowed area 300 feet east of Smith Brook Road. Ski the snow-covered road, coming to clear-cuts and switchbacks in 1.8 miles. Ahead and to the north lie the open southern slopes of Union Peak.

Either ski the road, or head directly north uphill toward Rainy Pass (sometimes called Nason Saddle, 4,600 feet, 3.5 miles from US 2). A direct approach avoids snow sloughs falling from Union Peak and shortens this distance somewhat. Rainy Pass is the broad saddle between Nason Ridge and Union Peak. From the right side of the saddle, the gleaming south ramp of Jove Peak is visible to the northwest.

From Rainy Pass, climb directly uphill, heading northwest and keeping to the ridge crest. The route meanders along this airy ridge, reaching the summit of Union Peak in 1.5 miles. Note the small, moderately steep bowls southeast of the peak that feed the Rainy Creek drainage. Once over the summit, continue north for 0.5 mile to a saddle and descend north for 200 feet, then ski the fall line to Lake Janus. (It is possible to ski the fall line from the saddle to the lake, but this is a very steep line.)

The outlet of Lake Janus lies at its southwestern end. Descend past the outlet south-southwest into the Rapid River drainage for 1.0 mile (3,600 feet), then climb east to Union Gap (0.9 mile, 4,470 feet). Descend southeast to Smith Brook Road and ski out. If snowshoers and snowmobilers who came behind you were considerate, you'll have a wonderful roller-coaster ride to your car.

Jove Peak

Start Point: Stevens Pass Highway (Smith Brook Road), 3,100 feet
High Point: Jove Peak, 6,007 feet
Best Time: December to April
Day Trip: 10 miles
Skiing Time: 8 hours
Skill Level: Advanced
Difficulty: High avalanche potential; permit/fee area; snowmobile traffic on approach road
Maps: USGS Labyrinth Mtn., 1:24,000

Jove Peak lies 1.7 miles north-northwest of Rainy Pass and is approached via Smith Brook Road. Its northwest and southeast shoulders can offer powder and corn on the same day! On the downside, afternoon slides from the south side of Union Peak and Jove Peak pose a significant threat to skiers.

Drive US 2 to the Smith Brook Road turnoff, 4.5 miles east of Stevens Pass.

Jove Peak (Photo by Rainer Burgdorfer)

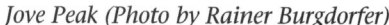

Ski Smith Brook Road through forests and clear-cuts for 1.8 miles, then climb to Rainy Pass. (See Union Peak Tour No. 44.)

Cross through the pass and descend the Rainy Creek drainage for 0.5 mile, heading due north. Near 4,000 feet, climb north-northwest heading toward Jove Peak. Gain the summit via its eastern ridge, keeping well clear of cornices that may form on either side. You may be forced to the steep southern slope for the summit climb.

From the summit of Jove, you may ski west to Lake Janus or head south back to Rainy Pass and out via the approach. From Lake Janus, you can make the loop back to Smith Brook Road via Union Gap (2 miles, 600 feet elevation gain, see previous tour).

Alternative Route: Another approach to Jove Peak involves climbing Union Peak from Rainy Pass, then traversing the connecting ridge between Union and Jove Peaks. If ridge conditions are unfavorable to complete this approach, you can still escape to Lake Janus and Union Gap.

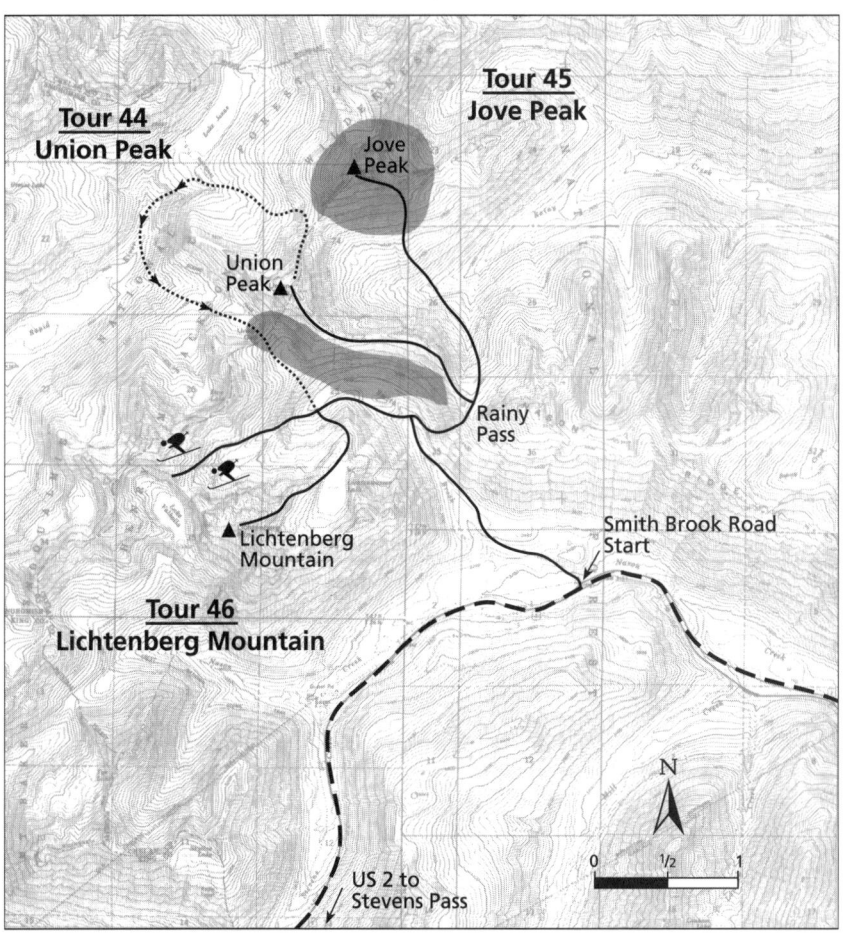

Lichtenberg Mountain

Start Point: Stevens Pass Highway (Smith Brook Road), 3,100 feet
High Point: Lichtenberg Mountain, 5,844 feet
Best Time: December to April
Day Trip: 8 miles
Skiing Time: 6 hours
Skill Level: Advanced
Difficulties: High avalanche potential; permit/fee area
Maps: USGS Labyrinth Mtn., 1:24,000

Lichtenberg Mountain lies 1.6 miles south of Union Peak, just across the Smith Brook Valley. In midwinter, the two basins to the northeast and northwest frequently hold powder snow for weeks after it falls.

The approach is similar to those for Union and Jove Peaks. Ski along Smith Brook Road, this time to the first switchback, 1.7 miles from US 2. Continue northwest for 0.5 miles, crossing Smith Brook at the most opportune place. Once you complete this leg, climb due south up a broad, partly wooded ridge to Lichtenwasser Lake (4,700 feet).

The ridge directly west of Lichtenwasser Lake leads to the summit of Lichtenberg Mountain. Alternately, you can cross the lake and climb the headwall to its south until you reach a saddle (0.9 mile, 900 feet), then continue until prudence suggests a halt.

From your high point, two different descents are possible. You can descend to Lake Valhalla via benches to the northwest or retrace your ascent route.

Jim Hill Mountain (Photo by William C. Shigley)

Jim Hill Mountain

Start Point: Mill Creek Road (Stevens Pass Nordic Center), 3,000 feet
High Point: Jim Hill Mountain, 6,765 feet
Best Time: January to April
Day Trip: 6 miles
Skiing Time: 9 hours
Skill Level: Advanced
Difficulties: High avalanche potential; routefinding required; permit/fee area
Maps: Green Trails No. 144, Benchmark Mountain; No. 145, Wenatchee Lake; No. 176, Stevens Pass; No. 177, Chiwaukum Mountains

Jim Hill Mountain takes its name from an early day railroad tycoon. The mountain is visible from US 2, just south of the highway near the Lanham Lake Sno-Park (now called the Stevens Pass Nordic Center). Jim Hill is the major peak west of the Chiwaukum Range and could be considered one of the better tours in this area.

Drive to the Stevens Pass Nordic Center 5.7 miles east of Stevens Pass on US 2. Park in the outer lot. (The inner lot will be blocked when the center closes for the day.) The Nordic Center may require you to purchase a trail pass.

Ski up (or alongside) Mill Creek Road for 0.1 mile and head due south at the Lanham Lake trailhead. Follow the trail or the creek bed of Lanham Creek to just short of Lanham Lake (4,120 feet) to an avalanche path. Climb this for 2,000 feet, enter the very steep forest, and work up benches to a saddle. From

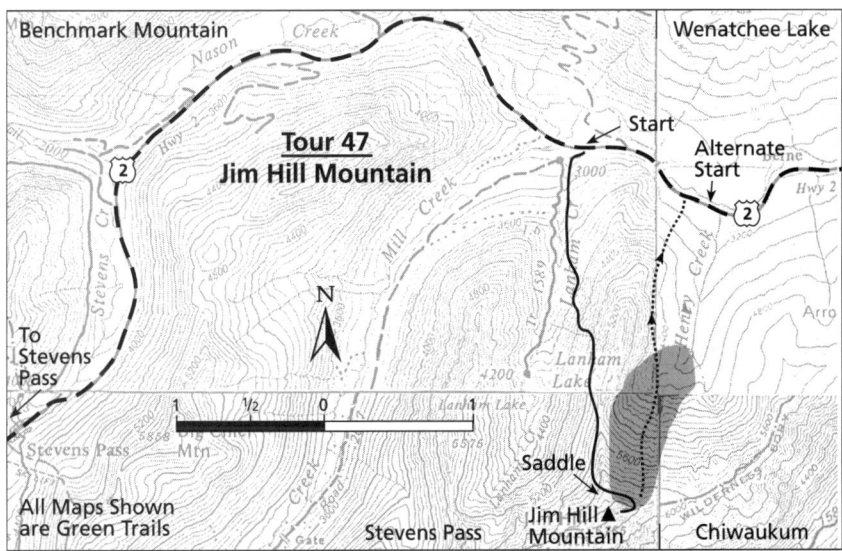

this saddle, you can either ski the bowl to the east, or climb to the summit.

An alternate approach to the north bowl of Jim Hill Mountain can be made via Henry Creek, the drainage 1.1 mile east of the Stevens Pass Nordic Center. Park at the plowed area near the east railroad tunnel entrance, and hike logging roads and clearcuts to gain the north bowl. Reverse the approach to return to the car.

Rock *48* Mountain

Start Point: Stevens Pass Highway, Rock Mountain Trailhead, 3,030 feet

High Point: Rock Mountain, 6,852 feet

Best Time: November to April

Day Trip: 9 miles

Skiing Time: 8 hours

Skill Level: Alpine

Difficulties: High avalanche potential; permit/fee area

Maps: Green Trails No. 145, Wenatchee Lake; No. 144, Benchmark Mtn.

Rapid access, a scenic hike, and open slopes make the Rock Mountain tour delightful after an early season snowfall. The heather benches and smooth scree slopes require little snow to provide excellent skiing. In midwinter, larger quantities of snow make parking and the approach more difficult. This approach is continuously steep and exposed, and would be extremely hazardous in unstable snow. Carry an ice ax and crampons.

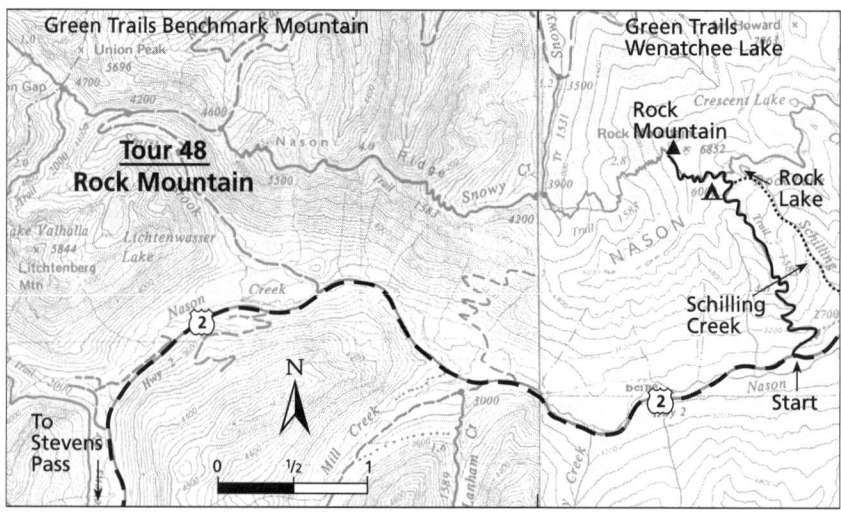

Drive US 2 over Stevens Pass, or head west from Tumwater Canyon. Rock Mountain Trail No. 1587 begins 8.6 miles east of the summit, on the north side of Highway 9, and climbs the north-trending ridge to Rock Lake Basin. Rock Lake Basin consists of open slopes facing north, south, and east. Surely you can find skiing on one of these slopes! When you tire of skiing these bowls, climb to the summit of Rock Mountain and drop into the northwestern ramp, which offers more than 2,000 feet of fall-line skiing.

The trouble is, you will have to climb back up to return to US 2. Be sure you allow enough time to hike out in daylight, because the trail crosses above cliffbands near the trailhead. Schilling Creek has been skied directly to the highway in exceptionally deep snowpack with stable conditions.

44
Mount Mastiff

Start Point: Merritt Lake Trail, 2,600 feet

High Point: Mount Mastiff, 6,741 feet

Best Time: April to May

Day Trip: 9 miles

Skiing Time: 10 hours

Skill Level: Alpine

Difficulties: High avalanche potential; routefinding required; permit/fee area

Maps: USGS Mt. Howard, 1:24,000

Mount Mastiff doesn't boast the altitude or the skiing of Mount Howard, but is a spectacular objective when approached via the Merritt Lake Trail. The return run offers great tree skiing in mid- and late winter. This is a long tour and makes an excellent overnight trip. One way to gauge the safety of this trip: if skiing in the trees is nice, the snow higher up is dangerous.

Drive US 2 to Merritt Lake Trailhead Road No. 657 (15 miles east of Stevens Pass, 8.7 miles west of Coles Corner). Head north on this road, driving it 1.6 miles to its end (3,030 feet). If the road is snow-covered, simply climb due north for 1 mile through steep forest and clear-cuts, topping a ridge near 4,600 feet. Once on the ridge, head northwest, climbing along a narrowing ridge toward the summit of Mount Mastiff.

From Point 6125, 0.8 mile southeast of Mount Mastiff, it may be necessary to descend to the east side of the narrow summit ridge, then climb the steep east slopes to the summit.

From the summit, start your descent by dropping northeast for 800 feet (0.2 mile), then descending east-southeast into Lost Lake Basin. From the southern end of the lake, make an east-ascending traverse for 0.2 mile, then climb due south to a small pass above tiny Merritt Lake. Descend to the lake, then

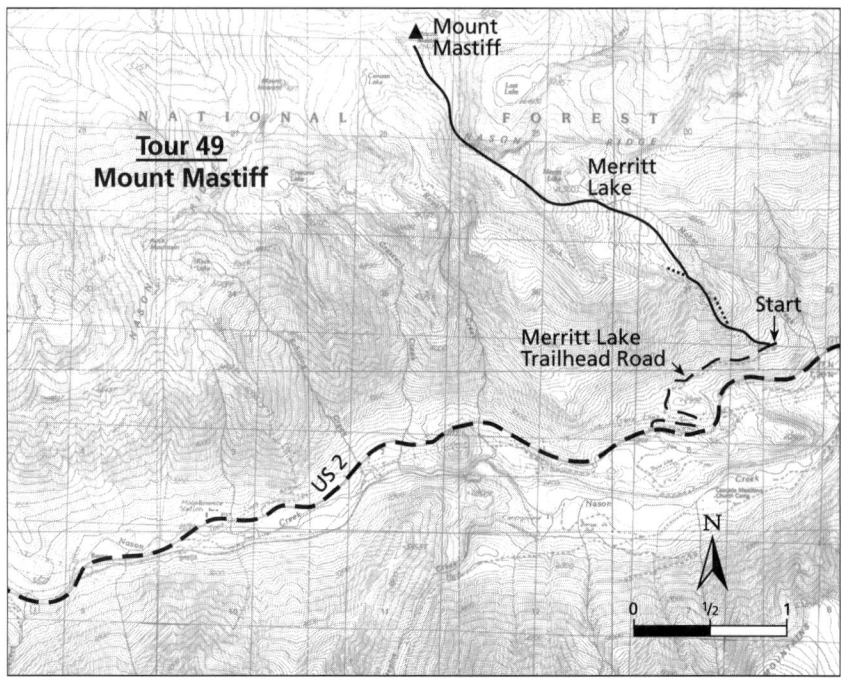

leave the basin, descending southeast along the route of the summer trail. Intersect the road and take it back to the highway.

Chiwaukum *50* Mountains

Start Point: White Pine Creek Road, 2,800 feet
High Point: Big Chiwaukum, 8,081 feet
Best Time: April to May
Day Trip/Overnight: 16 miles
Skiing Time: 12 hours
Skill Level: Advanced
Difficulties: High avalanche potential; routefinding required; permit/fee area; not recommended for snowboarders
Maps: Green Trails No. 145, Wenatchee Lake; No. 177, Chiwaukum Mountains

This approach to the Chiwaukum Range makes sense because it provides access to the heart of this high range via a scenic if lengthy approach. And there is parking, unlike the Coulter Ski Trail approach. The trail near the trailhead

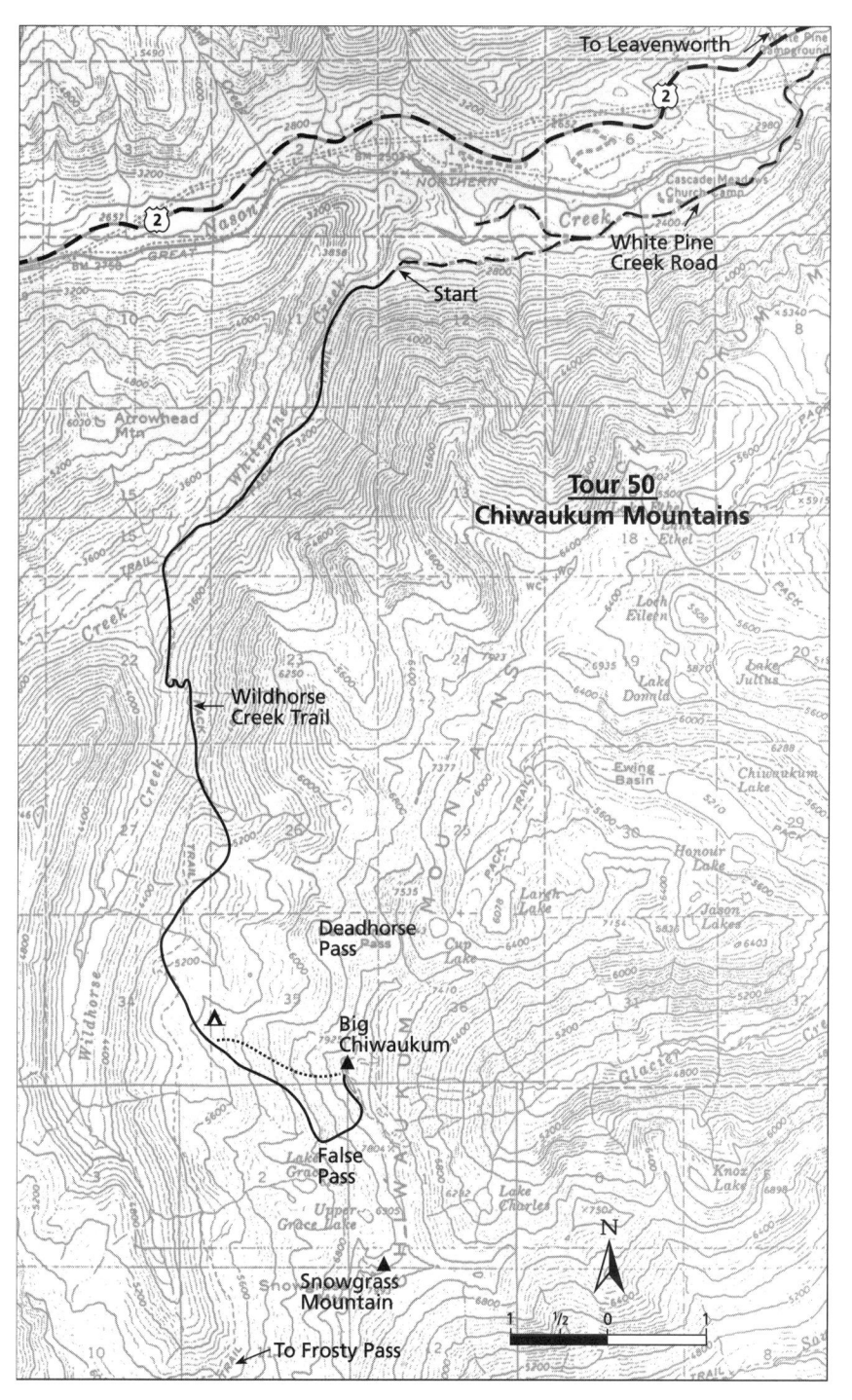

To Leavenworth

White Pine
Creek Road

Start

Tour 50
Chiwaukum Mountains

Wildhorse
Creek Trail

Deadhorse
Pass

Big
Chiwaukum

False
Pass

Snowgrass
Mountain

To Frosty Pass

N

Chiwaukum Mountains (Photo by William C. Shigley)

passes through a steep-sided gorge with White Pine Creek raging along its narrow floor. If snow covers the trail, the skier is faced with a long, steep traverse above the torrent. A climbing rope with the correct accessories might be just the thing here to make this tour comfortable in early season.

Drive US 2 to White Pine Creek Road No. 2638 (13.7 miles east of Stevens Pass). Ignore all side roads and drive under a railroad bridge to road's end at 3.2 miles (2,800 feet). Park here.

The trail heads southwest, staying close to White Pine Creek for 2.4 miles. Near 3,240 feet, climb due south for 2.5 miles. Near 4,950 feet, pass a buttress on your left, then continue south, climbing for 1 mile into a basin. Climb steepening slopes for nearly a mile to reach False Pass (6,600 feet), then head east until the terrain forces a northern route to the summit of Chiwaukum (0.8 mile to summit).

Descend to White Pine Creek and ski out along the river.

Alternative Route: The western slope of the Chiwaukums would keep a platoon of skiers occupied for a week. It is usually not practical to reach the eastern slopes of Big Chiwaukum, except by a very steep descent 0.2 mile south of the summit. This saddle leads to a traverse to Chiwaukum Creek drainage

(11 miles to the highway). It is also possible to ski over Frosty Pass and descend to upper Icicle Creek (11 miles to Icicle River Road, 7 miles upstream from Bridge Creek campground). This tour is wonderfully scenic.

51
Alpine Lookout

Start Point: US 2, 2,170 feet (Butcher Creek Road)
High Point: Alpine Lookout (Nason Ridge), 6,235 feet
Best Time: January to March
Day Trip/Overnight: 18 miles
Skiing Time: 12 hours
Skill Level: Intermediate
Difficulties: Moderate avalanche potential; routefinding required; long trip
Maps: USGS Lake Wenatchee, 1:24,000

Alpine Lookout lies 2.5 miles northwest of Round Mountain, the eastern end of Nason Ridge. Although this tour has a long approach, the descent is fairly fast because it is all downhill, and moderate in steepness.

Drive 17 miles east from Stevens Pass on US 2 (2.6 miles west from Coles

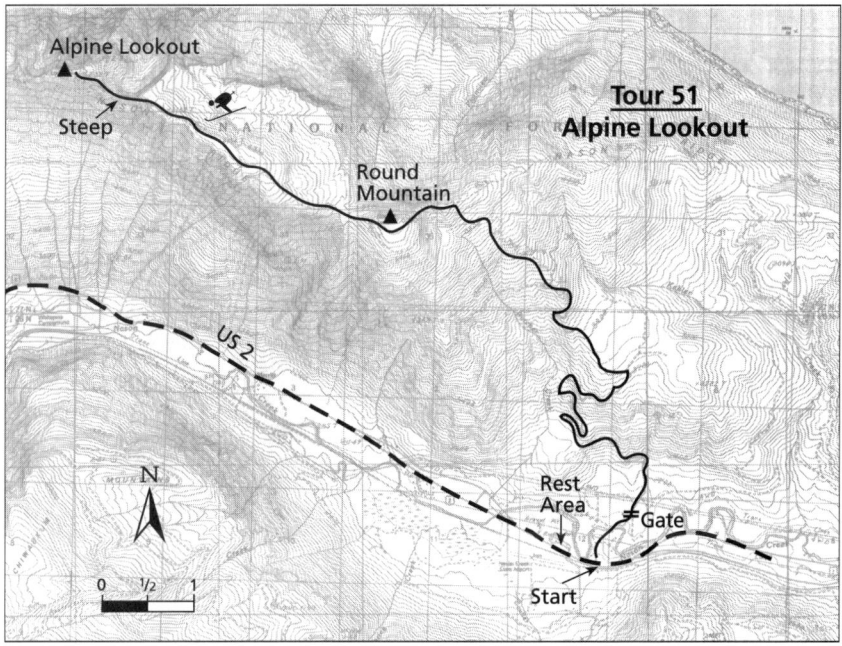

Corner). Butcher Creek Road heads north from the highway 0.2 mile east of the rest area. Parking can be difficult to find, especially in midwinter. By means of aggressive snow shoveling, you can sometimes make a place for your car. The parking lot across from the rest area is private—do not park there.

Drive or ski Butcher Creek Road, crossing Nason Creek in 0.3 mile. Continue on the road for 1 mile. If you're on foot, consider leaving the road here (2,500 feet) and climbing due north for 0.3 mile, intersecting the road at 3,100 feet. (This saves 1.2 miles of road skiing.) Once you regain the road, follow it for 1.7 miles to 3,960 feet, then leave the road and start skiing northwest along the summer trail. The trail switchbacks northwest over open slopes around the summit of Round Mountain (2 miles, 5,700 feet). This can be a good turn-around point.

From Round Mountain, head west for 1.6 miles, descending slightly to a broad ridge that narrows drastically. The gentle north-facing slopes northeast of this area offer fabulous short runs, if you can find a way through the cornices. Continue heading west until the ridge becomes a knife-edge and you are forced left to the southern side of Nason Ridge. The terrain eases in 0.3 mile and in 0.3 mile more, you arrive at Alpine Lookout. Retrace your approach to go home.

Alternative Route: A shorter but much steeper approach involves skiing the Merritt Lake Trail, and then climbing northeast from the lake to gain the ridge leading to Alpine Lookout. This route is 13 miles round trip.

Mount Maude

Start Point: Phelps Creek Road, 3,500 feet
High Point: Mount Maude, 9,082 feet
Best Time: April to May
Weekend: 18 miles
Skiing Time: 14 hours
Skill Level: Alpine
Difficulties: High avalanche potential; routefinding required; permit/fee area
Maps: Green Trails No. 113, Holden

The Entiat Mountains are rugged, remote, and tall. Mount Maude is one of the few non-volcanic peaks in the state higher than 9,000 feet. Its steep north face is a good ice climb, but the objective of this tour is the gentle south shoulder, which can be done in a long weekend if road conditions are suitable. Take an ice ax and crampons.

Drive US 2 to the Lake Wenatchee turnoff (19.5 miles east of Stevens Pass,

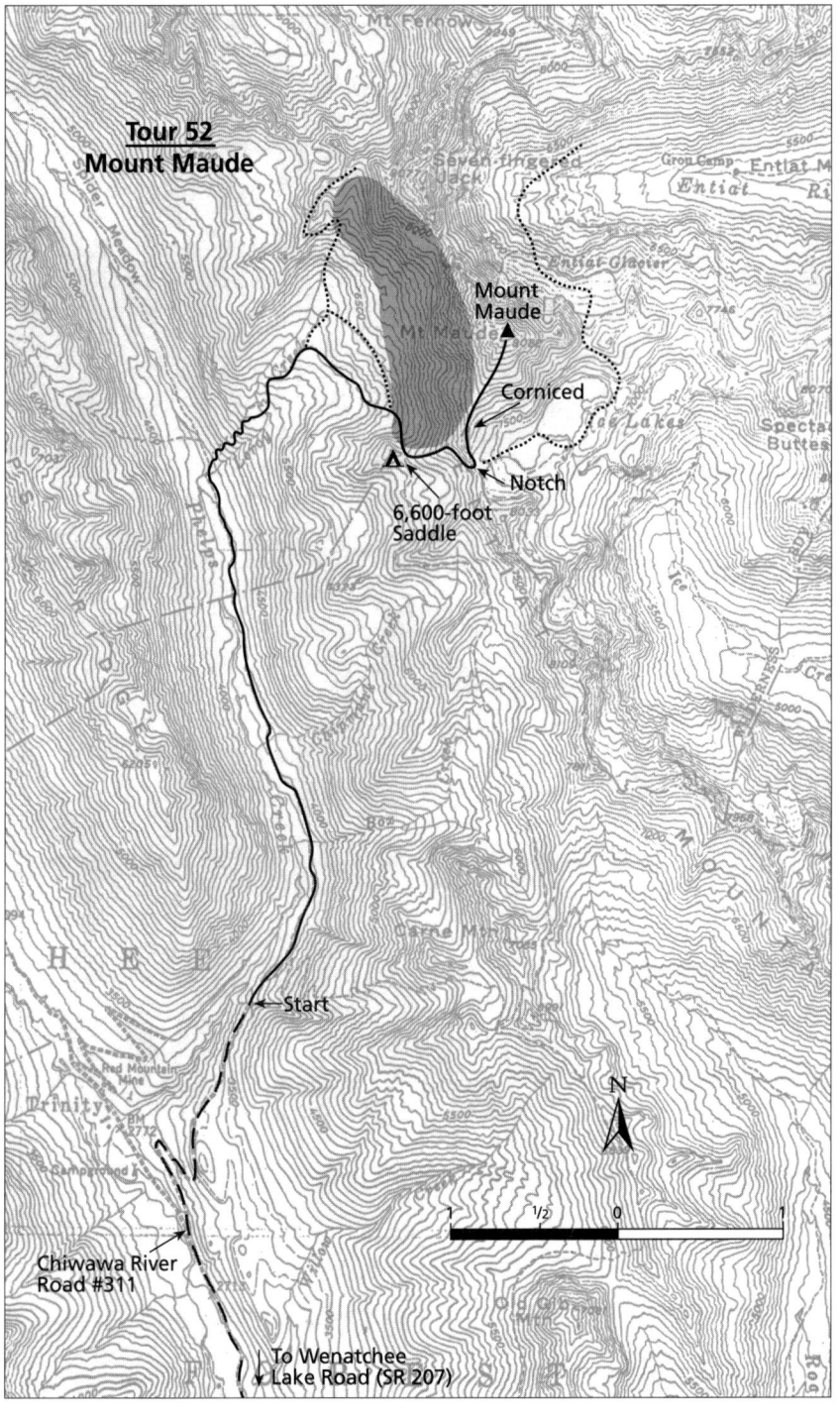

**Tour 52
Mount Maude**

Mount
Maude

Corniced

Notch

6,600-foot
Saddle

Start

N

½ 0 1

Chiwawa River
Road #311

To Wenatchee
Lake Road (SR 207)

16 miles west of Leavenworth) and turn northeast onto State Route 207 toward Lake Wenatchee State Park. Cross the Wenatchee River and 4.6 miles from US 2, turn right (east) onto Country Road No. 22. Drive for 1.4 miles and turn left onto Meadow Creek Road. Continue past Fish Lake and over the Chiwawa River. You will come to a fork in 3.3 miles; go left, heading north on Chiwawa River Road. (This intersection can also be reached by taking Plain Road from Leavenworth.)

Drive up the Chiwawa River Valley for 19.2 miles, or as far as road conditions permit. At 19.2 miles (2,760 feet) fork right to Phelps Creek Trailhead (2 miles, approximately 3,500 feet). Park at the trailhead. Look around to gain a sense of the size of the mountains in this range.

Hike the gently rolling Phelps Creek Trail for 3.3 miles to the Leroy Creek Trail (4,150 feet), just north of Leroy Creek. The Leroy Creek Trail will, with luck, be covered with snow. Ski or hike the steep shoulder north of the stream, heading east-northeast until the angle eases off near 5,000 feet. As you leave the thinning trees, you'll find yourself in a large cirque with the bulk of Mount Maude directly to the east and Seven-Fingered Jack to the northeast. There are benches with fine campsites in this cirque. Continue heading east for 0.5 mile to 6,000 feet, then climb southeast along a ridge that protrudes west from the south ramp of Mount Maude. At 6,600 feet, you'll come to a saddle, which makes a good, lofty camp. From there, make a climbing traverse to the east to the ridge above, bypassing a cliff on your left to gain the southern shoulder of Mount Maude. Ice Lakes lie just to the east, below the pass.

Climb north along the ridge to gain the summit—this is well worth doing for the views. Return to camp and your car via your approach.

 Chiwawa Mountain

Start Point: Phelps Creek Road, 3,500 feet
High Point: Chiwawa Mountain, 8,460 feet
Best Time: April to June
Weekend: 19 miles
Skiing Time: 15 hours
Skill Level: Alpine
Difficulties: High avalanche potential; routefinding required; permit/fee area
Maps: Green Trails No. 113, Holden

Chiwawa Mountain lies at the head of the Chiwawa River and offers good skiing and spectacular views of Bonanza Peak, the highest non-volcanic peak in Washington. The approach is the same as that of Mount Maude (see Tour

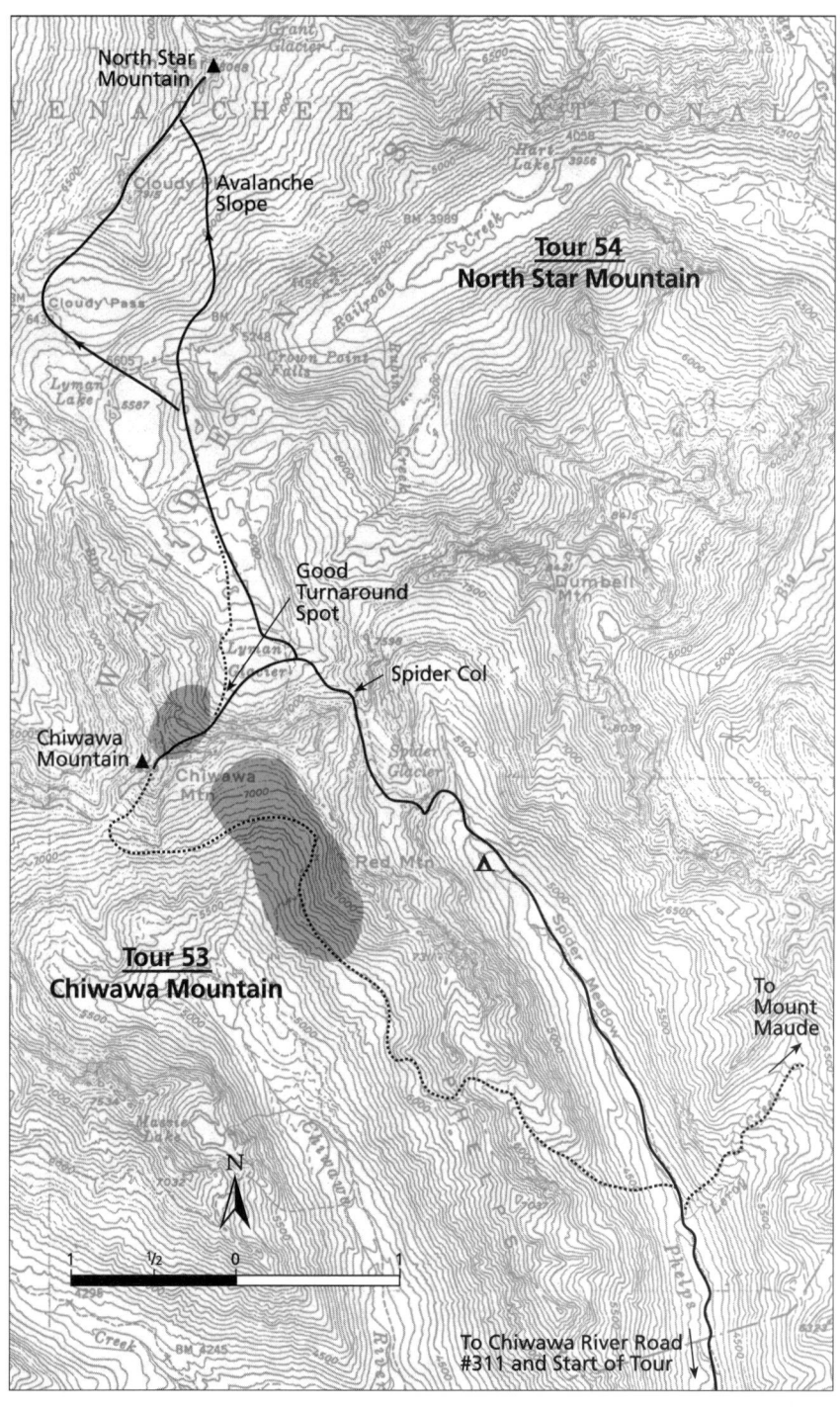

North Star Mountain

Avalanche Slope

Cloudy Pass

Lyman Lake

**Tour 54
North Star Mountain**

Good Turnaround Spot

Spider Col

Chiwawa Mountain

Dumbell Mtn

Red Mtn

**Tour 53
Chiwawa Mountain**

To Mount Maude

N

1   ½   0   1

To Chiwawa River Road #311 and Start of Tour

52), until you cross Leroy Creek. Bring an ice ax and crampons.

Continue past Leroy Creek, heading up Phelps Creek to Spider Meadow (5,000 feet), a broad valley bottom that gradually climbs northwest for more than a mile to a headwall. Camp here, or switchback up the headwall to the northwest and gain the Spider Glacier. Just left is a knoll (6,360 feet) that has level campsites. Camping or not, climb the Spider Glacier and reach its apex, Spider Col (7,100 feet) in 0.7 mile.

From the saddle, make a descending traverse northwest to 6,500 feet, then head southwest for 0.5 mile, dropping onto the Lyman Glacier. The terrain steepens at a step to the glacier, but the route continues directly to the summit in 0.7 mile. In most years, the summit requires a class 3 scramble. The view is well worth it. Return by retracing the approach. The descent through Spider Meadow is sheer delight, a moderate run in a wilderness setting over miles of rolling, generally downhill, skiing.

Alternative Route: For an adventurous return, descend the southwest shoulder of Chiwawa to 6,500 feet, then contour southeast along Red Mountain until you converge on an abandoned mining road (shown as a trail on maps). Follow the vestigial road back to the junction of Trinity and Phelps Creek Roads (9 miles from Chiwawa Summit).

North Star Mountain

Start Point: Phelps Creek Road, 3,500 feet
High Point: North Star Mountain, 8,096 feet
Best Time: April to June
Extended Trip: 3 to 4 days
Skiing Time: 26 hours
Skill Level: Advanced
Difficulties: Glacier travel; high avalanche potential; routefinding required; permit/fee area; not recommended for snowboarders
Maps: Green Trails No. 113, Holden

Close-up views of Bonanza Peak are among the attractions of this multiday tour. This classic ski tour was first done in 1938 via Phelps Creek Basin. Long runs in every direction and a downhill track from Spider Col to the car complete the package. When you return from this tour, you'll know you've been somewhere.

Start as for Chiwawa Mountain or Mount Maude. Climb to Spider Col (7,100 feet). Then descend 2.4 miles northeast to Lyman Lake (5,600 feet) and

The inherent stability of snowboards make them powerful tools for cruising difficult backcountry snow. (Photo by William C. Shigley)

cross to its northern shore. Climb gladed trees 0.9 mile north-northwest to Cloudy Pass (6,500 feet). From here, climb 1 mile northeast along the ridge over Cloudy Peak summit (7,915 feet) and continue 1 mile to the summit of North Star Mountain (8,068 feet).

Descents are possible on all three faces of this pyramid, including one to the Lutheran Retreat village of Holden (6.8 miles plus boat ride). Return to your car by retracing the approach.

55 Clark Mountain

Start Point: White River Road, 2,300 feet (Boulder Pass trailhead)

High Point: Clark Mountain, 8,576 feet

Best Time: March to June

Weekend: 24 miles

Skiing Time: 18 hours

Skill Level: Alpine

Difficulties: High avalanche potential; glacier travel; routefinding required; permit/fee area

Maps: USGS Holden, Wenatchee Lake, 1:24,000

Clark Mountain lies just north of the White River, a major tributary to Lake Wenatchee. It is the eastern terminus of a high route starting west of Glacier Peak and a magnificent objective in its own right. Take an ice ax, crampons, and rope.

Clark Mountain (Photo by Rainer Burgdorfer)

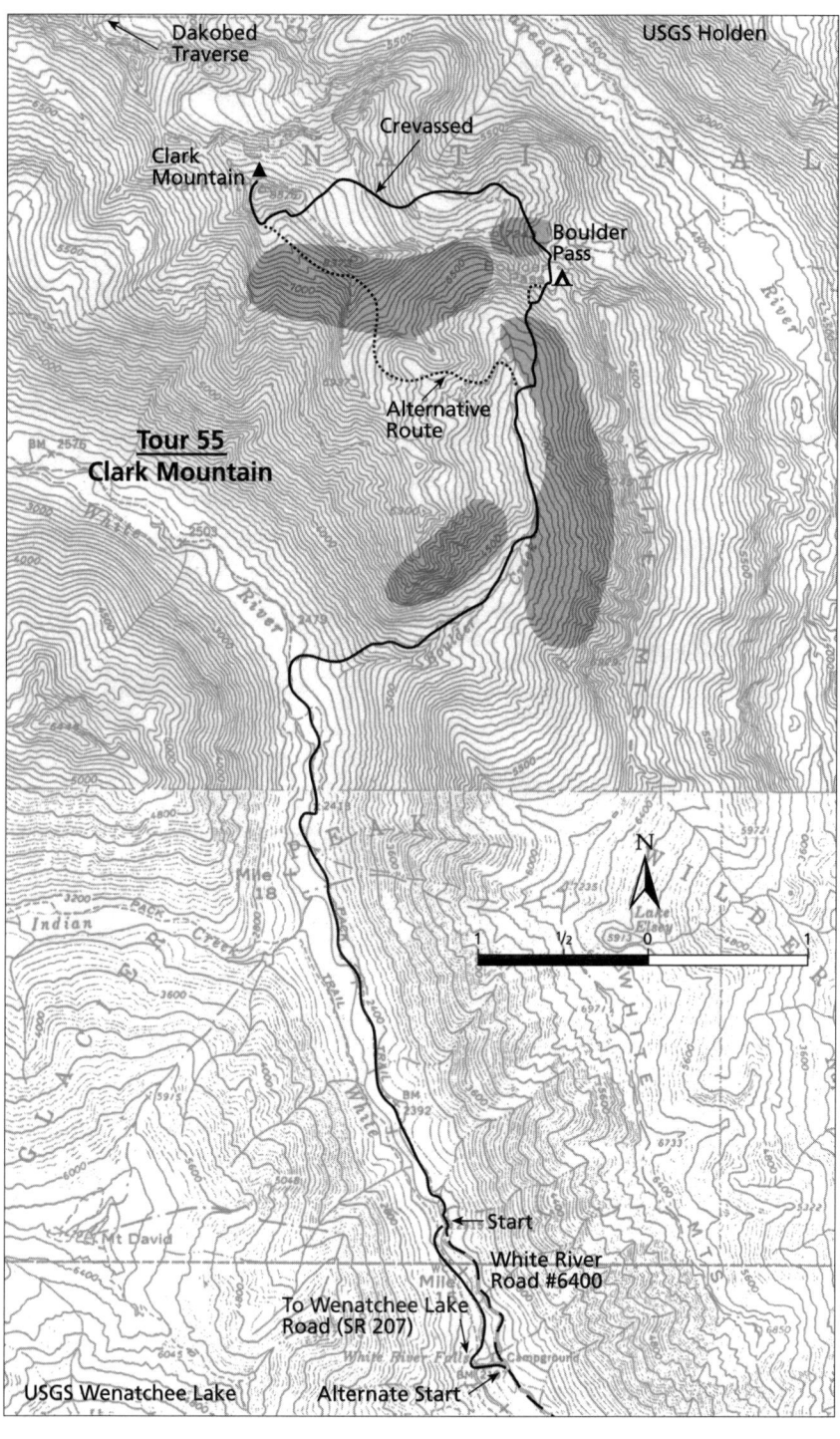

Dakobed Traverse

USGS Holden

Crevassed

Clark Mountain

Boulder Pass

**Tour 55
Clark Mountain**

Alternative Route

N

Start

White River Road #6400

To Wenatchee Lake Road (SR 207)

USGS Wenatchee Lake

Alternate Start

Drive US 2 to Wenatchee Lake Road and head north. Continue past the Lake Wenatchee ranger station and continue for 10.4 miles along White River Road past White River Falls to the end of the road (2,300 feet), or as far as road conditions allow. The Boulder Pass Trail crosses the White River via a timber bridge a short distance beyond the campground.

Hike the near-level trail 4 miles to its junction (2,540 feet) with the Boulder Pass Trail, 0.2 mile north of Boulder Creek. The steep trail switchbacks up Boulder Creek drainage to its source near Boulder Pass. The trail climbs east for the first 2.8 miles (to 4,200 feet), and then trends north for 3.5 miles to Boulder Pass (6,260 feet). The headwall below the pass is quite steep; it is easiest to climb through the small trees just east of the trail shown on the map.

Boulder Pass is a good place to camp and ski, even if you don't attempt to reach the summit of Clark Mountain. The high shoulder 0.7 mile northeast of Boulder Pass provides many outstanding runs, although some end in cliffs.

The approach to the summit of Clark Mountain leads over the moderately angled but active Walrus Glacier. Glacier-climbing equipment is recommended here, and late-season skiers may need some luck in crossing major crevasse systems.

From Boulder Pass, climb up a shoulder to the northwest. At 6,800 feet, contour around the shoulder to gain the Walrus Glacier. The flattest area of the glacier (not level by any means) at this elevation provides a crevasse-free ramp to the center of the glacier. The largest crevasses occur between 7,100 and 7,700 feet with a large bergschrund near 7,700 feet. Ski up the center or left-center of the glacier to the eastern ridge of the main peak. Cross over this ridge to the south slope and climb easily to the summit. Descend via the approach route.

Big Jim Mountain

Start Point: Hatchery Creek Trailhead, 2,800 feet

High Point: Big Jim Mountain, 7,763 feet

Best Time: March to May

Day Trip/Overnight: 14 miles

Skiing Time: 10 hours

Skill Level: Advanced

Difficulties: High avalanche potential; routefinding required; permit/fee area; not recommended for snowboarders

Maps: USGS Big Jim Mtn., 1:24,000

Big Jim Mountain is a tall, relatively gentle peak on the northeast corner of Icicle Ridge. The initial portions of the approach are steep. But even if you don't make a summit attempt, the larch basins make the climbing worthwhile.

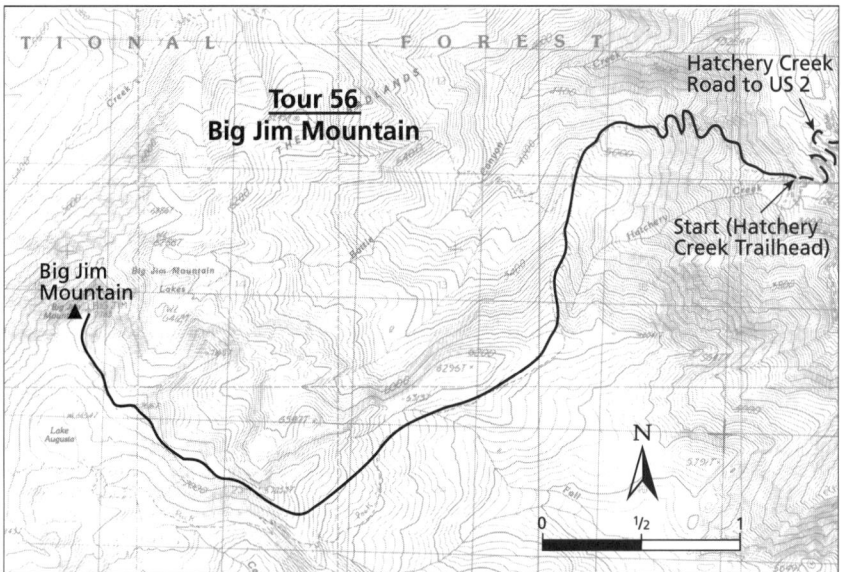

This area is seldom visited, perhaps because of the rigors of the approach.

Drive US 2 to the north end of Tumwater Canyon. At the north end of the Wenatchee River Bridge, a road leaves the highway heading southwest and uphill. Drive this road for 2.5 miles to the parking lot at its end, or as far as conditions permit.

The trail starts at the northwestern corner of the parking lot and climbs due west for 0.6 mile, immediately adjacent to clear-cuts for the first few hundred yards. For the next 1.2 miles, the trail switchbacks slightly northwest through steep forest. As the angle eases off, the trail turns south, reaching a junction in 0.6 mile (5,240 feet). The right (west) fork leads to Big Jim Mountain Lakes in 2.8 miles. The left (east) fork leads, via connecting ridges, to the south ramp of Big Jim Mountain in 4.5 miles.

To reach the lakes, take the right fork and climb southwest for 0.2 mile. Near 5,280 feet, climb west, crossing Canyon Creek in 0.4 mile, until you come to a dome in 1.2 miles (1.8 miles from the junction, 6,245 feet). Climb southwest to reach the lakes (1 mile, 6,288 feet). It is feasible to climb Big Jim from this basin, but the trail is quite steep. To reach the southern ramp of Big Jim, head due south from the knoll, passing to the east of a pinnacle southeast of the lakes, then climb southwest to connect to the southern approach.

The left fork climbs due south for 0.9 mile above the headwaters of Hatchery Creek and enters a large basin (6,040 feet). Here the trail climbs southwest for 1.1 miles, turning south again, then west to gain the ridge crest (0.7 mile, 6,700 feet). The summit of Big Jim Mountain lies 1.7 miles northwest along narrow connecting ridges. Return via the approach.

57
Icicle Ridge

Start Point: Icicle River Road, 1,200 feet

High Point: Icicle Ridge, 6,696 feet

Best Time: December to February

Day Trip/Overnight: 14 miles

Skiing Time: 9 hours

Skill Level: Intermediate (Loop Tour is advanced)

Difficulties: Moderate avalanche potential; permit/fee area; not recommended for snowboarders

Maps: Green Trails No. 177, Chiwaukum Mountains; No. 178, Leavenworth

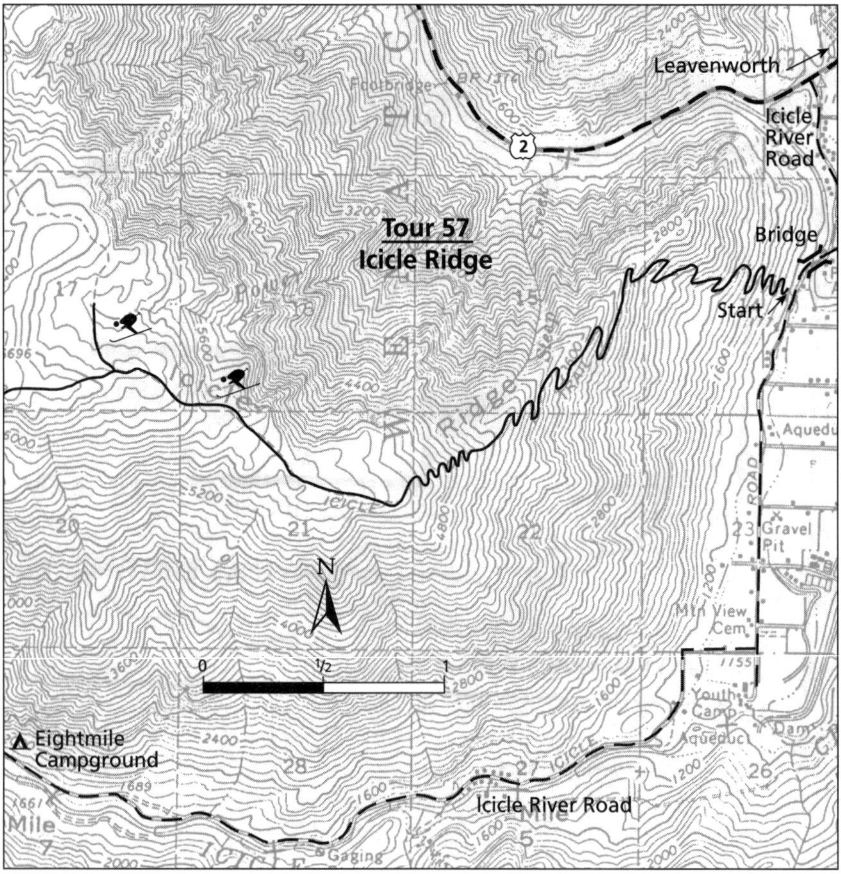

"Icicle" is an interpretation of the native word "nasikelt" meaning "steep-sided canyon." The ridge forming the northern boundary of Icicle Canyon is indeed

steep-sided, but by climbing it lengthwise from east to west, you can avoid some of the steepness. Adequate snow cover is essential for an enjoyable tour, as are an early start and a high level of fitness.

Drive US 2 (or Plain Road) to Leavenworth. On the west end of town, head south on Icicle River Road for 1.4 miles and turn right (west) at the intersection. The road turns south and terminates in 0.1 mile.

Hike or ski the trail north for 0.3 mile, then switchback 1.9 miles to the ridge crest above (3,000 feet). The forest is fairly open and there are views of the valley below. Although the summer trail keeps to the east of the ridge, in winter it is easier to ski near or on the crest. Follow the crest southwest for 1.8 miles until the ridge broadens and turns to the northwest (5,252 feet). Continue climbing northwest, reaching the high point of 6,696 feet in 1.9 miles. Return via the approach.

Dragontail Peak

Start Point: Stuart Lake Trailhead (Mountaineer Creek Trail), 3,400 feet

High Point: Dragontail Peak, 8,840 feet

Best Time: March to May

Day Trip/Overnight: 14 miles

Skiing Time: 9 hours

Skill Level: Advanced

Difficulties: High avalanche potential; routefinding required; permit/fee area

Maps: USGS Mt. Stuart, Chiwaukum Mtns., 1:24,000

Dragontail Peak is the second-highest summit in the Stuart Range. A "ski ascent" is possible from the east side, via the 2,500-foot slope from Colchuck Lake to Asgaard Pass, because the road to the trailhead melts out long before the skiing deteriorates. Crampons and ice axes are advisable, and both user fees and entry permits may be required.

Drive Icicle River Road from Leavenworth to Bridge Creek Campground (14 miles), and cross the Icicle River on a concrete bridge. Continue up the road for 4 miles, and park at a broad elbow in the road.

Hike Lake Stuart Trail No. 1599 for 2.5 miles to a level valley drained by beaver-dammed Mountaineer Creek. The Colchuck Lake Trail forks left in this area. Cross Mountaineer Creek on a bridge and hike south among boulders to the trail. The trail switchbacks up and over buttresses to approach Colchuck Lake (5,570 feet). The safest campsites are west of the lake, well away from the shore.

Circle the lake counterclockwise, climbing over small humps, and ski through the woods on the southwestern shore. Come out to an open basin

south of the lake. The northwest wall of Dragontail looms ahead and Colchuck Peak lies ahead. Your objective is the pass just left of Dragontail.

At this point, it may be easier to ski along the frozen lake, rather than to wander through the nearby boulder field. Either way, hike up the long slope toward Asgaard Pass (7,800 feet). Keep to the left to 7,200 feet, then cross right to a moraine to avoid cliffs above. The view begins to open up as you approach the pass and you'll get glimpses of the innards of the huge couloirs dividing the faces of Dragontail.

From the pass, begin heading southwest toward a steep glacier headwall. Climb the glacier via its easiest side to the saddle. From the saddle, a gentle spur leads to the summit area 300 feet above. The summit is an undistinguished lump with extraordinary views.

To descend, retrace your ascent. If the steep portions of Asgaard's apron are icy, you may need to crampon down.

Alternative Route: It is possible to exit through the Enchantment Lakes basin, down Trauma Rib, past Snow and Nada Lakes, and out the Snow Lakes Trail. This route requires ideal conditions and expert planning.

Colchuck Glacier is a good side trip if you have an extra afternoon. Instead of heading up Asgaard Pass, climb the steep slopes of the terminal moraine below the glacier, then continue to Colchuck Col (8,000 feet) above. The glacier segment below Colchuck Peak is crevassed—keep left close (but not too close) to Dragontail. The far side of Colchuck Col is the source of Porcupine Creek, a tour accessible from US 97.

54
Cashmere Mountain

Start Point: Eightmile Lake Trailhead, 3,300 feet
High Point: Cashmere Mountain, 8,501 feet
Best Time: January to June
Overnight: 18 miles
Skiing Time: 14 hours
Skill Level: Alpine
Difficulties: High avalanche potential; routefinding required; permit/fee area
Maps: USGS Mt. Stuart, Chiwaukum Mtns., 1:24,000

Cashmere Mountain is another enigmatic giant of the Cascades: tall, beautiful, and remote. Because of its location, the mountain, named after the region in Asia, does not host many alpine enthusiasts.

Colchuck Peak and Glacier (Photo by Rainer Burgdorfer)

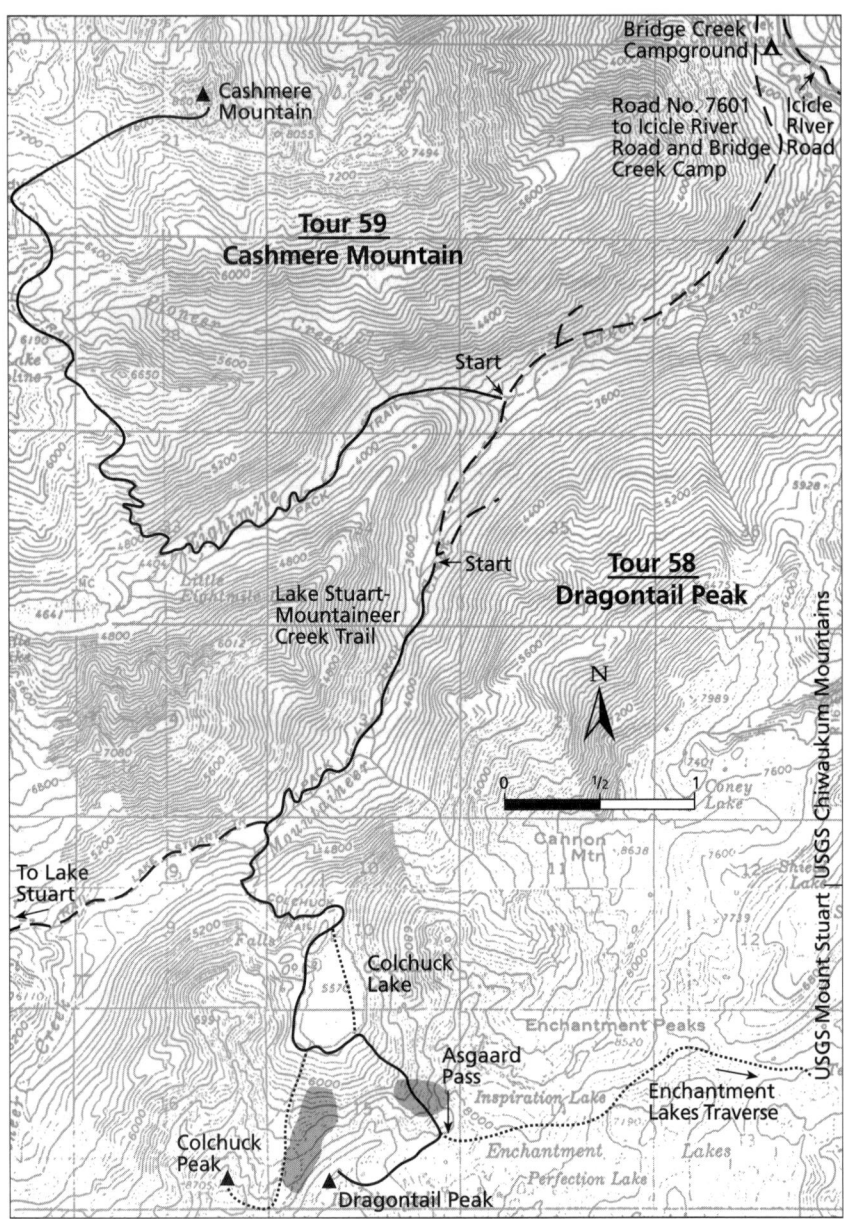

Drive Icicle River Road to Bridge Creek Campground (14 miles), and cross the Icicle River on the concrete bridge. Drive the former logging road for 2.8 miles and park near the Eightmile Lake trailhead.

The trail follows a gated road heading west up the Eightmile Creek drainage. Head west-southwest along the creek. You will arrive at Little Eightmile Lake in 3.0 miles (4,400 feet). Ski to the northwestern shore of the lake and climb directly northwest to the ridge crest above Lake Caroline (2.5 miles, 6,400 feet).

Descend to Lake Caroline and cross to the northern shore. Then continue north-northwest 2.0 miles to Windy Pass (7,260 feet). From the pass, head northeast, and then east to the summit area of Cashmere Mountain (1.5 miles). The view from the summit is worth the scramble.

Delightful descents can be made down the north, west, and southwest sides. (The northeast and east basins are hard to enter from their flanks, and cliff bands near 6,000 feet don't offer much promise for fluid runs.) The north, northwest, west, and southwest basins offer much easier access and more "vertical," including one-way, traverses.

Return to your car by retracing the approach.

Wedge Mountain

Start Point: Mountain Home Road, 2,725 feet

High Point: Wedge Mountain, 6,885 feet

Best Time: December to April

Day Trip: 10 miles

Skiing Time: 7 hours

Skill Level: Intermediate

Difficulties: Moderate avalanche potential; routefinding required; parking (you may have to dig)

Maps: USGS Leavenworth, 1:24,000

Wedge Mountain is the high point of the ridge immediately east of Nada and Snow Lakes and Snow Creek. This tour's virtues lie in its gentle skiing terrain (steeper if you look for it) and its overlook of the Stuart Range and Snow and Nada Lakes. Some maps identify Wedge Mountain as a lower point near 5,836 feet. "Popular terminology and logic make the choice the 6,885-foot summit," writes Fred Beckey in his *Cascade Alpine Guide*, vol. 1.

Drive US 2 to Leavenworth. At the east end of town, just east of the Wenatchee River Bridge, turn south at the first intersection and turn left onto Mountain Home Road in 400 feet. Drive this road for 4 miles and park at an intersection (2,725 feet). You may have to carve a parking spot for your vehicle with snow shovels. (If this seems a daunting task, consider that someday you may have to move at least that much snow to uncover an avalanche victim who is buried 6 feet deep. Practice never hurts.)

Mountain Home Road can also be approached from US 97. Four miles south of the US 2 junction, head west from US 97 onto a side road. Take this road southwest for 0.2 mile, and then turn right onto Mountain Home Road. Follow Mountain Home Road for 3.2 miles and park as before.

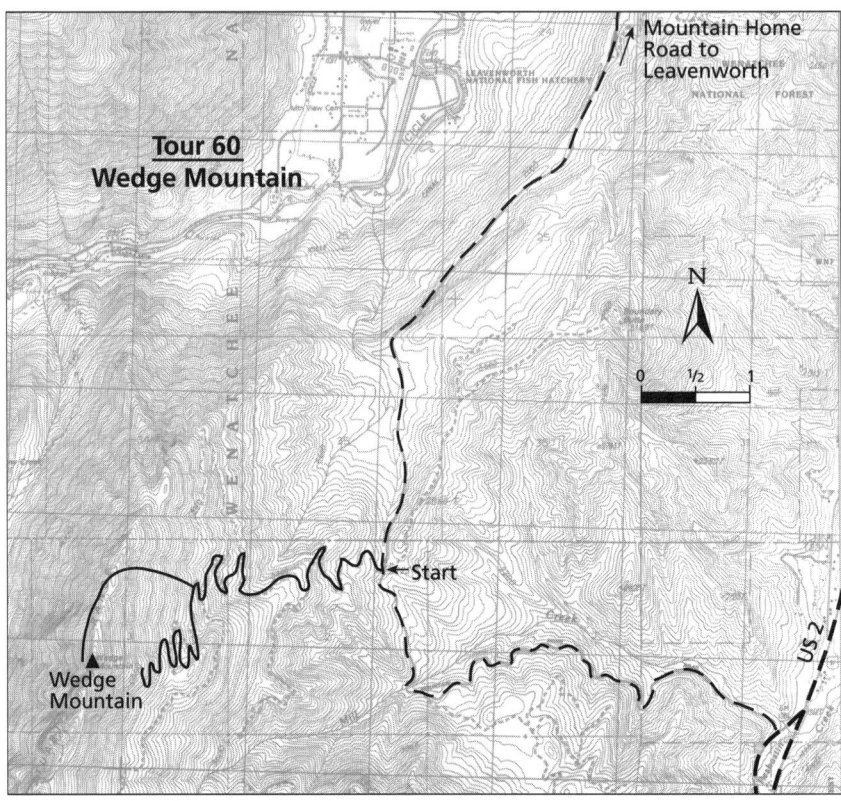

The trail trends west for 0.8 mile, switchbacking up open slopes. Near 3,200 feet, the trail heads south for 0.2 mile and forks. The right fork switchbacks toward the ridge crest and terminates in 2.2 miles (4,500 feet). False-Wedge Mountain lies 0.6 mile above (5,836 feet). Skiers can climb the ridge crest to the summit of Wedge Mountain (2 miles, 6,885 feet). The left fork climbs south, terminating in 1.2 miles near 3,300 feet. Continue south for 2.8 miles, then head 1.7 miles west as the terrain permits, up a rib to the ridge and summit. The open pine forests, burns, and meadows offer excellent skiing when conditions are right. Retrace your approach to return to your car. There is snowmobile traffic in this area.

BLEWETT PASS HIGHWAY, US 97

Highway 97 is the major north-south highway east of the Cascade Crest. North of US 2 and south of I-90, the highway lies well to the east of the Cascades, but in the area bordered by these two east-west corridors, US 97 provides access into the heart of the Stuart Range.

Porcupine Creek

Start Point: Ingalls Creek Trailhead, 1,950 feet
High Point: Colchuck Col, 8,000 feet
Best Time: January to May
Overnight: 22 miles
Skiing Time: 16 hours
Skill Level: Advanced
Difficulties: High avalanche potential; routefinding required; long hike; permit/fee area
Maps: Green Trails No. 209, Mount Stuart

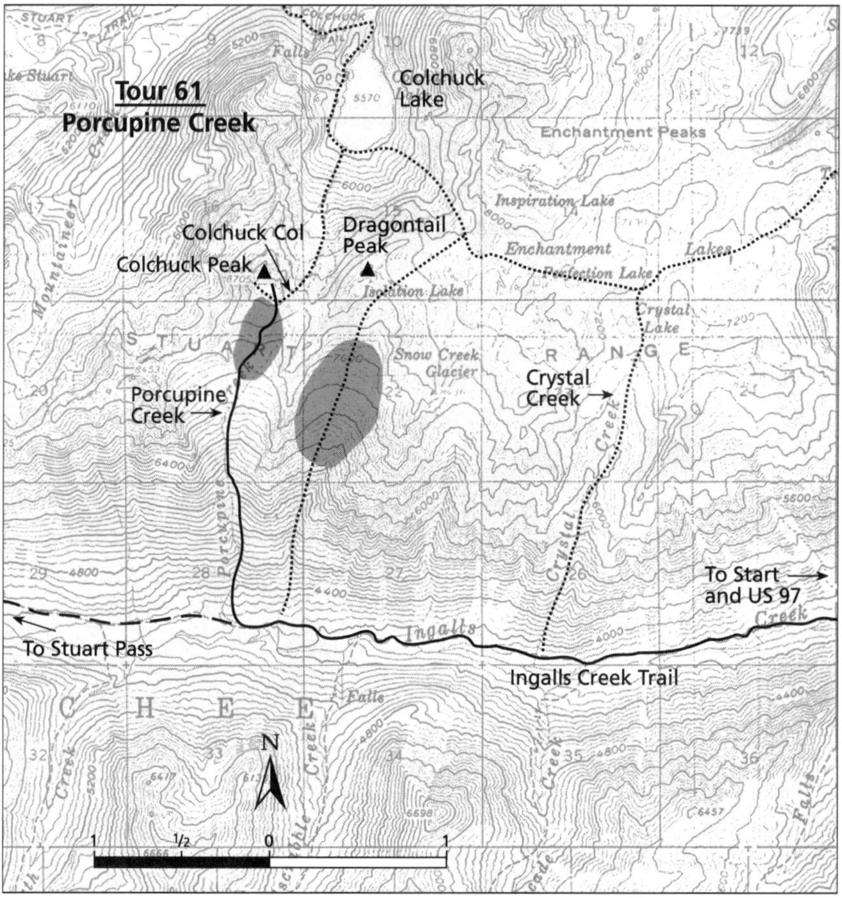

The long Ingalls Creek Valley forms both the southern boundary of the Stuart Range and a reasonable winter access route to this area. Ingalls Creek receives many tributaries from flanking mountainsides. One of these drainages, Porcupine Creek, is noteworthy because it not only offers good skiing, but also tops out in an interesting place, Colchuck Col. Take ice ax and crampons.

Drive US 97 to the Ingalls Creek Trail access road, 7 miles south of the US 2–US 97 junction. Turn right and drive 1.2 miles to road's end or as far as conditions permit. Ski directly up the valley for 9.1 miles, keeping to the north side of the stream. Camp near the confluence of Ingalls and Porcupine Creeks in trees, well away from open slopes, near 4,150 feet.

From camp, look up toward the abrupt south ridge of Dragontail Peak. The Porcupine basin lies just to the left. Ascend this straight on. Near 6,600 feet, the basin turns slightly northeast. Above 7,800 feet the angle lessens and soon you are at the col. Colchuck Lake lies below and to the north. In spring conditions, time your descent so that you ski just as the sun begins to soften the snow. Descend quickly before melting progresses too far. This is basically a steep 3,000-foot ski run in the fall line.

The descent along Ingalls Creek is straightforward.

62
Diamond Head

Start Point: Swauk Pass/Blewett Pass Sno-Park, 4,120 feet
High Point: Diamond Head, 5,915 feet
Best Time: January to March
Day Trip: 5 miles
Skiing Time: 5 hours
Skill Level: Advanced
Difficulties: Moderate avalanche potential (high in gullies); permit/fee area
Maps: USGS Blewett Pass, 1:24,000

The high point of US 97 between US 2 and Interstate 90 is called "Swauk" by the USFS and "Blewett" by WSDOT. While the terrain near here does not offer large-scale descents, the snow quality and better weather make for worthwhile visits. Diamond Head, just 1.7 miles southeast of Swauk/Blewett Pass, has short but steep gullies on its western bulwark, a nice run on its northern side, and gentler forested and clear-cut slopes on its southern and southeastern aprons.

Drive US 97 to Swauk Pass summit. Park at the Sno-Park at the pass. If this lot is full, drive 0.8 mile north on US 97 to Tronsen Campground Sno-Park or head for the Pipe Creek Sno-Park just east of the pass.

From Swauk Pass, ski south along Forest Road No. 9716 for about 2 miles. Pass under the west face of Diamond Head. Climb it directly, gaining the summit in 0.6 mile. This is where the runs are. Retrace the approach to go home

Alternative Route: It is possible to continue south on a loop tour. Near

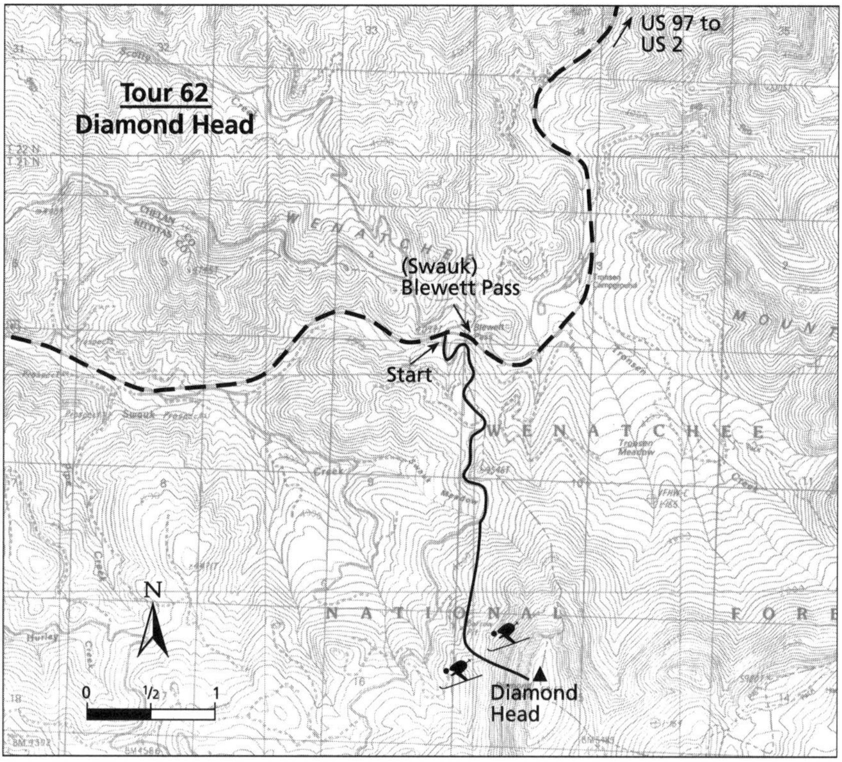

5,100 feet, you will intersect a multiple-use road, which loops around the south ridge of Diamond Head. Ski north to rejoin US 97. (Travel off-road to avoid snowmobiles.)

Ingalls Peak

Start Point: North Fork Teanaway River Road, 4,240 feet

High Point: North-South Peak Col, 7,400 feet

Best Time: April to June

Day Trip/Overnight: 11 miles

Skiing Time: 8 hours

Skill Level: Advanced

Difficulties: High avalanche potential; routefinding required; permit/fee area

Maps: Green Trails No. 209, Mount Stuart

Ingalls Peak lies 2 miles west of Mount Stuart in a scenic, easily accessible area. Crowded in summer, the area is less populous in winter—the snow cover markedly diminishes the number of visitors. The open slopes above and below Ingalls Lake and Ingalls Creek offer a seeming infinity of ski runs. A snowmobile lift to Longs Pass or the end of the road makes this tour feasible in winter. The approach crosses steep, open slopes.

Drive US 97 to Teanaway River Road, 7 miles from Interstate 90. Drive Teanaway River Road for 23 miles to the north fork of the Teanaway River (4,240 feet), or as far as conditions permit.

The trail heads north from road's end for 0.5 mile, then turns right up the hill, switchbacking numerous times to 5,360 feet and a junction (buried under 6 feet of snow). Head north for 1.4 miles, contouring to Ingalls Pass (6,460 feet).

Another approach to Ingalls Lake and Peak continues 0.9 mile east to Longs

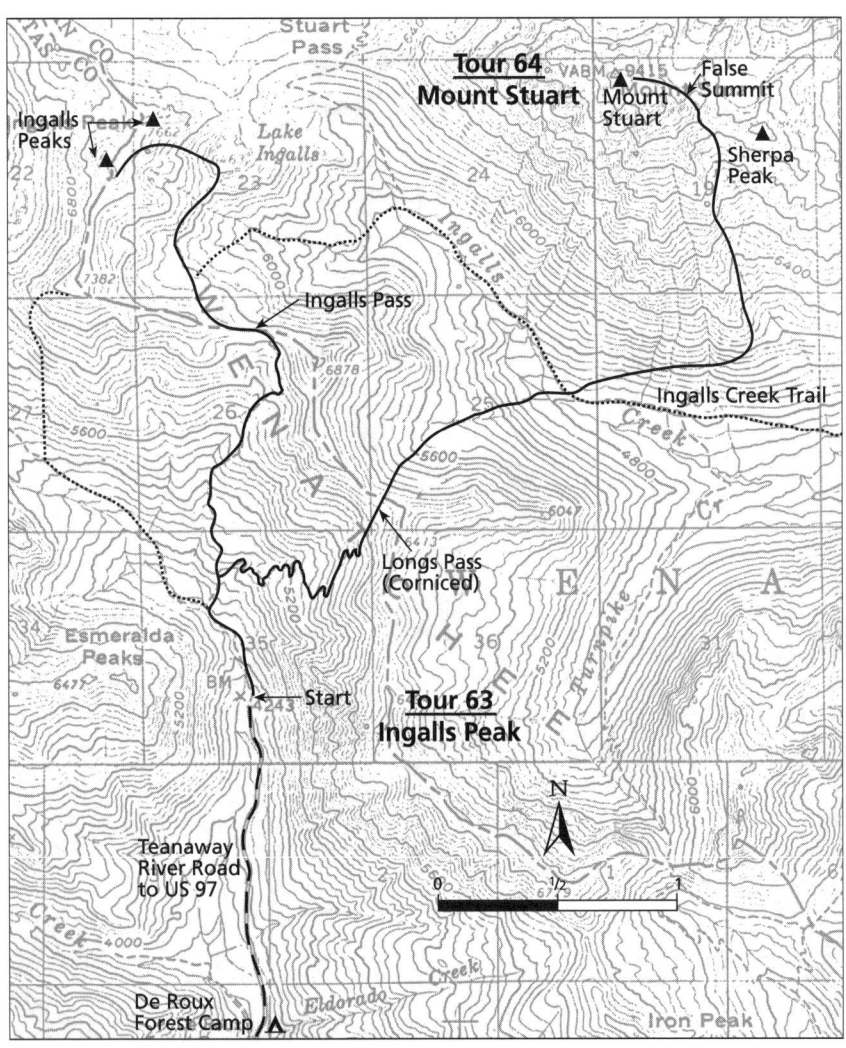

Ingalls Peak country (Photo by Harry Hendon)

Pass (6,200 feet). From the pass, head 0.9 mile north along a ridge around cornices to Ingalls Pass.

From Ingalls Pass, ski 0.8 mile northwest, passing over rolling terrain before dropping into the basin of Ingalls Lake (6,463 feet). The high point of the tour is the col just west of Ingalls Lake (0.8 mile, 7,370 feet). It is possible to ski the lesser Ingalls Peak, which lies south of the col. Other diversions include a ridge traverse to Goat Pass (1.6 miles, 7,900 feet) via Stuart Pass, and descents from Stuart Pass to Jack Creek and Ingalls Creek.

Return to the car by skiing the approach route.

Mount Stuart

Start Point: North Fork Teanaway River Road, 4,240 feet
High Point: Mount Stuart False Summit, 9,160 feet
Best Time: March to April
Overnight: 14 miles
Skiing Time: 10 hours
Skill Level: Alpine
Difficulties: High avalanche potential; routefinding required; permit/fee area
Maps: Green Trails No. 209, Mount Stuart

Mount Stuart and the Enchantment Plateau are visible to the north from Interstate 90 between Ellensburg and Thorp. The long snowfield that descends left

Aerial view of Mount Stuart, with Longs Pass visible left of the wing strut (Photo by Rainer Burgdorfer)

to right from the false summit of Mount Stuart is the southeastern shoulder. This broad slope is steep in only a few sections near the top. This is a good tour; it has a reasonable and varying approach, large-scale skiing is possible on both the northern and southern faces, and it offers spectacular views. Ice axes and crampons are suggested.

Drive to the end of North Fork Teanaway River Road, and hike the Ingalls Way Trail to Longs Pass (2.7 miles, 6,200 feet). Mount Stuart beckons to the east. Take a moment to plan both your route down from Longs Pass, and your approach to Mount Stuart. Your route will follow the eastern flank on the southern rib of the false summit.

Bypassing the cornices at Longs Pass may take some exploration. Descend 1,200 feet to cross Ingalls Creek and head northeast along the gladed valley floor for 0.4 mile toward the southeast shoulder of Mount Stuart. Camp in the woods, well away from avalanche runouts.

The southeast shoulder terminates in a broad avalanche fan to the east of both Ulrichs and Cascadian Couloirs. Although these gullies offer the shortest route to the summit, they are avalanche accumulators.

The southeast shoulder is slightly longer, but not as entrapping. Ski directly up this ramp for 4,000 feet to the false summit. The true summit lies 0.2 mile to the west; in winter conditions, it is a serious climb.

Descend the route of ascent. Once back in the valley, climb back to Longs Pass and descend to the car.

Alternative Route: An optional return route heads upstream to the headwall above Ingalls Creek, then climbs to Ingalls Lake (2.4 miles) and out to the car.

INTERSTATE 90

The primary east-west corridor through the Cascades, Interstate 90 also provides rapid access to tours in these mountains. Tours reached directly from I-90 are accessible year-round, but routes starting from secondary roads may not be feasible until late spring.

This area has a history of snow recreation dating from the nineteenth century, when Norwegian miners first skied the slopes behind the town of Cle Elum. Foot- and gravity-powered recreationists and snowmobilers continue this tradition today. The region has sufficient snow cover for ski tours from December to May. Many of the tours in this area depart from ski-area parking lots. During the ski season, backcountry skiers may be asked to pay a parking fee.

If the weather is particularly foul near Cascade Crest, more benign conditions may sometimes be found near Amabilis Mountain or even farther east, say near Salmon La Sac. (See Jeff Renner's *Northwest Mountain Weather*.)

Mount Daniel

Start Point: Cle Elum River Road, 3,350 feet
High Point: Mount Daniel's East Summit, 7,899 feet
Best Time: April to June
Overnight: 14 miles
Skiing Time: 8 hours
Skill Level: Advanced
Difficulties: High avalanche potential; glacier travel; routefinding required; permit/fee area
Maps: USGS Mt. Daniel, The Cradle, 1:24,000

Mount Daniel's massive, gently sloping shoulders support acres of snow ideally suited for ski touring and snowboarding. Its main drawback is the lack of convenient access; Cle Elum River Road is snow-covered late into spring. The trick to making Mount Daniel a successful tour is to get there just when the road melts out, or to hire a snowmobile operator to give you a lift to the trailhead. An occasional obstacle blocking the last 3 miles of road is the Scatter Creek crossing, which becomes impassable when meltwater rushing across the road is too deep to drive through. Bring a towrope, in case you get stuck. (Or, better yet, examine the situation before you commit!) This tour is a leisurely overnighter, but can be an athletic day trip. Take ice axes and crampons.

Take Interstate 90 to the Roslyn interchange 3 miles west of Cle Elum. Drive through the town of Roslyn, past Salmon La Sac, to the end of the road at 3,350 feet, about 33 miles from Roslyn. Parking lies at the left side of the

The route to Mount Daniel can be seen going directly up the center of this photograph. (Photo by Bryan Scott)

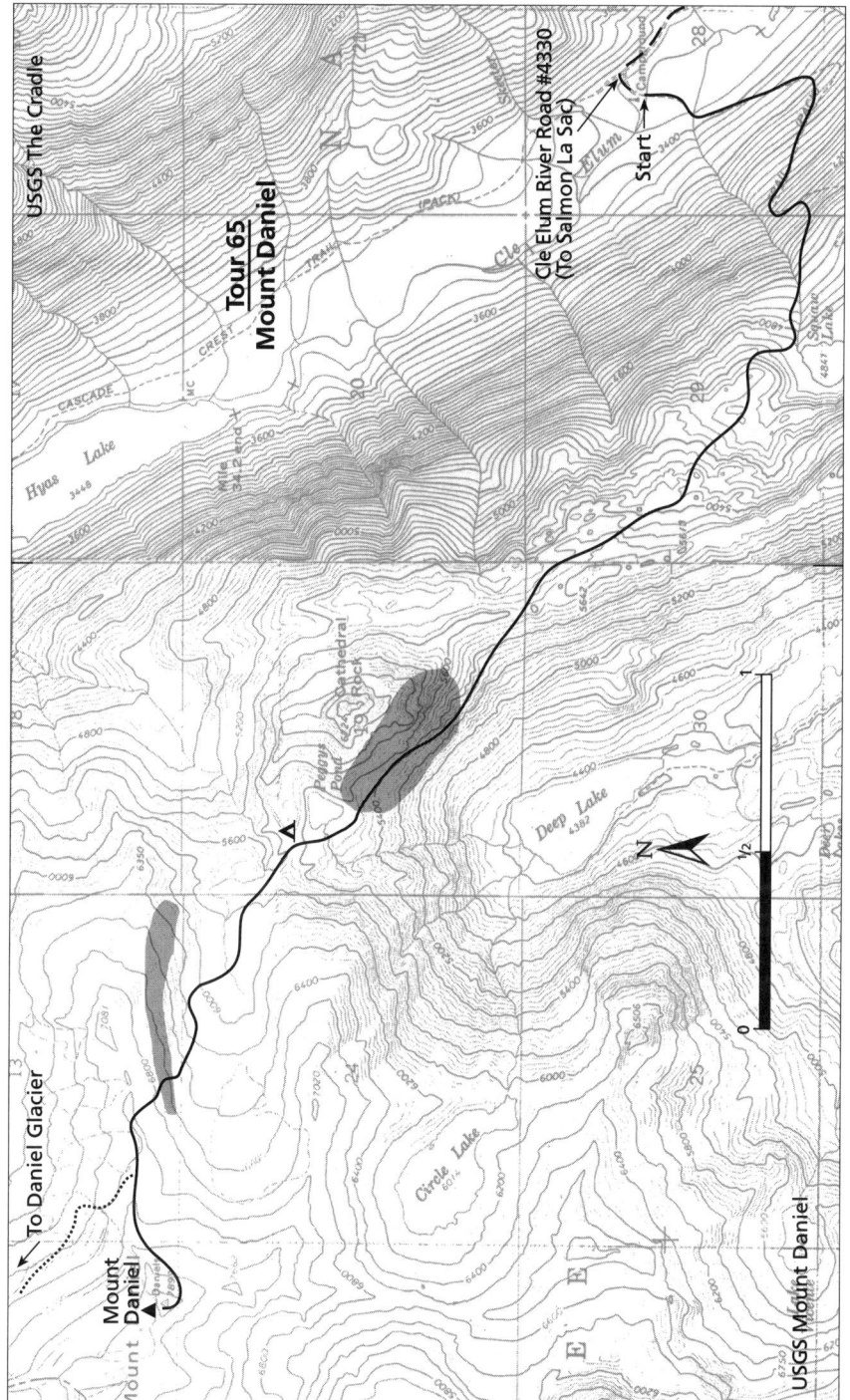

main road. Cathedral Rock is visible to the northwest. Your objective is to reach Peggys Pond just west of the tower.

Hike trail No. 1345 south and then west, gaining 1,000 feet in 1.8 miles. When the ridge begins to flatten, turn northwest over rolling terrain and climb through glades toward the south ridge of Cathedral Rock. Stay above Squaw Lake. Continue for 2.5 miles, heading just left of Cathedral Rock. As you approach the mountain, the terrain will force you to ski left onto a steepening hillside. Cathedral Rock now towers on your right, while Deep Lake lies frozen below. Continue traversing north, climbing a few hundred feet until you see Peggys Pond (5,600 feet). Camp on snow, southwest of the lake, or on a rise to the west. This is a high-use area; stay on the snow or on trails to minimize "meadow busting."

The route to the east summit of Daniel is straightforward and evident from Peggys Pond. Head northwest to the summit, which is visible from the lake; find your route through cliff bands and crevasses. From the pond, climb west into a basin. In 0.3 mile, the angle eases off for a bit, then steepens again to reach the Hyas Creek Glacier. The lower portion of this stagnant ice body is fairly level, and in some years, a lake forms just above the glacier's terminal moraine.

From the eastern end of the glacier, climb directly north onto Mount Daniel's broad east ridge. Ski west to the summit, past a small spire near 7,700 feet. Descend via the approach.

Alternative Route: It is easy to reach Daniel and Lynch Glaciers from Peggys Pond by traversing high on the north side of Mount Daniel. This route provides access to the middle and western summits of Mount Daniel, as well as Mount Hinman beyond. Both glaciers are moderately steep and have extensive crevasse systems.

Jolly *66* Mountain

Start Point: Salmon La Sac, 2,400 feet
High Point: Jolly Mountain, 6,440 feet
Best Time: January to April
Day Trip: 12 miles
Skiing Time: 7 hours
Skill Level: Intermediate
Difficulties: Moderate avalanche potential; permit/fee area; not recommended for snowboarders
Maps: Green Trails No. 208, Kachess Lake

Jolly Mountain is located northeast of Cle Elum Lake. It is an easy, albeit long, tour and affords wonderful views of the Mount Stuart and Dutch Miller Gap areas. The weather tends to be better here than on the west side of the mountains; in recent years, the road has been kept open all the way to Salmon La Sac to provide access to Sno-Park users.

Drive Interstate 90 to Exit 80. Take State Route 903 through Roslyn, past Cle Elum Lake to the Salmon La Sac guard station. Jolly Mountain Trail No. 1307 climbs out of the bottom of the valley behind the stables east of the guard station. At first, the trail climbs through forest. It then switchbacks through clear-cuts for 1.5 miles to a wooded ridge near 4,500 feet. Climb around this buttress on its left, passing a level ridge top near 5,140 feet, then head east to the crest (6,000 feet, 0.9 mile).

Head south along the ridge to the summit of Jolly Mountain (0.7 mile, 6,440 feet). Retrace the approach.

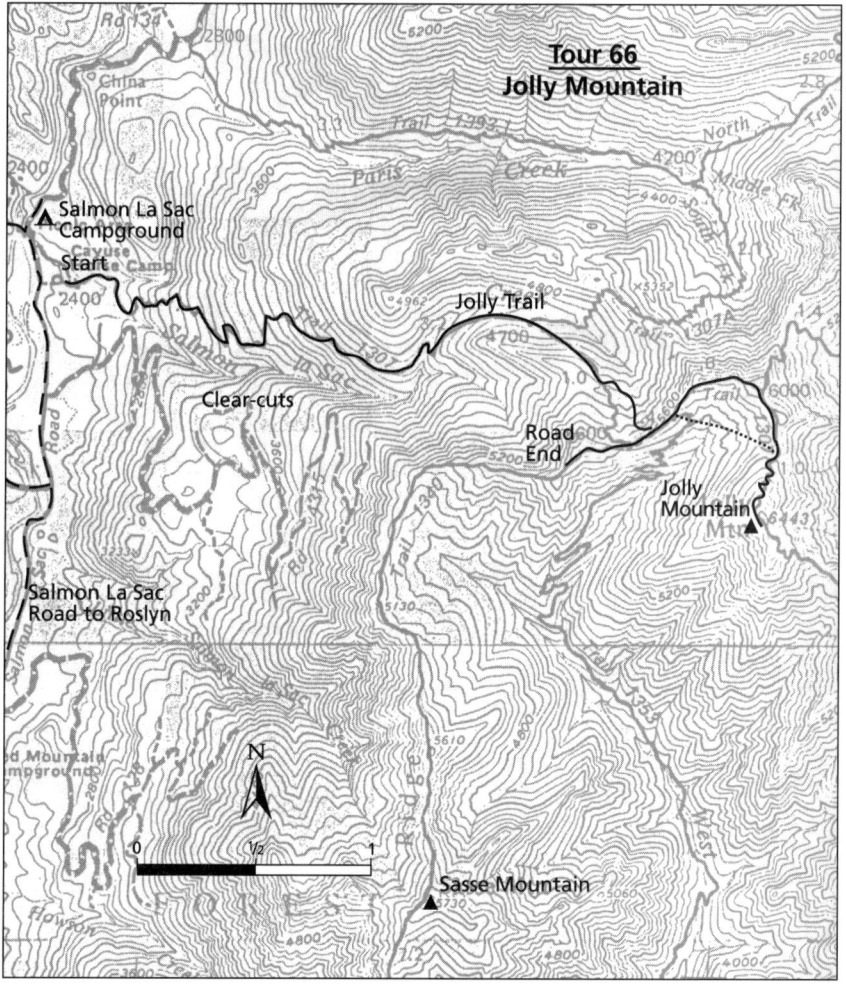

Amabilis Mountain

Start Point: Cabin Creek Sno-Park (I-90 Exit 63, 2,300 feet)
High Point: Amabilis Mountain, 4,500 feet
Best Time: December to March
Day Trip: 8 miles
Skiing Time: 4 to 6 hours
Skill Level: Intermediate
Difficulties: Low avalanche potential; permit/fee area
Maps: Green Trails No. 207, Snoqualmie Pass

Amabilis Mountain offers an aerobic ascent to a broad summit with sweeping views and minor runs on its north and south slopes. This tour is best suited to Nordic equipment because of the moderate terrain. This is a popular area, so arrive early to find a place to park. Snowshoers, please stay out of skiers' tracks.

Drive Interstate 90 to Exit 63, the Cabin Creek exit. Park in the Sno-Park west of the highway and walk across the overpass to Cabin Creek Road.

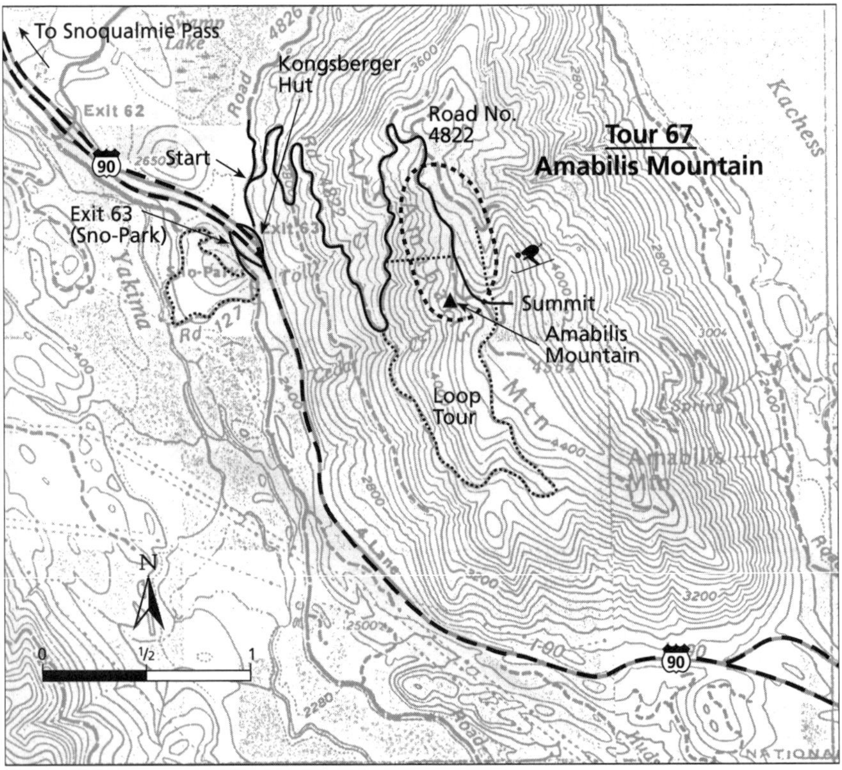

Ski the road past the Kongsberger Ski Club, a Nordic racing club, and turn right (uphill) onto Amabilis Mountain Road. The road crosses the Kongsberger racetrack twice: be sure to look both ways to avoid interfering with racers. Climb the road for 2 miles. At 3,300 feet there is a junction. The right fork makes a loop and returns to the left fork. (From the Sno-Park, the round-trip distance for this tour is 8 miles.)

Take the left fork for better views and more interesting skiing. Climb through switchbacks to the 1.3-mile-long summit ridge. Peer down the eastern side of the ridge for skiing possibilities—there are gullies and glades there to challenge adventurous skiers. If you descend far enough, you'll intersect log roads that circle the mountain and bring you back to the start. You'll probably meet snowmobiles, too.

The summit hump lies near the southern end of the ridge. There are four possible descent routes. The first is to reverse the approach. The second option is to descend the northeastern side and follow log roads to the start. The third is to find the southern branch of the loop and follow it to the intersection below. Finally, it is possible to ski the fall line along the southern slope through clear-cuts and then follow a road back to the start.

Mount Margaret

Start Point: Gold Creek Sno-Park, 2,700 feet
High Point: Mount Margaret, 5,531 feet
Best Time: December to March
Day Trip: 15 miles
Skiing Time: 6 hours
Skill Level: Intermediate
Difficulties: Moderate avalanche potential; permit/fee area
Maps: Green Trails No. 207, Snoqualmie Pass

The huge, gleaming slope southeast of the Gold Creek Sno-Park is the southern terminus of Rampart Ridge. Mount Margaret lies to the east, separated from Rampart by Rocky Run (a creek). This tour has a flavor similar to the Amabilis tour, with the bonus of better skiing higher up. While wax makes skiing the road easy, climbing skins make the ascent to the high point a delight (as much as this is possible).

Drive Interstate 90 to Exit 54, the Rocky Run exit. Drive to Gold Creek Sno-Park and continue south as far as possible. (A Sno-Park permit is required.)

Ski the road south for 2 miles, paralleling Interstate 90 and passing some homes. When the road turns left and starts to climb, follow it for 3 miles. Keep right at the first intersection. In 0.6 mile you'll come to another intersection: take

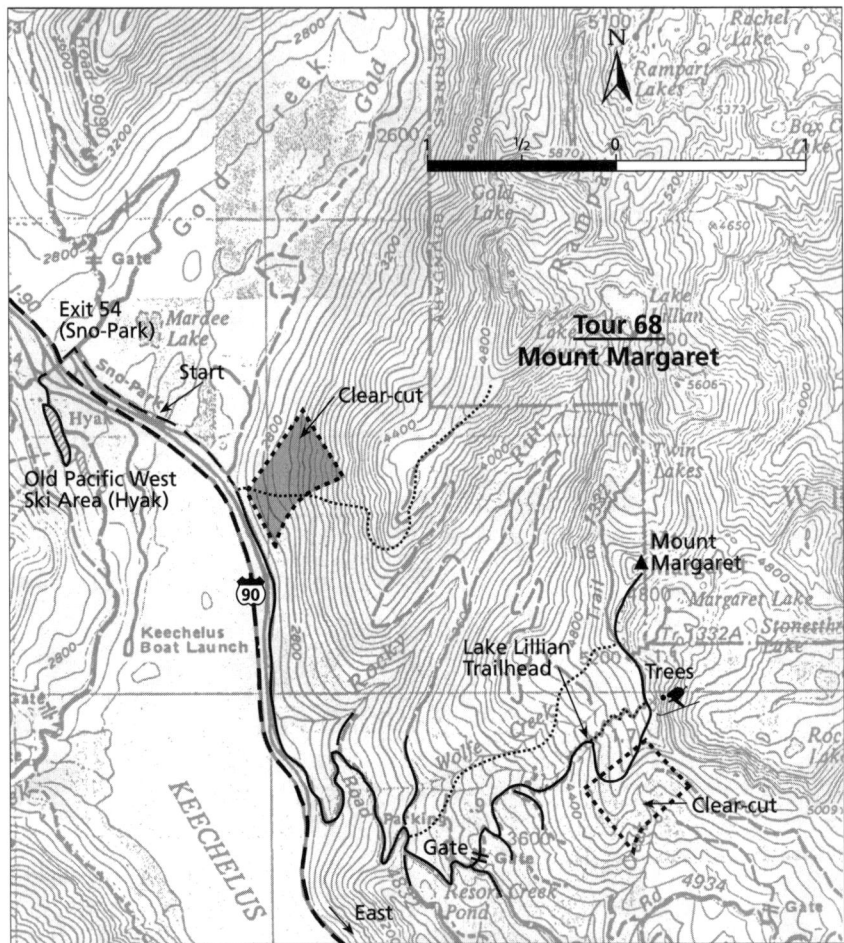

a left fork and continue climbing for 1 mile to the Lake Lillian Trailhead (3,600 feet). Head northeast from the south end of the trailhead (the road peters out), climbing steeply across a branch of Wolfe Creek and up a giant clear-cut, bordered on the distant left by mature forest.

Continue climbing to the ridge crest (5,000+ feet), then look over the east side. Good descents can be made in the various gullies that divide the east slope. Other treasures await higher up. Head north along the ridge and enter the forest. Continue climbing in the trees to the summit of Mount Margaret (0.8 mile, 5,531 feet). The forest remnant near the summit of Mount Margaret often acts as a powder cache long after the passage of winter storms. In these conditions, it's fun to set a track and yo-yo ski this fine powder repeatedly. To return to the car, reverse the approach.

Alternative Route: From the summit of Mount Margaret, you can ski along the northern ridge to Twin Lakes. Retrace your route to return to the car.

Moist marine air produces deep snowpacks; looking south from Mount Margaret. (Photo by Joe Catellani)

Kendall Ridge

Start Point: Gold Creek Sno-Park, 2,700 feet
High Point: Kendall Ridge, 4,800 feet
Best Time: January to March
Day Trip: 8 miles
Skiing Time: 4 hours
Skill Level: Intermediate
Difficulties: Moderate avalanche potential; permit/fee area
Maps: Green Trails No. 207, Snoqualmie Pass

The Kendall Ridge tour ascends part of the southern flank of Kendall Peak. It is a short trip, ideal if you have only a morning but would like a little exercise and some fun skiing. This is a good tour for Nordic equipment.

Drive Interstate 90 to the Hyak–Rocky Run exit. Gold Creek is just east of the highway. Park at the Sno-Park.

From the Sno-Park, head northeast on the snow-covered road. Within 0.2 mile there is a fork: take the left road and follow it through switchbacks to a forested section (1.5 miles). Continue along the forested road, crossing a clear-cut

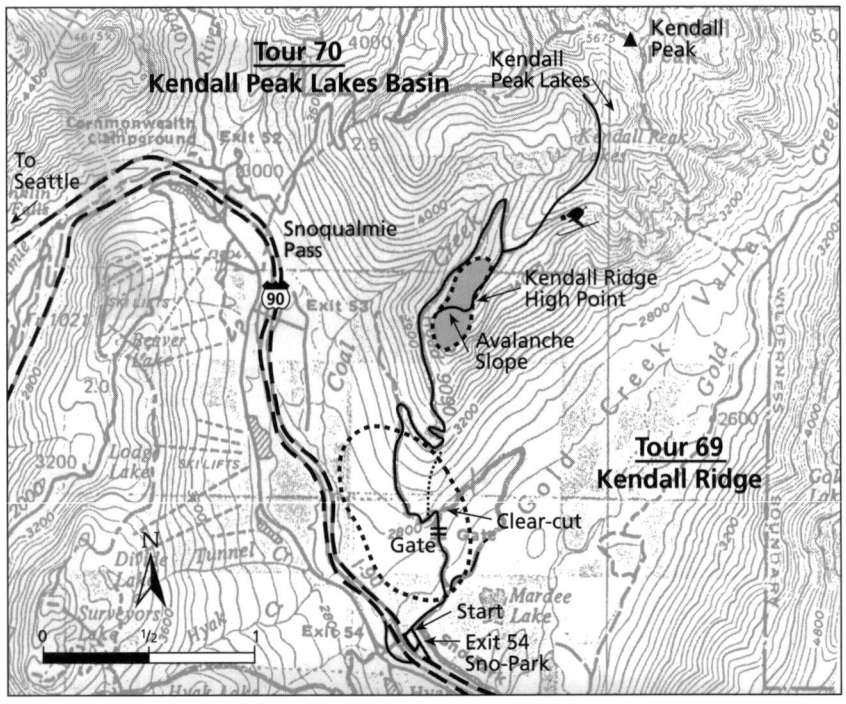

Mid-season at Kendall Ridge (Photo by Rainer Burgdorfer)

beneath a minor buttress. This feature was the site of an avalanche accident in the late '80s—the party successfully rescued itself with transceivers, shovels, and savvy.

Continue, following the curving road to the top of the clear-cut. From the ridge crest, head northeast into the woods for 1 mile to a knoll just south of Kendall Peak Lakes. Trees provide shelter for a lunch spot. Clear-cut slopes and glades on the northeastern shoulder of Kendall Ridge offer good runs.

Head back to Kendall Knoll, and then descend south-southwest through dense trees to rejoin the road below.

70
Kendall Peak Lakes Basin

Start Point: Gold Creek Sno-Park, 2,700 feet
High Point: Kendall Ridge, 4,800 feet
Best Time: December to March
Day Trip: 8 miles
Skiing Time: 6 hours
Skill Level: Intermediate
Difficulties: High avalanche potential; permit/fee area
Maps: Green Trails No. 207, Snoqualmie Pass

Kendall Peak Lakes Basin lies 1.7 miles northeast-east of Snoqualmie Pass, but is reached via the Kendall Ridge approach.

The complex slopes surrounding the basin provide numerous runs of varying steepness up to a mile long with 1,200 feet of elevation gain.

From the Gold Creek Sno-Park, ski the road to Kendall Ridge. From the knoll at 4,250 feet, head northeast for 0.5 mile. Near 4,400 feet, keep left of the ridge as you traverse 0.5 mile to lower Kendall Peak Lakes (4,465 feet). It is another 0.2 mile to upper Kendall Peak Lakes (4,700 feet).

Ski the gullies and ridges along the north rim of the basin, then return via the approach.

71
Red Mountain

Start Point: Alpental Road, 3,000 feet
High Point: Red Mountain, 5,890 feet
Best Time: January to April
Day Trip: 10 miles
Skiing Time: 7 hours
Skill Level: Advanced
Difficulties: High avalanche potential
Maps: Green Trails No. 207, Snoqualmie Pass

Red Mountain is located at the head of the upper east fork of Commonwealth Creek, 1.3 miles east of Mount Snoqualmie. The peak is also visible from the

The Kendall Peak Lakes Basin in foreground (Photo by Rainer Burgdorfer)

Descending the west face of Red Mountain (Photo by Brian Povolny)

slopes of Snoqualmie Summit ski area, its gleaming west face showing just to the right of Guye Peak. Take an ice ax and crampons. Time your descent so that only the top inch of snow is soft—this is a steep run.

Drive I-90 to Exit 52, the Snoqualmie West exit. Park at the west end of the Snoqualmie Summit ski area parking lot. (Do not park in the Sahale Ski Club parking lot north of I-90.)

Walk north under the freeway bridge, and then begin skiing northeast immediately across the road from the westbound on-ramp. Climb for 0.8 mile and cross Commonwealth Creek near 3,600 feet.

Continue north-northeast for 1 mile to the southwest ridge of Red Mountain (4,000 feet) and climb it directly to the summit (0.8 mile, 5,890 feet). Enjoy the views and get ready for a ride! Descend quickly to the valley floor and ski the fall line to Alpental Road. Walk back to the car.

Mount Snoqualmie

Start Point: Alpental Road, 3,000 feet
High Point: Mount Snoqualmie Summit, 6,280 feet
Best Time: December to April
Day Trip: 6 miles
Skiing Time: 8 hours
Skill Level: Advanced
Difficulties: High avalanche potential; routefinding required
Maps: Green Trails No. 207, Snoqualmie Pass

This is a view tour, with a panoramic vista ranging from Mount Baker to Mount Rainier. The skiing is quite good, too. Recoilless rifles are sometimes used to release snow buildup on Cave Ridge; check with Alpental snow controllers before beginning a tour in this area. If you see any unusual object (e.g., something that might be a projectile) lying on the ground or snow, do not approach it! Mark the general location and report it to the snow controllers. This tour is steep: take an ice ax and crampons.

Leave I-90 at the West Snoqualmie Summit exit and park near the western end of the ski area parking lot.

Hike under the freeway and climb northeast from the road, as in the Red Mountain tour. Climb for 0.8 mile and cross Commonwealth Creek near 3,600 feet. Ski due north now, curving around the north wall of Guye Peak for 0.5 mile. Then climb northeast, gaining Cave Ridge near 4,600 feet near the Guye-Snoqualmie saddle. From the saddle, ski due north for 0.5 mile toward the summit of Mount Snoqualmie.

Traverse the gully that leads to the southwest ridge of Mount Snoqualmie and ascend the steep, gradually easing ridge to the summit. Descend by reversing the summit portion of the climb, then either retracing the approach or heading down the northeastern portion of Cave Ridge.

Alternative Route: Direct ascents of Snoqualmie have been made from the Alpental side but cliff bands make routefinding uncertain.

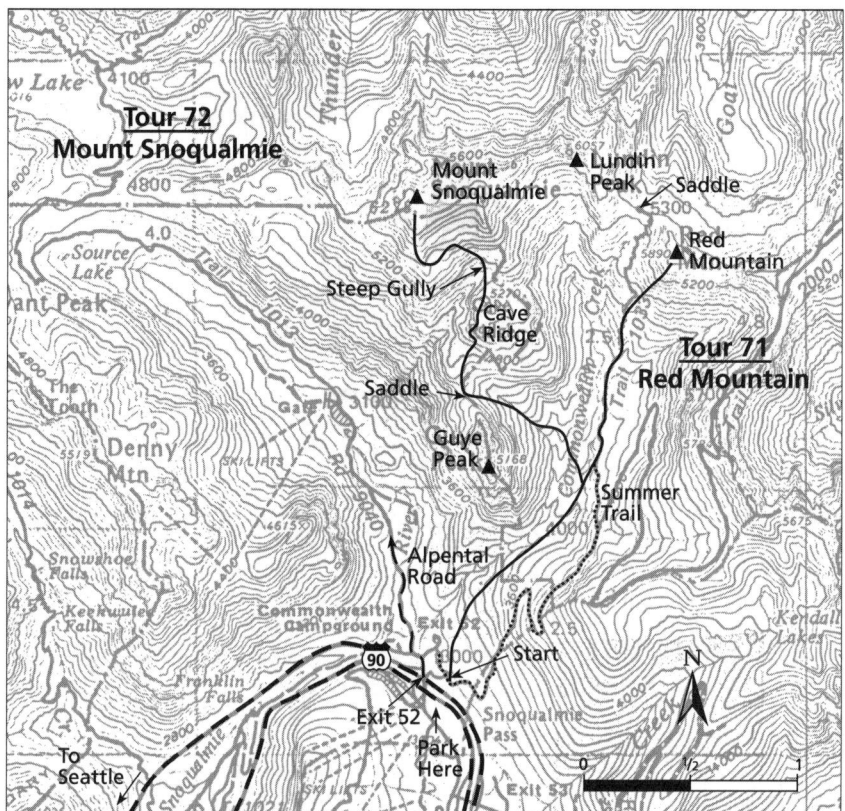

73
Chair Peak Basin

Start Point: Alpental parking lot, 3,260 feet
High Point: Chair Peak East shoulder, 5,440 feet
Best Time: December to May
Day Trip: 5 miles
Skiing Time: 5 hours
Skill Level: Alpine
Difficulties: High avalanche potential
Maps: Green Trails No. 207, Snoqualmie Pass

The Alpental Basin offers short but entertaining tours with plenty of variety. The skiing tends to be steep and the setting intimate—no huge mountains here, just pretty peaks and charming hanging valleys.

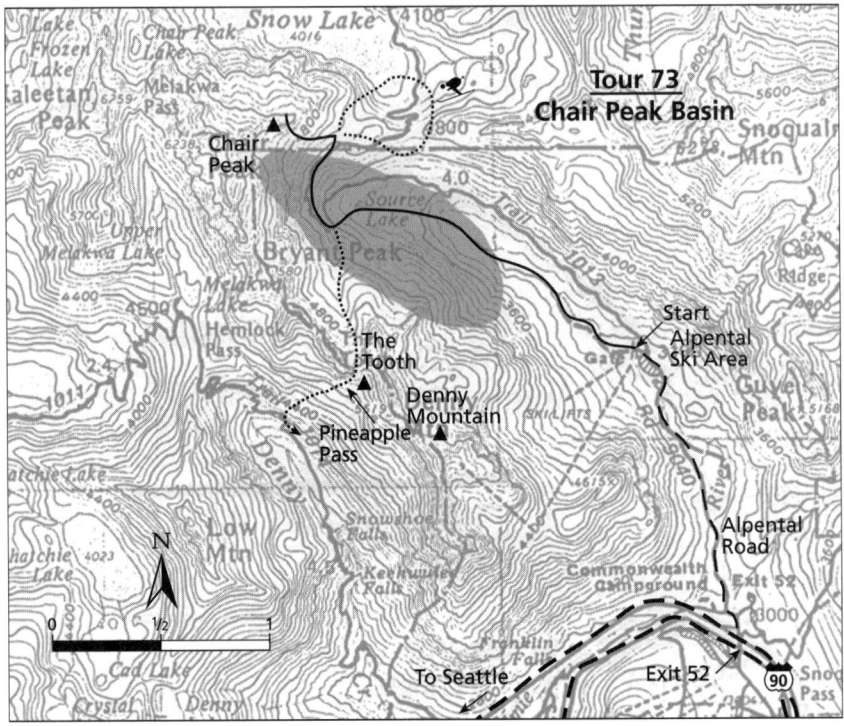

Drive I-90 to Snoqualmie Pass, take the Alpental exit, and drive Alpental Road to the uppermost ski area parking lot.

From the parking lot, ski northwest along the valley bottom for 0.6 mile, climbing up a groomed road. Watch out for descending skiers, especially when the lifts are running. Keep generally to the left. When the terrain steepens, climb northwest-west to Source Lake (0.5 mile, 3,760 feet).

From Source Lake, climb northwest into the Chair Peak basin and gain the ridge just to the right of the mountain (0.7 mile, 5,400 feet). Short, steep runs can be made to the north (beware of the cliff bands below), but the major portion of the skiing lies along the ascent route.

To return to the car, reverse the ascent.

Alternate Route: A scenic side trip heads due east down Chair Peak Basin and over a shoulder into Snow Lake Basin.

Another variation, since discovered in reverse by downhill skiers from Alpental/Denny Mountain, is made by climbing to Pineapple Pass, the notch just south of the Tooth. Ski up the Source Lake drainage. From the lake, climb due south to a hanging valley (4,800 feet). Pineapple Pass lies at the head of the valley.

Chair Peak Basin (Photo by Brian Sullivan)

Silver Peak

Start Point: Keechelus Sno-Park, 2,500 feet
High Point: Silver Peak, 5,620 feet
Best Time: December to March
Day Trip: 8 miles
Skiing Time: 7 hours
Skill Level: Advanced
Difficulties: High avalanche potential; routefinding required; permit/fee area
Maps: Green Trails No. 207, Snoqualmie Pass

Silver Peak was among the first of the Snoqualmie peaks to be climbed on skis and remains a popular objective. A scenic approach, suitable for skis or

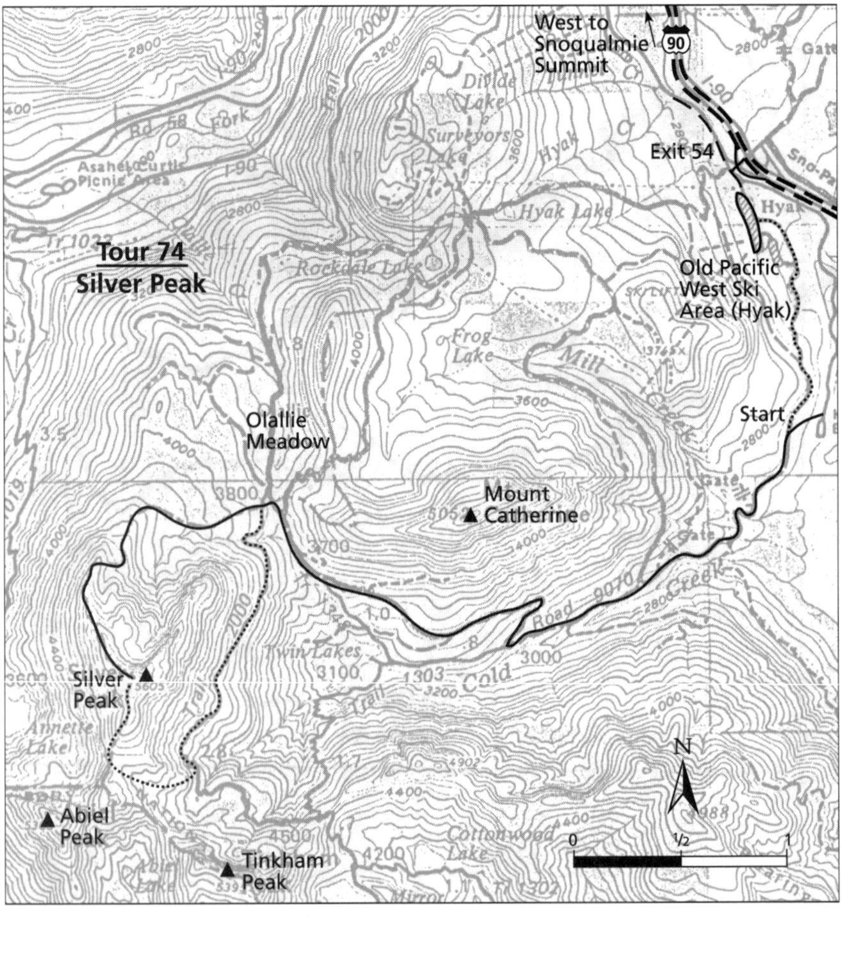

Silver Peak (Photo by Rainer Burgdorfer)

snowshoes, can be made from the Hyak/Pacific West ski area or from the Keechelus Sno-Park, 1.5 miles south of Exit 54. The latter point of departure avoids interference with the Nordic ski operation at Hyak.

Drive Interstate 90 to Hyak, Exit 54. The road to Hyak hamlet and beyond is in the southeast quadrant of the interchange. Drive this road for 1.6 miles to the Keechelus Sno-Park. Park at the boat-launch site. If the road to the Sno-Park is not plowed, park at Hyak/Pacific West ski area, then ski along the road clockwise to start the tour.

Ski southwest up the Cold Creek drainage on Forest Road 2219, skirting the southern flank of Mount Catherine. Snowshoers should stay out of skiers' tracks. Switchback to stay on the west slope of Mount Catherine, then head northwest to Windy Pass (4.2 miles, 3,700 feet).

From Windy Pass, follow a winding road west, or head directly southwest-west for 0.8 mile. Turn south near 4,200 feet, gaining the summit of Silver Peak in 1 mile (5,620 feet). The final section is quite steep. Descend via the approach.

Humpback Mountain

Start Point: Exit 47, Interstate 90, 1,800 feet
High Point: Humpback Mountain, south ridge, 5,170 feet
Best Time: February to March
Day Trip: 9 miles
Skiing Time: 6 hours
Skill Level: Intermediate
Difficulties: Moderate avalanche potential; permit/fee area
Maps: Green Trails No. 206, Bandera; No. 207, Snoqualmie Pass

Humpback Mountain rises 3,000 feet above the Interstate 90 corridor, but its public face doesn't display its virtue. It is the southwest shoulder that sometimes offers reasonable skiing in spring conditions.

On Granite Mountain; Humpback Mountain lies in the immediate background. (Photo by Brian Sullivan)

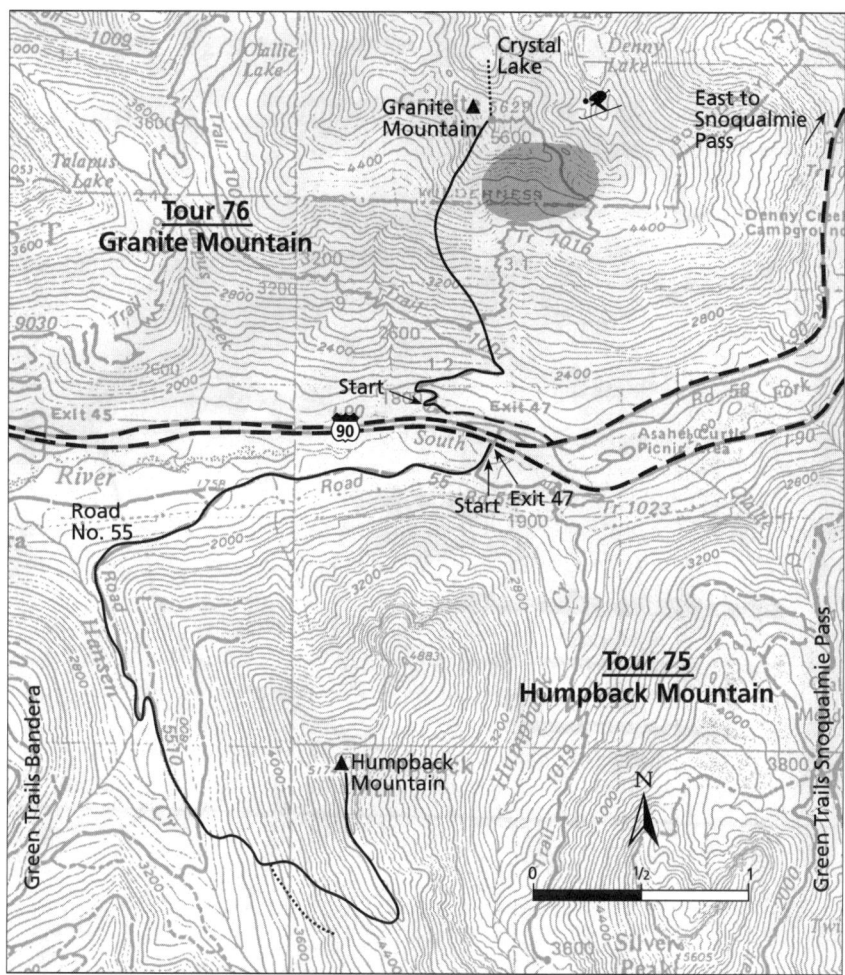

Drive Interstate 90 to Exit 47, the Granite Mountain exit, and head south for 0.2 mile, parking at the T intersection.

Ski the right road and follow it for 1.4 miles to a junction. Go left and begin contouring around Humpback Mountain. In 0.7 mile, you are in the Hansen Creek drainage. Pass under an old railroad bridge and continue heading south as the road makes a left, then a right switchback. When the road approaches Hansen Creek, leave it at any convenient place and begin climbing through slide alder, trees, and cliff bands. Continue climbing southeast, heading for the ridge crest at 4,600 feet. Climb the ridge north to the summit if conditions and inclinations allow. Reverse the approach to go home.

The hillsides across Hansen Creek also offer nice runs. For either tour, a small wax kit eases the long, nearly level return along the bottom of the valley.

Granite Mountain

Start Point: Exit 47, Interstate 90, 1,800 feet

High Point: Granite Mountain, 5,600 feet

Best Time: January to April

Day Trip: 8 miles

Skiing Time: 6 hours

Skill Level: Advanced

Difficulties: High avalanche potential; permit/fee area

Maps: Green Trails No. 207, Snoqualmie Pass; No. 206, Bandera

Granite Mountain is that gleaming bulk across Interstate 90 from Humpback Mountain. This is the premier tour in the Snoqualmie Pass area because of its huge south-side runs of varying difficulty, its numerous and complex northern descents, and its short approach. When Snoqualmie Summit is cloaked in the dreaded Snoqualmie ice fog, Granite Mountain often enjoys spring-like sunshine and corn snow.

Drive I-90 to Exit 47 and park at the trailhead parking lot north of the highway.

Follow the trail through forest as it switchbacks east and west to 2,250 feet. Once out of the trees, begin a climbing traverse. Head generally north, staying on the broad ridge west of the major gully system. The summer trail traverses east near 4,000 feet—don't go this way. Rather, stay out of the gullies.

When convenient, start climbing north-northwest to gain the windswept

Granite Mountain (Photo by Rainer Burgdorfer)

ridge that leads to the summit. Look for a convex snow formation on the south side, just below the summit. Make a mental note to avoid it on the descent. From the summit, you can make runs to the north toward Crystal, Denny, and Tuscohatchie Lakes. Or, if you prefer, you can head down the broad southwestern ridge (often graced with corn snow) back to the car.

McClellan Butte

Start Point: McClellan Butte Trail, 1,800 feet
High Point: McClellan Butte west shoulder, 4,400 feet
Best Time: January to March
Day Trip: 7 miles
Skiing Time: 6 hours
Skill Level: Advanced
Difficulties: High avalanche potential; permit/fee area
Maps: USGS Chester Morse Lake, Bandera, 1:24,000

McClellan Butte is the pointed, alpine-looking mountain just south of I-90, 6 miles east of the Edgewick Road exit. The glades on the west slope of the peak, with their easy access, offer a change of pace from high mountain skiing. The gullies on the freeway side have been skied.

Drive I-90 to the McClellan Butte exit and head south, driving the access

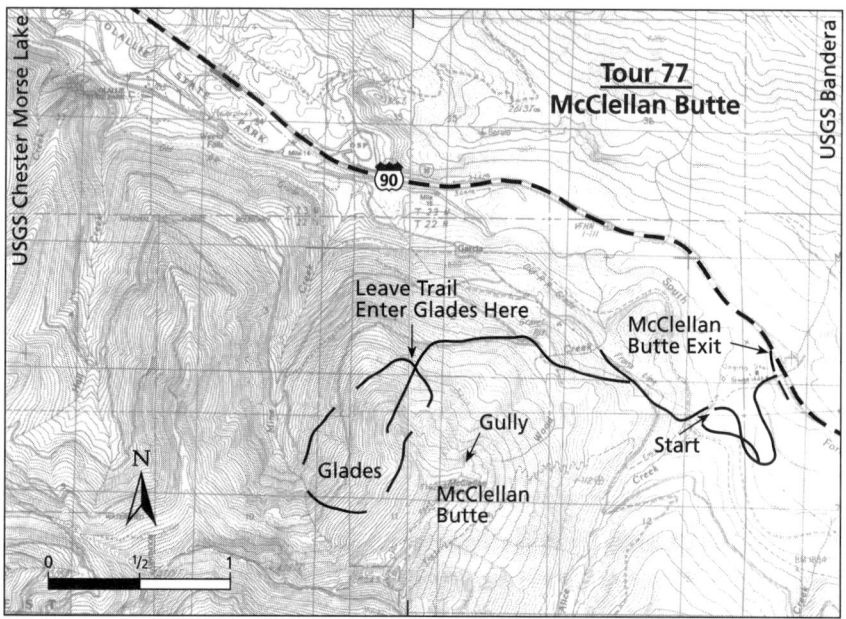

McClellan Butte (Photo by Rainer Burgdorfer)

road to the trailhead. The trail climbs through much-thinned forest and crosses former logging roads and railway right of way. Your objective is to reach the northwest shoulder, where open areas sweep from the summit cliffs to 2,500 feet.

Follow the trail until you converge onto the bottom of a glade, then climb directly to its apex. Traverse east or west to link up with more gullies (east) and glades (west). Reverse the approach to return to the trailhead.

MOUNT RAINIER AND AREAS SOUTH

The southern Washington Cascades, with the exception of the volcanoes, lack the rugged alpine aspect of the northern range. Nevertheless, challenging tours abound. This section covers three general areas: the area accessible from the north side of Mount Rainier via State Route 410; the area accessible from the west and south sides of Mount Rainier National Park via State Routes 165 and 7; and, finally, the areas south of the park.

State Route 410 leads to the Crystal Mountain ski area, the White River entrance to the park, and to the Chinook–Cayuse Pass area. Chinook Pass closes early in the season, but Cayuse stays open a few weeks longer. When both passes are finally closed for the winter, the highway is gated at the Crystal Mountain turnoff. This unfortunate closure turns midwinter day tours into major expeditions.

Large elk herds live in this area. It is sometimes possible to see these magnificent animals grazing along the banks of the White River.

Norse Peak

Start Point: Crystal Mountain Ski Area, 4,400 feet
High Point: Norse Peak, 6,860 feet
Best Time: January to April
Day Trip: 7 miles
Skiing Time: 6 hours
Skill Level: Advanced
Difficulties: High avalanche potential
Maps: Green Trails No. 271, Bumping Lake

Crystal Mountain's skiing potential is largely undeveloped, a fact that backcountry skiers familiar with the area fully appreciate. Norse Peak is the mountain on your left as you enter the resort valley. Big Crow Basin and Lake Basin are two drainage areas east of Norse Peak that are accessible from the summit area. These two basins often hold powder for many days after a snowfall. Parents of young children take note: the ski area operates a daycare center.

Drive State Route 410 to the Crystal Mountain Road. Take this road to the ski area. Park on the eastern side of the parking lot if possible.

Ski directly southeast for 2.5 miles past Bullion Basin, reaching the ridge crest near 6,600 feet. Once on the ridge, head north to the summit of Norse Peak. From here, head north for 0.2 mile to descend to Big Crow Basin or head directly east for 0.2 mile, then south to ski into Lake Basin.

Reverse your descent to regain Norse Peak, then ski the west face to return to the car.

Union Creek

Start Point: Crystal Mountain Ski Area, 4,400 feet
High Point: Norse Peak (south ridge), 6,200 feet
Best Time: January to April
Day Trip: 9 miles
Skiing Time: 7 hours
Skill Level: Advanced
Difficulties: High avalanche potential
Maps: Green Trails No. 271, Bumping Lake

Union Creek is the collector for streams draining from the Lake and Cement Basins. Highway 410 crosses the creek 9.4 miles east of Chinook Pass. This tour

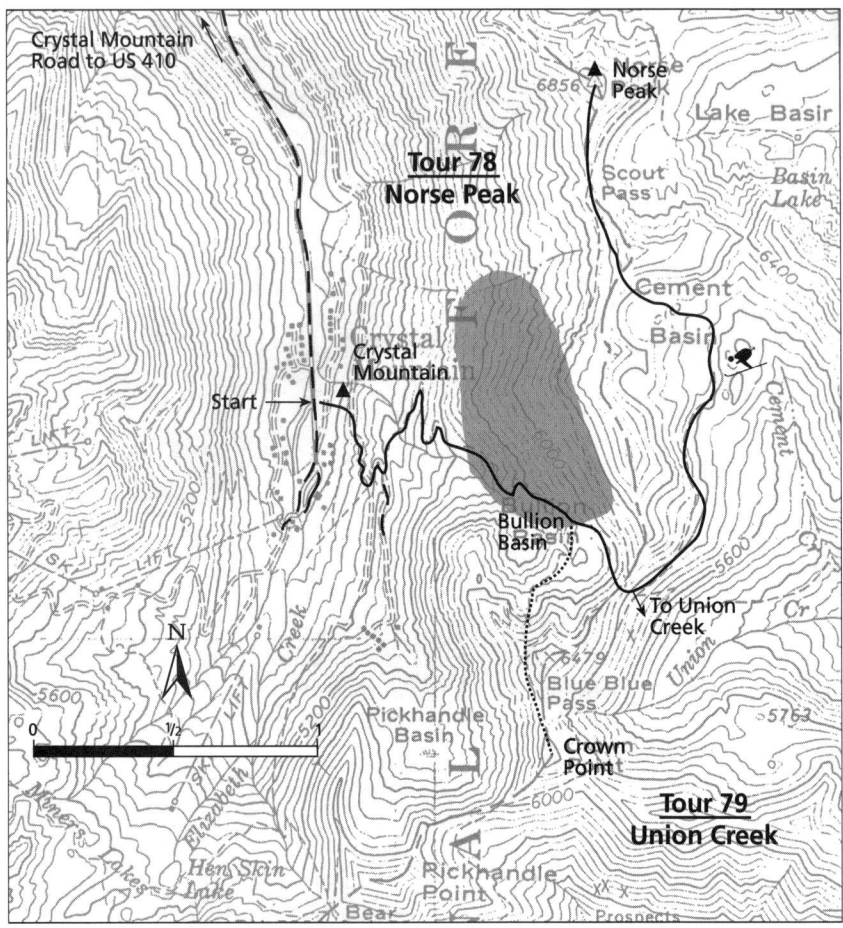

leaves from Crystal Mountain and drops into Union Creek from the head of Bullion Basin.

Drive to Crystal Mountain ski area and park.

From the upper parking area, climb the left edge of the children's ski area east of the chapel. Locate the road, which climbs north through trees near 4,800 feet, and follow it to the Bullion Basin trailhead. Ski north for 0.1 mile, crossing the stream, then switchback southeast along the treeline (follow the summer trail if visible), staying above the streambed.

Enter the basin in 1 mile and gain the saddle (6,100 feet), avoiding avalanche slopes crossed by the trail. Head south along the ridge for a short distance, then drop east onto the Union Creek slope for 500-foot runs. From Union Creek, contour to the ridge above Bullion Basin and descend to the ski area.

Silver King

Start Point: Crystal Mountain Ski Area, 4,400 feet
High Point: Silver King, 7,000 feet
Best Time: January to April
Day Trip: 5 miles
Skiing Time: 4 hours
Skill Level: Advanced
Difficulties: High avalanche potential
Maps: Green Trails No. 271, Bumping Lake

Directly south of the Crystal Mountain ski area are three basins: Silver, Campbell, and Crystal. Slopes in these basins provide fine skiing. Silver Basin is now fully incorporated into the Crystal Mountain ski area. This basin is only suitable for a backcountry tour when the lifts are not running. Then overnight tours are feasible, with safe campsites available in all three basins. If you do plan an

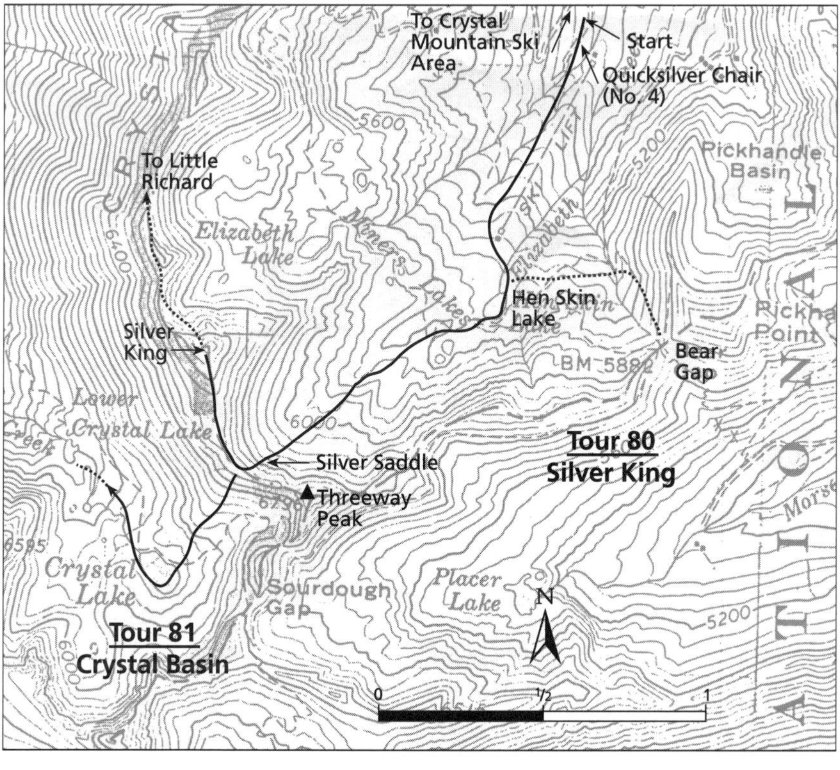

Approaching Camp Muir (Photo by Craig Miller)

overnight tour, park in the designated overnight area. Sign in with the ski patrol for all backcountry tours.

From Enumclaw, drive State Route 410 to Crystal Mountain. From the base area, climb south-southwest under Chair 4 (Quicksilver), staying well off the run. At the head of the lift, continue south along a groomed trail past Hen Skin and Miners Lakes. Start climbing west to reach the Silver King–Three Way Peak saddle (1.1 mile from Hen Skin, 6,460 feet). Climb north to reach the summit of Silver King (0.4 mile, 7,000 feet).

Descend Silver King via its eastern or southeastern slope. Connect traverses back to Silver Basin. From Silver Basin, simply reverse the approach to the car. When you return to the ski area, sign out with the Ski Patrol.

Avalanche Basin, to the north of Silver King, is extremely steep on its southern slope (the Silver King side). The solitude of this basin has been degraded slightly by alpine skiers making ridge traverses to Silver King, then skiing out to Chair 4.

Crystal Basin

Start Point: Crystal Mountain Ski Area, 4,400 feet
High Point: Silver King Saddle, 6,500 feet
Best Time: January to April
Day Trip: 6 miles
Skiing Time: 5 hours
Skill Level: Advanced
Difficulties: High avalanche potential
Maps: Green Trails No. 271, Bumping Lake

Crystal Basin lies directly west of Silver Saddle. This tour is excellent in spring, when days are longer and corn snow has had a chance to develop. It is possible to descend all the way to State Route 410 (2.4 miles), and then to ski or hike the highway to the Crystal Mountain turnoff (4.1 miles). This is a very steep run.

Ski from the top of Chair 4 past Hen Skin Lake to Silver Saddle. Descend open slopes southwest to upper Crystal Lake (5,828 feet), and then continue down, heading northwest to lower Crystal Lake into forest.

Climb back to Silver Saddle and out to Hen Skin Lake when so inclined.

To descend to Highway 410, continue descending northwest until you come to an open area. Ski this directly to the highway, avoiding a small buttress on the descent. Hike or ski out to the Crystal Mountain Road junction and wait for your ride.

Aerial view of Crystal Mountain (Photo by Rainer Burgdorfer)

Chinook Pass to Crystal Mountain Traverse

Start Point: Chinook Pass, 5,450 feet; or Cayuse Pass, 4,700 feet
High Point: Sourdough Gap, 6,500 feet
Best Time: January to April
Day Trip: 6 miles
Skiing Time: 9 hours
Skill Level: Advanced
Difficulties: High avalanche potential; routefinding required
Maps: Green Trails No. 271, Bumping Lake; No. 270, Mount Rainier East

This challenging winter tour offers stimulating skiing on seldom-traveled terrain. The route travels just east of the Cascade Crest along the Crest Trail, which runs between Cayuse Pass and the Crystal Mountain ski area.

Begin from either Cayuse Pass or Chinook Pass. If you start at Cayuse, ski east at Tipsoo Lakes to Chinook Pass. Once through Chinook Pass, head northeast toward a patch of timber, climbing above the road.

About 1.3 miles (5,300 feet) from Chinook Pass, start climbing north into

Looking from Chinook Pass to Crystal Mountain, with Yakima Peak in the left foreground (Photo by Rainer Burgdorfer)

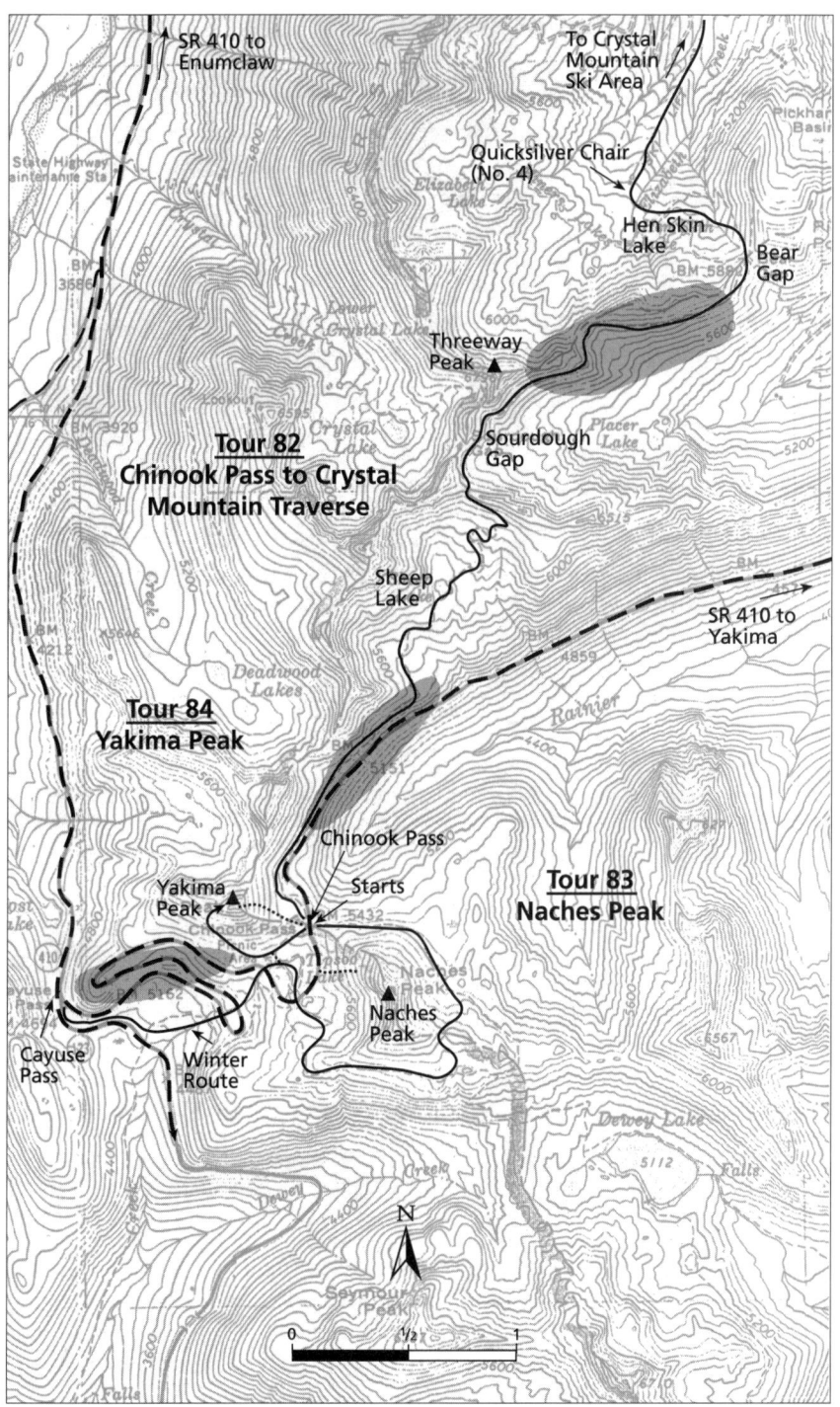

the basin that holds Sheep Lake (5,800 feet). Continue climbing, northeast now, to Sourdough Gap (6,500 feet, 2.9 miles from Chinook Pass), the first pass of the traverse.

From Sourdough Gap, descend a few hundred feet in a north-northeastern traverse. Continue northeast for 1.9 miles from the pass, contouring above the Morse Creek basin to Bear Gap (5,882 feet). Ski through the pass and descend 0.6 mile northwest to the top of Chair 4 at Crystal Mountain. Ski down the hill and meet your friends below.

Alternative Route: When the road to Cayuse Pass is blocked, it makes more sense to do this route in reverse. Be sure to take the road shortcuts above Cayuse Pass and be prepared for a 6-mile road ski, much of it downhill.

Naches Peak

Start Point: Chinook Pass, 5,450 feet; or Cayuse Pass, 4,700 feet
High Point: Naches Peak, 6,460 feet
Best Time: November; April
Day Trip: 2 miles
Skiing Time: 2 hours
Skill Level: Intermediate
Difficulties: Moderate avalanche potential
Maps: Green Trails No. 270, Mount Rainier East

Naches Peak is the southern guardian of Chinook Pass. Its proximity to a major highway and its gentle eastern bowls make it a worthy early season objective. In clear weather, the views alone make this trip worth the drive.

Drive State Route 410 to Chinook Pass, and park your car.

Head east from the road, just east of the pass in a clockwise contour around Naches Peak. In 0.5 mile, the route turns southwest and climbs the eastern bowls of Naches Peak. Continue due south, reaching a crest in 0.5 mile. Follow this crest north for 0.4 mile to gain the summit of Naches (ice ax recommended). The bowls on the eastern flank of the peak offer skiing on open slopes, especially when the southern slopes are too windswept.

To ski tree-sheltered glades, continue around Naches Peak and ski glades on the west side of the peak above Tipsoo Lakes Basin. Continue your circle to return to the car.

Alternative Route: If Chinook Pass is closed, park at Cayuse Pass. Ski east along the road to Chinook Pass for 1 mile (or descend to the open slopes just south of the road and ski east for 0.8 mile to rejoin the road at a switchback near 5,000 feet). From the eastern side of the switchback, climb directly east for 0.4 mile to the Tipsoo Lake Basin and Chinook Pass beyond.

Yakima Peak

Start Point: Chinook Pass, 5,450 feet; or Cayuse Pass, 4,700 feet
High Point: Yakima Peak, 6,226 feet
Best Time: November; April
Day Trip: 2 miles
Skiing Time: 2 hours
Skill Level: Advanced
Difficulties: Moderate avalanche potential
Maps: Green Trails No. 270, Mount Rainier East

Yakima Peak forms the northwestern sentinel at Chinook Pass and sometimes offers a refuge from the hordes of early season backcountry skiers at Naches Peak.

From Chinook Pass, head west into the Tipsoo Lakes Basin. Make a climbing traverse, west through forest to the southwestern slopes of Yakima Peak. When you come to glades, climb to their high points and ski. Trees here often protect snow from wind damage.

To reach the summit of Yakima Peak, head north about 0.8 mile west of Chinook Pass until you gain the western ridge (0.1 mile). Then turn right and climb 0.2 mile to the summit. An ice ax is required for the summit pitch.

Alternative Route: Good skiing lies on the northern side of Yakima Peak, too. To reach this area, climb northwest from Chinook Pass and circle clockwise around Yakima Peak.

Naches Peak and Chinook Pass (Photo by Rainer Burgdorfer)

Just another incredibly beautiful glade (Photo by Rainer Burgdorfer)

85 Summerland

Start Point: Frying Pan Creek, 3,900 feet
High Point: Summerland, 5,440 feet; Frying Pan Glacier, 8,600 feet
Best Time: October to November; April to June
Day Trip: 9 miles
Skiing Time: 8 hours
Skill Level: Advanced
Difficulties: High avalanche potential; glacier travel above Summerland; routefinding required; permit/fee area
Maps: USGS 7.5-minute series, Mount Rainier East

A sense of remoteness, 2,000-foot runs, and better-than-average weather characterize the Summerland tour. Ice axes and crampons are suggested for this tour. For all tours in Mount Rainier National Park, call (360) 569-2211 for weather and road information. Permit and fee requirements include a vehicle/tourist entry fee, backcountry permit/campsite reservations for overnight stays, and summit fees for skiing above stated elevations. The Code of Federal Regulations forbids solo (unroped) travel on glaciers. (Why rangers seem to be immune from this proscription is a mystery.)

Enter Mount Rainier National Park via the White River entrance (State Route 410) and drive to the Frying Pan Creek trailhead, 4 miles past the White River ranger station. The trail starts across the road from the parking lot, west of Frying Pan Creek. The trail climbs gently southwest for the first 2 miles, then, near 4,200 feet, switchbacks steeply and continues due west up the valley. By now you are out of the forest. Follow the main stream branch right to an open bowl below the Frying Pan Glacier.

From here (3.3 miles, 5,800 feet), you can see a small knoll (6,000 feet) to the south. Head directly for this bump and find a small stone shelter 0.1 mile southwest of this knoll. This shelter is frequently filled with snow and always filled with rodents, which, according to the Center for Disease Control, may carry the dreaded hantavirus. Bring a tent if you plan to spend the night.

Frying Pan Glacier, southwest of Summerland, offers excellent skiing. To reach the Frying Pan Glacier, climb directly up steep snow or rock just west of Meany Crest, then continue climbing southwest past Point 7573.

The small glaciers (6,400–7,400 feet) that lie 0.8 mile south of the shelter provide a closer destination. Good early season skiing can often be found on old névé covered with fresh snow.

Reverse the approach to return to the car.

Summerland on Mount Rainier (Photo by Rainer Burgdorfer)

Cowlitz Chimneys

Start Point: Frying Pan Creek, 3,900 feet

High Point: Sarvant Glacier, 6,900 feet

Best Time: April to June

Day Trip: 13 miles

Skiing Time: 10 hours

Skill Level: Advanced

Difficulties: High avalanche potential; glacier travel; routefinding required; permit/fee area

Maps: USGS 7.5-minute series, Mount Rainier East

The Cowlitz Chimneys, a group of prominent rock towers, dominate the skyline east of Mount Rainier when seen from Sunrise. The Chimneys are set among glaciers with 1,000 feet of local relief. This is a challenging tour because of the long approach, but the unique character of this area may interest the adventurous backcountry skier. Ice axes are recommended.

Enter Mount Rainier National Park via the White River entrance and drive to the Frying Pan Creek trailhead.

Hike the Frying Pan Creek Trail to Summerland. From the rise near the shelter, head southeast for 1 mile, climbing to the notch (6,740 feet) just left of Panhandle Gap. Climb through the notch and continue southeast along the

The Cowlitz Chimneys and the Sarvant Glaciers (Photo by Rainer Burgdorfer)

southern flank of Banshee Peak for 1 mile. Round the ridge of Banshee Peak near 6,900 feet. One of the Sarvant Glaciers lies at your feet. Connect gullies and ramps to ski the snowfields surrounding the Chimneys. To go home, reverse the approach.

Alternative Route: Other approaches include a midwinter ascent up Wright Creek and a more direct approach to Banshee Peak via a snow gully from the 2.5-mile area of Frying Pan Creek. These have not been tested by the author, although an early spring fly-over suggested this shortcut could work.

Interglacier

Start Point: White River Campground, 4,400 feet
High Point: Steamboat Prow, 9,700 feet
Best Time: April to June
Day Trip: 12 miles
Skiing Time: 8 hours
Skill Level: Advanced
Difficulties: Moderate avalanche potential; glacier travel; permit/ fee area
Maps: USGS 7.5-minute series, Mount Rainier East; Sunrise

A huge fall line run, manageable crevasse risk, and reasonable access (so long as the White River Road is open) make the Interglacier an outstanding snowboard tour.

Drive State Route 410 to the White River entrance and continue to White River Campground (6.5 miles), or as close as road conditions allow. At times the National Park Service (NPS) permits snowmobile traffic on this road.

The trail leaves the western end of the campground and follows the right side of the White River, climbing gradually for 3 miles. A steeper section is climbed in two switchbacks and Glacier Basin is gained in another 0.5 mile. Reservations are required for the campsites here (6,000 feet).

Continue up the valley along its right side until it becomes possible to traverse to the middle of the Interglacier. Crevasses near 7,800 feet mark the head of an initial steep section. Pass these on the western side, climbing between the Scylla of rockfall on the right and the Charybdis of crevasses on the left. Mark unobvious crevasse crossings to ease your descent. Climb the next 500 feet, crossing another crevasse band at 8,800 feet to the more gently sloping glacier above. From here, ski directly toward the high point above, or ski slightly east to the ridge and follow it to the highpoint of Steamboat Prow. The nearly level area east of the Prow (8,600 feet), but still on the crest, is called Camp Curtis.

To descend, simply ski the route of ascent—a 4,000-foot run down the Interglacier.

Alternative Route: A slight variation on the ascent is to keep to the right rim of Steamboat Prow. Gain this skywalk by climbing past the pinnacles on the uphill side of Saint Elmos Pass. This detour costs no time and offers spectacular views of the Winthrop Glacier far below. Other excellent downhill runs are found on the north-facing gullies of lower Mount Ruth. For the very energetic, the smooth section of the Emmons Glacier above Emmons "Flats" sometimes has excellent skiing. Its only drawback is the loose, steep pumice that makes for a wretched descent from the prow to the Flats.

Goat Island

Start Point: Frying Pan Creek, 3,900 feet

High Point: Goat Island Mountain, 7,288 feet

Best Time: April to June

Day Trip: 14 miles

Skiing Time: 10 hours

Skill Level: Advanced

Difficulties: High avalanche potential; routefinding required; permit/fee area

Maps: USGS 7.5-minute series, Mount Rainier East

Goat Island is the huge rocky summit that blocks views of Mount Rainier from White River Campground. It is easily accessible from the snowfields northwest of Summerland and offers an unusual view of Mount Rainier, along with some excellent skiing.

Emmons Glacier, Mount Rainier (Photo by Rainer Burgdorfer)

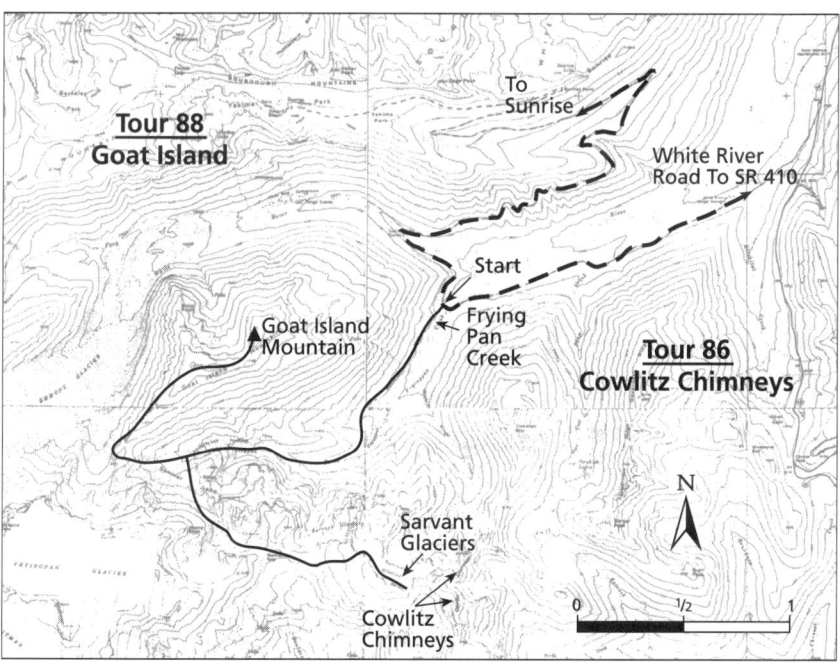

Goat Island Mountain and Meany Crest with Little Tahoma in the background (Photo by Rainer Burgdorfer)

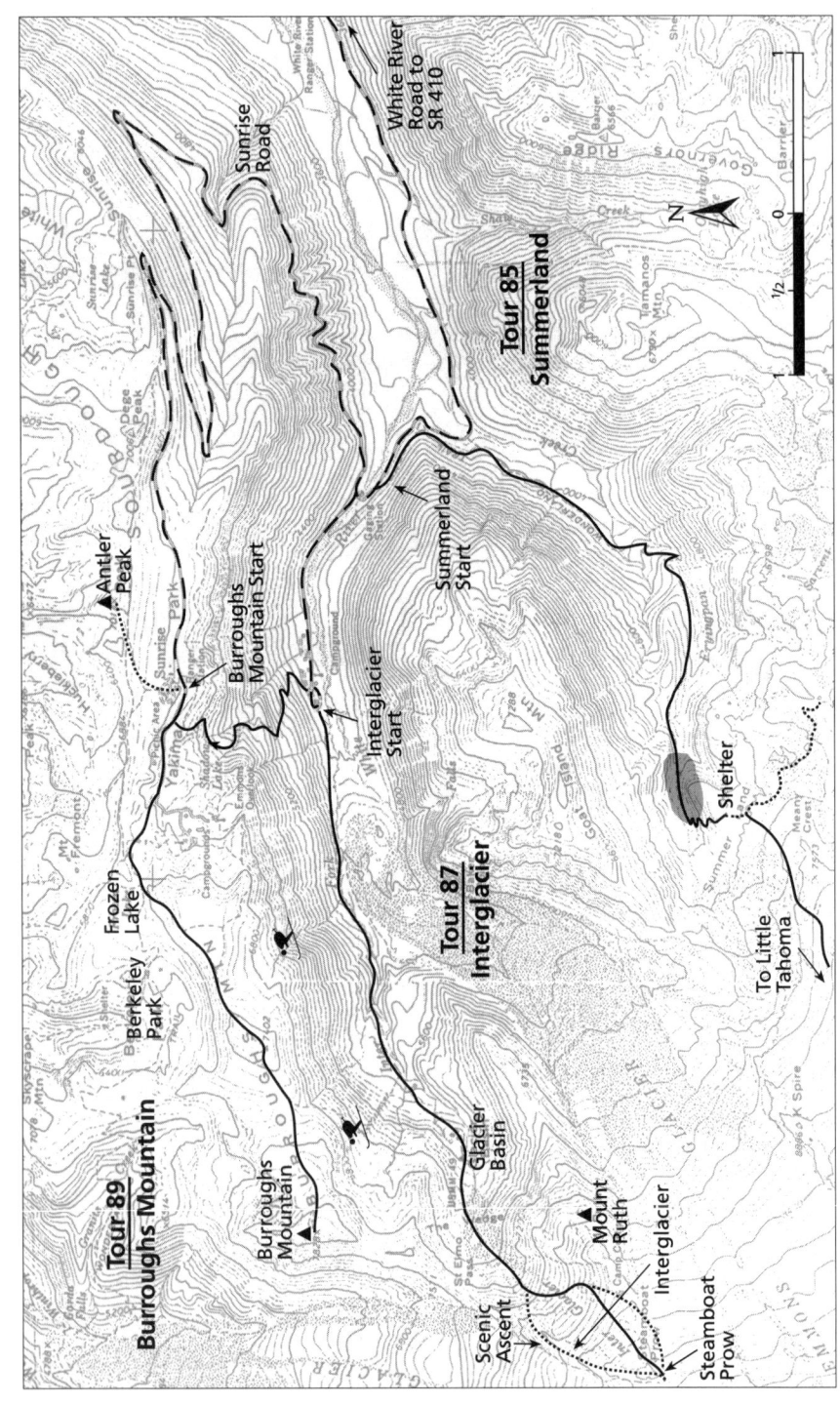

Enter Mount Rainier National Park through the White River entrance and park at the Frying Pan Creek trailhead.

Hike the Frying Pan Creek Trail, as for the Summerland tour, until you are due north of the 6,000-foot knoll (5,340 feet). Climb directly east for 0.8 mile, gaining the saddle at 6,380 feet. Turn right and climb a ridge northeast to the summit of Goat Island Mountain (1.8 miles, 7,288 feet). Goat Island Mountain is truly an island, with no easy way off other than the route of ascent. Reverse your climb to the saddle and take runs down to the Emmons Glacier, then ski Frying Pan Creek out to the road.

89
Burroughs Mountain

Start Point: Sunrise Parking Lot, 6,400 feet or White River Campground, 4,400 feet
High Point: Burroughs Mountain, 7,830 feet
Best Time: November; May to June
Day Trip: 8 miles
Skiing Time: 6 hours
Skill Level: Advanced
Difficulties: High avalanche potential; routefinding required; permit/fee area
Maps: USGS 7.5-minute series, Mount Rainier East; White River Park

Sunrise Park is slightly removed from Mount Rainier and has better views (not to mention better weather) because of it. The only requirement for this tour is road access to White River Campground. The only difference between the two starts is that one puts the climb at the beginning of the tour and the other puts it at the end.

West side of Burroughs Mountain (Photo by Rainer Burgdorfer)

From Sunrise, find the access road to the walk-in campground. It begins near the western end of the parking lot on its south side. In 0.7 mile, just past a streambed descending from Frozen Lake, the road turns southwest. Leave the road and head uphill, keeping to the right of a gentle ridge. The slope quickly becomes steeper. Climb 300 feet to the Frozen Lake Basin, then turn left and begin skiing west along the broad back of Burroughs Mountain. This area has near-tundra vegetation that's both beautiful and fragile: keep to the trails and stay on the snow as you head southwest to the summit of Burroughs Mountain.

Alternative Route: There are numerous options for the descent. The first is to reverse the approach. Another possibility is to descend northeast to Berkeley Park and ski out via Frozen Lake. You could ski southwest to Saint Elmos Pass and out to White River Campground. Another option is to descend the steep snow-covered rockslides on the southeast flank of Burroughs Mountain. (This last alternative requires that you ski southwest near 6,600 feet into a drainage to avoid cliff bands below.)

If the road to Sunrise is closed, the last two descent options can be connected from White River Campground. Climb to Saint Elmos Pass. From here, climb 0.9 mile to the summit of Burroughs Mountain and past it for 0.7 mile. Find the start of a broad snow gully that drops to the southeast and descend to 6,600 feet. Traverse southwest through trees into a drainage, and ski through glades to the White River Trail below.

Carbon Glacier
90

Start Point: Ipsut Creek Campground, 2,460 feet
High Point: Carbon Glacier, 7,830 feet
Best Time: April to June
Day Trip/Overnight: 10 miles
Skiing Time: 12 hours
Skill Level: Intermediate
Difficulties: High avalanche potential; glacier travel; permit/fee area
Maps: USGS 7.5-minute series, Mowich Lake

This is a marathon view tour, well suited to Nordic skis. A long approach up a glacier-fed river valley and a gentle, broad glacier puts the skier right into "The Hall of the Mountain King." This is a better overnight tour than a day trip; with more time, skiers can approach the north wall of Rainier more closely (but not *too* closely).

Drive State Route 165 from Buckley toward the Carbon River entrance of Mount Rainier National Park. Drive as far as conditions permit (the road is often gated well before the park entrance).

Hike the road past Ipsut Creek Campground and find the trail.

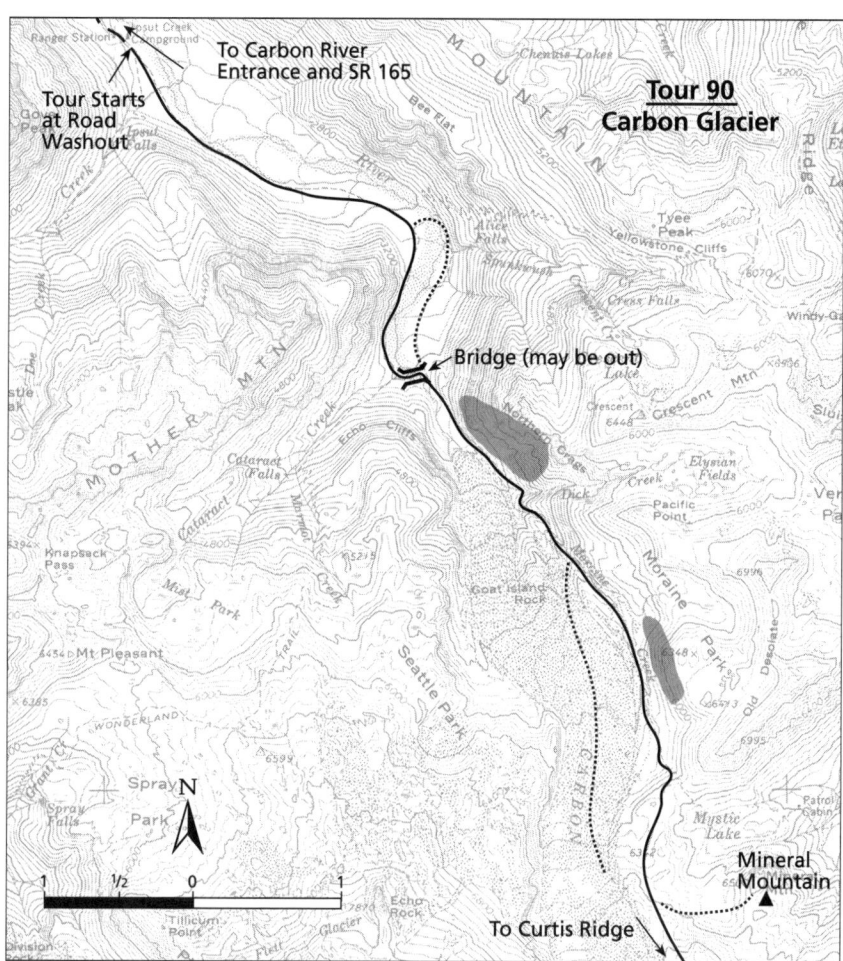

The trail leaves the campground at its upstream end. Hike through forest along the Carbon River until you come out of the woods at river's edge. Cross (ford) the stream where convenient. There are suspension bridges at 2,840 and 3,440 feet, but these may be closed for the winter season. If the bridges are not passable, it may be difficult to cross at this elevation. In winter, the river is typically low and may be crossed near 3,000 feet by boulder hopping. During spring runoff, you must use the bridges. Once across, continue upstream along the eastern bank to the narrow gorge that contains the glacier's snout. Scurry under the Northern Crags and make the steep traverse above the glacier, climbing steadily.

Cross Dick Creek, skirting the lateral moraine on its left side. Cross over this moraine and get on the glacier near 5,500 feet, 1.5 miles from its snout. The glacier slopes gently here and routefinding is straightforward.

Continue heading uphill for 2 miles until you come to a steep, broken section near 6,800 feet. Pass this on the right, and then turn southeast toward Curtis Ridge. The glacier steepens and is more broken here. Ski along the lower slopes of Curtis Ridge to make an end run around crevasses near 8,000 feet, then head right to the base of Liberty Ridge and high camp.

Descend by reversing the approach.

Alternative Route: A late-season option is to follow the trail to Mystic Lake or Curtis Ridge instead of skiing the glacier. Curtis Ridge is reached from the basin below (west of) Mystic Lake Saddle (6,000 feet). Ski due south, routefinding through the steep section above 6,400 feet. Once this cliffy section is passed, the gentler east shoulder of Curtis Ridge provides few obstacles to 8,000 feet. Descend by reversing the approach.

91
Russell Glacier

Start Point: Mowich Lake Parking Lot, 4,980 feet
High Point: Russell Glacier, 10,000 feet
Best Time: June to July, earlier if you can get up the road
Day Trip/Overnight: 10 miles
Skiing Time: 12 hours
Skill Level: Advanced
Difficulties: Moderate avalanche potential; glacier travel; routefinding required; permit/fee area
Maps: USGS 7.5-minute series, Mowich Lake

This is the ultimate midsummer tour for skiers and snowboarders alike. A brief trail approach through forest launches the climber onto snow-covered ridges and meadows that terminate at the top of a steep headwall at 10,000 feet. The most delightful aspect of this tour is that the top 3,000 feet of the downhill run are plainly visible from Seattle, so that the memory of this tour is refreshed whenever Mount Rainier is not obscured by clouds.

Drive State Route 165 from Buckley to the Carbon River Bridge and beyond to a junction. Take the right fork to the Mowich Lake entrance of Mount Rainier National Park. There is a gate at this entrance—call ahead to ensure it is open. The road to Mowich Lake is 11 miles long. With luck, you'll be able to drive all the way to the lake.

With less luck, you can ski or mountain-bike the road. About 3 miles from the gate is the first of two shortcuts that save a few miles of road skiing. The trail leaves the road, heading southwest along the left of a creek (4,360 feet). Follow the metal flags that mark the trail. The trail soon re-crosses the road at an S curve and continues on the other side, rejoining the road near Mowich Lake.

On Russell Glacier at 9,000 feet (Photo by Rainer Burgdorfer)

When the second section of trail rejoins the road, follow it left to Mowich Lake. If the snow is deep, use the Knapsack Pass approach to Spray Park. If not, use the hiking approach. To reach Knapsack Pass, ski counterclockwise around Mowich Lake until just beyond the ranger station, then climb east into an open basin north of Fay Peak. This basin is headed on its east side by Knapsack Pass (6,200 feet).

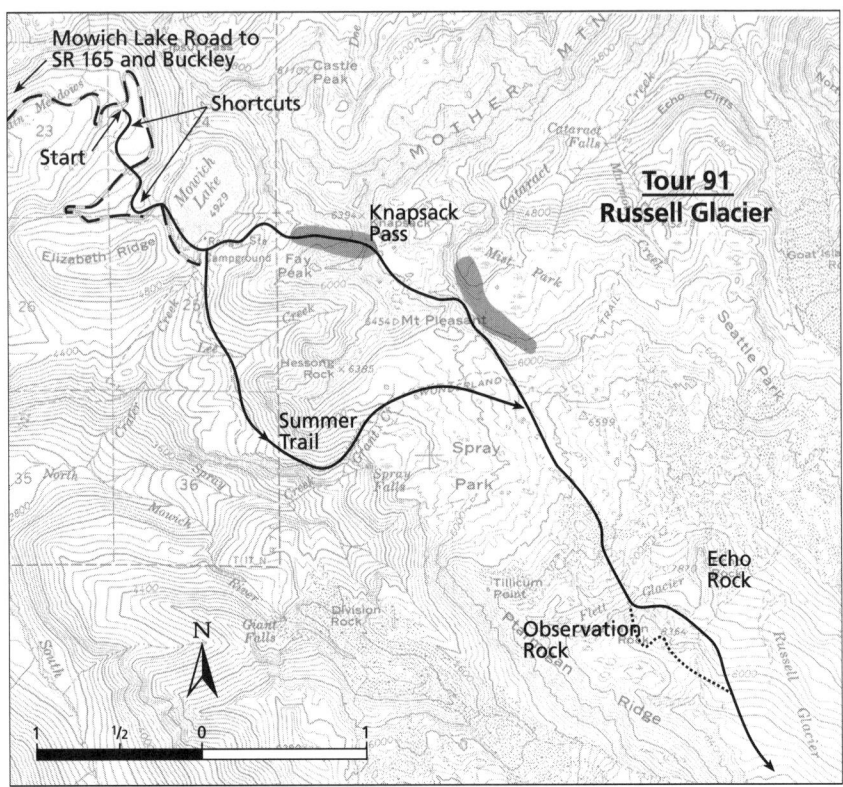

From the pass, make a descending traverse to the right (southeast) to a bench and cross a small rib (0.6 mile, 6,100 feet). Remember this spot for the return. Now climb the undulating slopes of Spray Park for about 2.5 miles to the southeast. Observation Rock (8,360 feet), a prominent feature, can be seen to the right of Echo Rock (7,870 feet). These landmarks are visible from Puget Sound on clear days.

The Flett Glacier (directly below Observation Rock) is mildly crevassed. Avoid its very steep upper section by traversing left, then heading right again to bypass Observation Rock.

Ski through a notch on the north side of Observation Rock to gain the Russell Glacier. Climb the right side of Russell Glacier to 10,000 feet. If the steep headwall lacks appeal, stop for lunch on the rocky crest of lower Ptarmigan Ridge and begin your descent from here.

On the return, keep in mind that you must find Knapsack Pass to return to Mowich Lake. Another approach (or exit) takes the summer hiking trail heading south from Mowich Lake. This approach is about 1 mile longer, but it avoids the steep climb over Knapsack Pass.

Puyallup Cleaver

Start Point: West Side Road, 2,200 feet
High Point: Puyallup Cleaver, 9,200 feet
Best Time: April to July, earlier if you can get up the road
Extended Tour: 11 miles (plus 11.5 miles by mountain bike)
Skiing Time: 16 hours
Skill Level: Advanced
Difficulties: Moderate avalanche potential; glacier travel; routefinding required; bike ride; permit/fee area
Maps: USGS 7.5-minute series, Mount Rainier West; Mount Wow

The Puyallup Cleaver divides the Puyallup Glacier from the Tahoma Glacier. This route brings the skier high on the mountain with minimal glacier travel. Since NPS closed West Side Road, this area has become even more remote. Mountain goats frequent the area.

Drive State Route 706 to the Nisqually (Longmire) entrance of Mount Rainier National Park. One mile past the entrance, turn onto West Side Road. Take this as far as possible. Either hike or bicycle 11.5 miles to the Klapatche Park trailhead (3,700 feet). Secure your bike. (Does anyone know how to discourage rodents from chewing sweat-soaked handlebar cushions?) Then hike or ski the trail to Klapatche Park (2.5 miles, 5,500 feet). Continue east to Saint Andrews Park (0.7 mile) and its lake.

From Saint Andrews Lake, head east up the valley to Tokaloo Spire (1.3 miles, 7,680 feet). Climb along the ridge uphill of the spire until you can gain the north shoulder of the Puyallup Cleaver. Continue climbing along this cleaver over steep subridges that intersect the cleaver at right angles. Near 9,000 feet, a large buttress requires an end run and a saddle appears on its uphill shoulder.

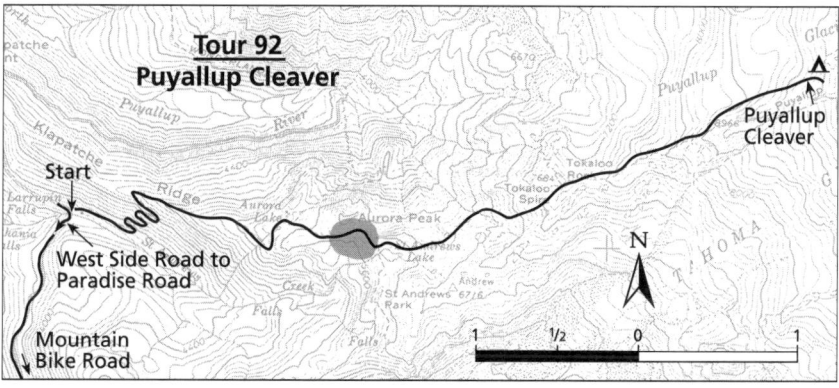

This is the classic high camp for summit attempts over the Tahoma Glacier. North of camp, there are unbroken portions of the Puyallup Glacier, which look appealing. Be advised that this ice body conceals huge crevasses. Much safer skiing is possible below 8,000 feet on both flanks of the Cleaver.

Return via the approach.

 Sunset Park

Start Point: West Side Road, 2,200 feet
High Point: Sunset Park, 5,713 feet
Best Time: April to June, earlier if you can get up the road
Extended Tour: 7 miles (plus 15 miles one way by mountain bike)
Skiing Time: 12 hours
Skill Level: Advanced
Difficulties: Moderate avalanche potential; routefinding required; bike ride; permit/fee area
Maps: USGS 7.5-minute series, Mount Rainier West; Mount Wow

What makes this tour worthwhile is seeing the unbroken sweep of the west faces of Rainier rising from the meadows of Sunset Park in evening light. The slopes in this area vary from minor to heroic. The approach is Homerian, thanks to the West Side Road closure.

Enter Mount Rainier Park via the Nisqually entrance. Take the West Side Road turnoff and drive as far as conditions permit. Bicycle 15 miles to road's

Below the Puyallup Cleaver (Photo by William C. Shigley)

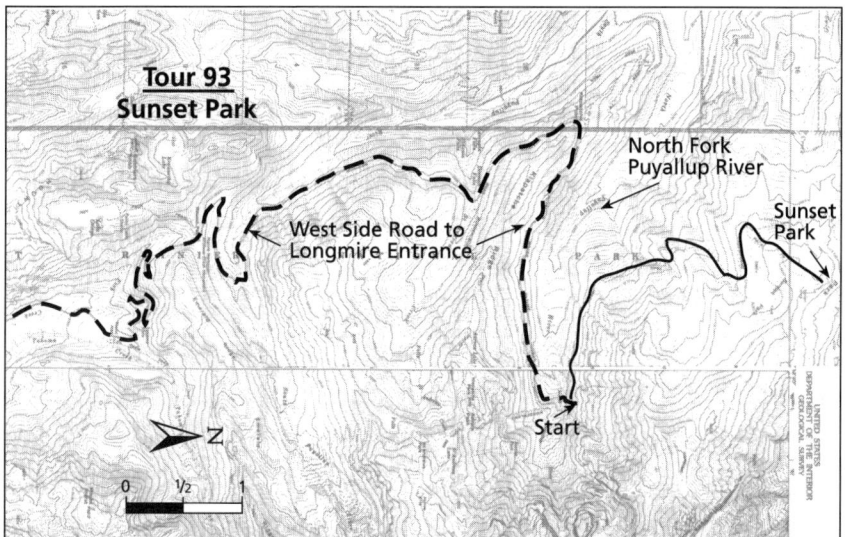

**Tour 93
Sunset Park**

North Fork
Puyallup River

Sunset
Park

West Side Road to
Longmire Entrance

Start

0 ½ 1

end (3,717 feet), dismounting and crossing snow patches as required.

From road's end, cross the North Fork of the Puyallup River, then follow the trail north, then west, climbing through forest for 1.3 miles. The trail turns north, continuing to climb for 0.7 mile, then switchbacks southwest and north again to 5,000 feet. Here the trail jogs west for 0.5 miles, then climbs to Sunset Park. Make camp and begin exploring. The open slopes below Sunset Park offer runs of varying lengths, but the mountain above is the real draw. The beauty is you don't have to leave today. When you finally have to leave, retrace the approach.

Van Trump Park
94

Start Point: Christine Falls, 3,670 feet; or Nisqually Bridge, 4,000 feet
High Point: Van Trump Glaciers, 9,500 feet
Best Time: December to April
Day Trip: 8 miles
Skiing Time: 8 hours
Skill Level: Advanced
Difficulties: High avalanche potential; glacier travel; routefinding required; permit/fee area
Maps: USGS 7.5-minute series, Mount Rainier West; Mount Wow

The Van Trump Park tour is a fine alternative to "Oh, no! Not Muir again!" Its remoteness and good skiing give the tour a distinctly different flavor from the carnival of Paradise with minimal glacier skiing.

Enter the park via the Nisqually entrance and drive to the Christine Falls trailhead, about 3 miles above Longmire.

The trail crosses Van Trump Creek 0.3 miles above the road and continues up the right side of the creek. From here to Comet Falls (another mile), the trail contours along a steep hillside above Van Trump Creek. About 200 yards below the falls, climb a steep hillside to the right (east) of the falls for 700 feet. You have arrived in Van Trump Park.

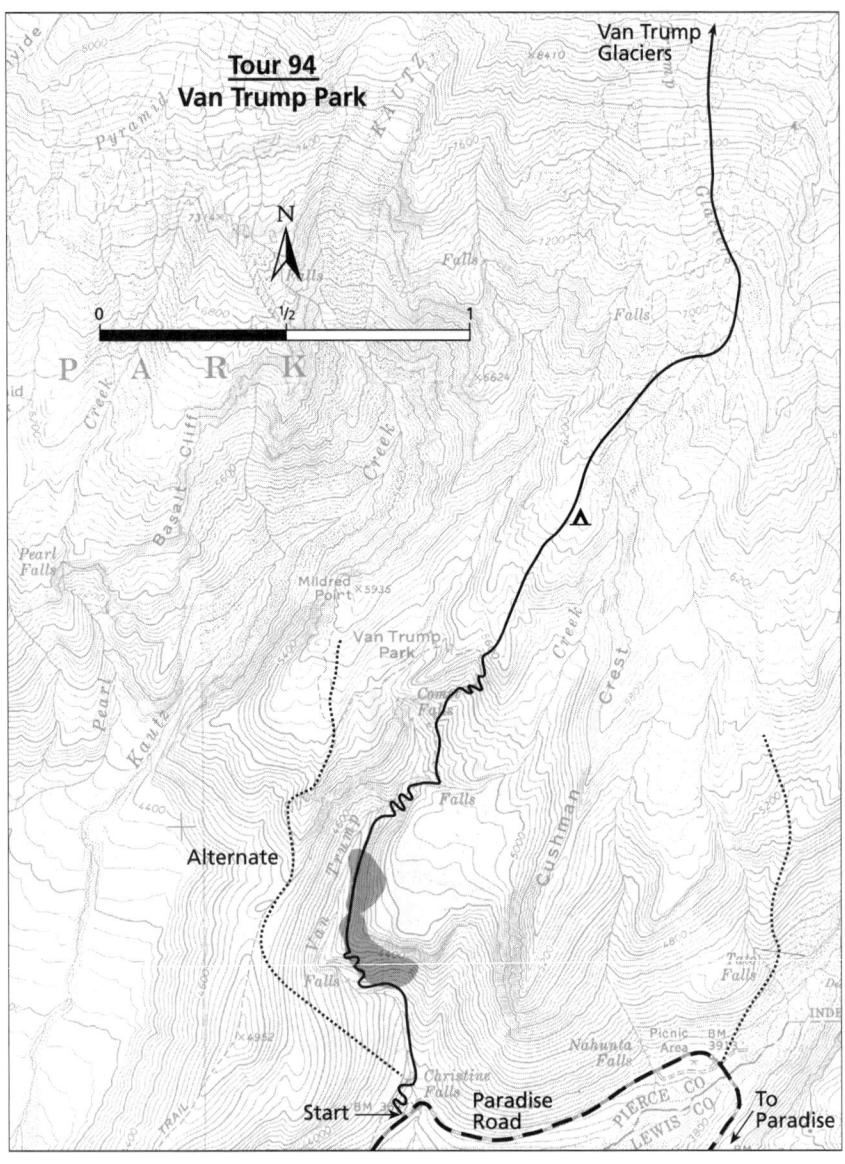

**Tour 94
Van Trump Park**

Van Trump Park on Mount Rainier's west side (Photo by Joe Catellani)

Good skiing is possible all the way to 10,000 feet. This side of the mountain is generally more sheltered from the wind than the Muir snowfield. Consequently, the snow tends to be less wind damaged.

Descend via the approach. Avoid being seduced into the Kautz Creek drainage by luscious gullies. They are hard to reverse and will force you into hiking out through the Kautz Creek drainage.

Alternative Route: When there is a deep snowpack, another approach becomes feasible. Ski northwest from Christine Falls for 0.5 mile, gaining 1,000 feet in the process. Near 4,500 feet, ski north until you reach Van Trump Park in 1 mile.

Tatoosh Range

Start Point: Narada Falls Parking Lot, 4,570 feet
High Point: Castle Saddle, 6,200 feet
Best Time: December to May
Day Trip: 4 miles
Skiing Time: 6 to 8 hours
Skill Level: Advanced
Difficulties: High avalanche potential; permit/fee area
Maps: USGS 7.5-minute series, Mount Rainier East; Packwood

This tour provides access to the north and south slopes of the Tatoosh Range. Outstanding skiing can be found below the notch between the Castle and Unicorn Peak.

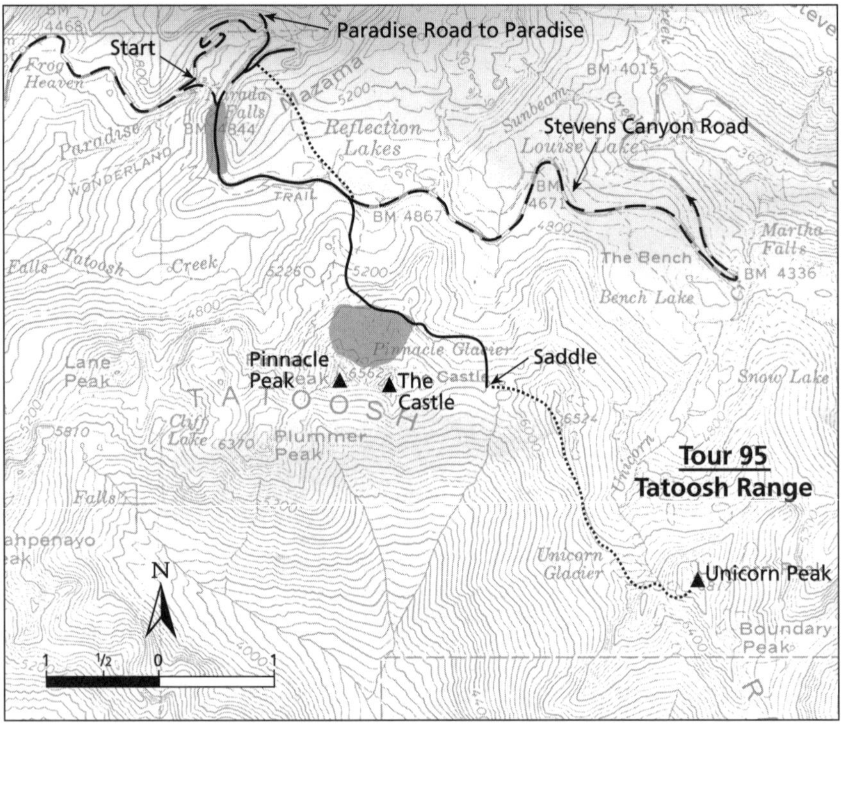

Descending the north side of the Unicorn-Castle saddle (Photo by Harry Hendon)

From the Nisqually entrance of Mount Rainier National Park, drive the road past Longmire to Narada Falls viewpoint and park your car. Water and heated restrooms are available here.

If a National Park Service sign informs you that the open slopes above the east end of the parking lot are "Closed to Skiers," hike 0.3 mile up the road to the junction of Stevens Canyon Road. Turn right and ski another 0.2 mile along this road to an intersection. Leave the road here and climb southeast over a 5,150-foot pass to Reflection Lakes.

If there is no sign and your assessment indicates the slope is stable, climb the hill behind the comfort station up to Stevens Canyon Road. Either way, ski the gentle downhill grade to Reflection Lakes Basin for 1.5 miles.

Looking directly south to the Tatoosh Range, you will see pointed Pinnacle Peak and, to the left, the Castle (the reason for its name is obvious) and distant Unicorn Peak. Avoid the steep slopes below Pinnacle Peak. From the road, make a climbing traverse southeast to the tree-studded ridge that runs northwest from the Castle. Climb this ridge and the bowl above it to the broad saddle to the left of the Castle.

From the saddle, there are numerous possibilities. Unicorn Peak lies over a mile to the southeast along a ridgeline; runs can be made into every drainage. The northern slope of the saddle has cliff bands that can be breached via steep gullies. Conservative skiers can retrace their tracks to the road and out.

Muir Snowfield

Start Point: Paradise Parking Lot, 5,450 feet
High Point: Camp Muir, 10,000 feet
Best Time: October to June
Day Trip: 9 miles
Skiing Time: 6 hours
Skill Level: Intermediate
Difficulties: Moderate avalanche potential; routefinding required; permit/fee area
Maps: USGS 7.5-minute series, Mount Rainier East

The broad, low-angle southern apron of Mount Rainier rises from Paradise at 5,440 feet to Camp Muir at 10,060 feet. Early season tours (October to November) offer the best combination of snow conditions, weather, and entertainment value on the Muir Snowfield. Navigation skills (and the requisite equipment) are required for this tour; whiteouts occur frequently, and the descent takes place on a broad, curving ridge with cliffs on either side. Keep a log, mental or otherwise, so you can find your way down in fog.

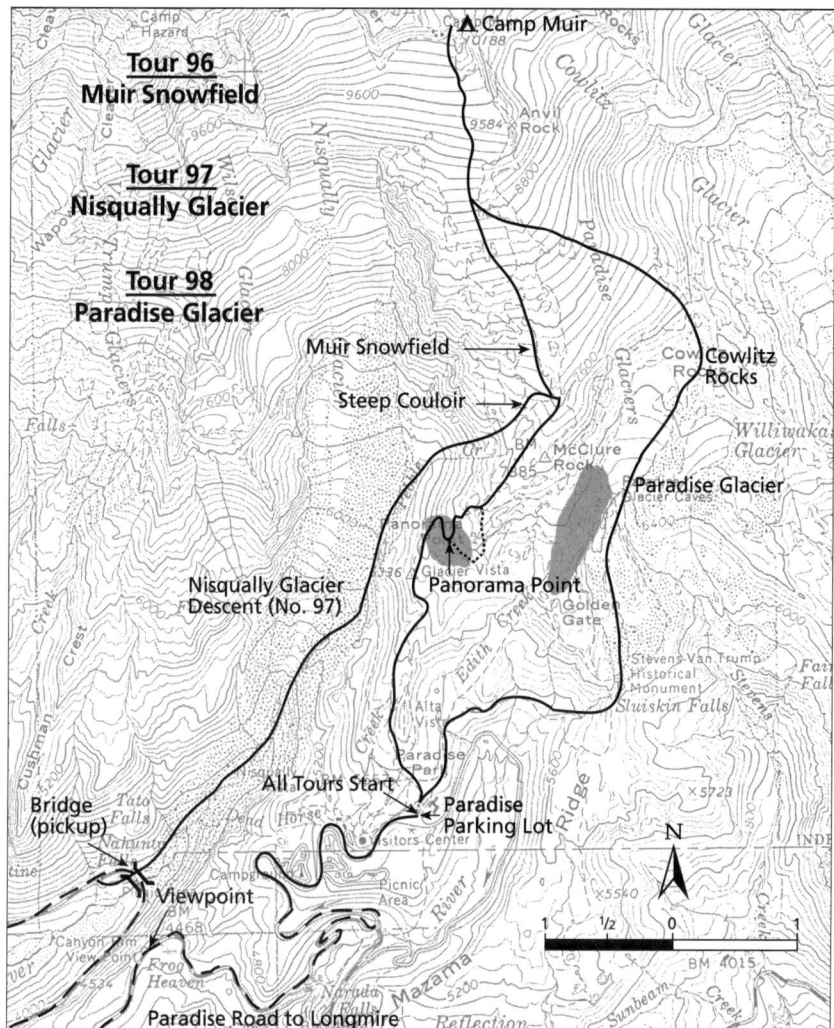

Tour 96
Muir Snowfield

Tour 97
Nisqually Glacier

Tour 98
Paradise Glacier

Drive State Route 706 to the Nisqually entrance to Mount Rainier National Park. Continue to the Paradise parking lot adjacent to the ranger station. (No overnight camping is permitted in the parking lot.)

Climb the open slopes above the parking lot, keeping left of Alta Vista. In low-snow conditions, stay on designated trails to protect alpine vegetation. Ascend the broad, rolling ridge to the steep face of Panorama Point. If the trail is visible, climb it to the top of Panorama Point (6,950 feet). Otherwise, climb the slope on the windswept side.

From Panorama Point, continue up the ridge heading north. Cross Pebble Creek (6,700 feet), skirting its windroll on either side, and continue past Anvil

Camp Muir (Photo by Craig Miller)

Rock (9,850 feet), keeping it well on your right. By now you can see the notch where Camp Muir is located, so scamper up to the saddle for lunch and the Rainier Mountaineering, Inc. (RMI) show.

If clouds begin moving in, consider an immediate descent, because skiing—not to mention routefinding—in whiteout conditions is dangerous. Despite the occasional circus-like atmosphere, this is a serious tour. It requires mountaineering skills, equipment, and attitude.

97
Nisqually Glacier

Start Point: Paradise Parking Lot, 5,450 feet
High Point: Above Pebble Creek, 7,600 feet
Best Time: January to April
Day Trip: 9 miles
Skiing Time: 8 hours
Skill Level: Advanced
Difficulties: High avalanche potential; routefinding required; permit/fee area
Maps: USGS 7.5-minute series, Mount Rainier East and West

This tour is basically a one-way descent of a mighty glacier, the Nisqually. Generally, it is feasible only in midwinter, when heavy snowfall has covered the crevasses on the lower glacier and smoothed the rubble fields below the glacier's snout. A good overview of the lower route is possible from Canyon

Tour 97 descends the snow slopes connecting the Muir Snowfield with the Nisqually Glacier (upper right). (Photo by Fred Veatch, USGS)

Rim Viewpoint. The exit and pickup take place on the Paradise Highway at the bridge that crosses the Nisqually River just east of Nahunta Falls. For this tour, visibility must be good.

Drive to Paradise and park. Climb over Panorama Point and McClure Rock to Sugarloaf, a promontory above Pebble Creek. Head west from Sugarloaf, looking for a couloir that descends to the Nisqually Moraine. Ski this steep 1,500-foot slope, keeping to the left, and do not venture far out onto the Nisqually. (For a shorter tour, ascend only to Panorama Point and descend directly to the Nisqually.)

Ski along the left (east) edge of the glacier until terrain forces you to the main glacier surface. If there is insufficient snow near the snout, you may have to descend to the north side and hike out the last 0.5 mile.

Paradise Glacier

Start Point: Paradise Parking Lot, 5,450 feet
High Point: Cowlitz Rock or beyond, 7,450 feet
Best Time: January to June
Day Trip: 7 miles
Skiing Time: 6 hours
Skill Level: Advanced
Difficulties: High avalanche potential; routefinding required; permit/fee area
Maps: USGS 7.5-minute series, Mount Rainier East

The Paradise Glacier lies just east of the Muir Snowfield and south of the massive Cowlitz Glacier. The Paradise Glacier is the site of the famous Paradise Ice Caves. In past years, the National Park Service would dynamite the caves to allow access for spectacle-hungry tourists. These caves have been closed in recent years, but the glacier still offers excellent skiing. This tour gives the skier a novel view of the south shoulder of Rainier and a chance to escape the hordes at Paradise and on the Muir Snowfield. The Paradise Glacier is frequently not as wind-blown as the Muir Snowfield; the terrain and exposure are well suited to spring touring.

Drive to the Paradise parking lot. Behind the ranger station is a trail leading right (northeast) to the Edith Creek Basin. Cross Edith Creek and head northeast across the basin, past the rightmost stream. Climb the ridge on the right side of the stream to gain gentler terrain above. Head north for 1 mile, skiing up the valley toward the snout of the glacier. Keep to the right here. Climb a steep rise between 6,900 and 7,400 feet, keeping close to Cowlitz Rocks, then climb to the upper Paradise Glacier. Descend by reversing the approach.

Alternative Route: A loop can be made by crossing the Paradise Glacier above Cowlitz Rocks and skiing northwest along various ramps to the Muir Snowfield between 8,000 and 9,000 feet. Skiers have descended the Cowlitz Glacier from Camp Muir. This is a significant undertaking.

White Pass

Start Point: White Pass, 4,470 feet
High Point: Hogback Mountain, 6,790 feet
Best Time: December to April
Day Trip: 6 miles
Skiing Time: 4 hours
Skill Level: Intermediate
Difficulties: Moderate avalanche potential; routefinding required; permit/fee area
Maps: Green Trails No. 303, White Pass

Hogback Mountain is a gentle summit adjacent to the White Pass ski area. It is possible that by the time this book sees print, the ski area will have absorbed

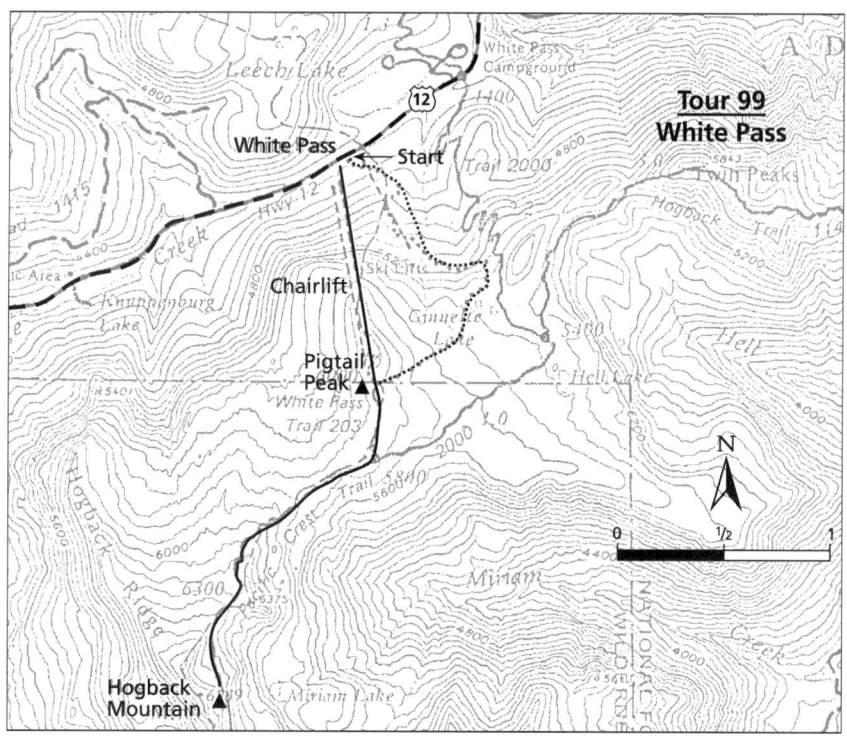

this nice mountain with its miles of hills and grand views of Mount Rainier and Goat Rocks.

Drive US 12 to the White Pass ski area. Park in the ski-area lot and sign out at the ticket booth. Unless you seek an early start or are broke, ride the chair lift to the top of Pigtail Peak. It is definitely worth the expense of the lift ticket to save your strength for the skiing ahead. From the top of the lift, ski straight ahead (south) to the start of the Holiday Run, descending 0.3 mile to a saddle (5,820 feet). (If you opt not to ride the chair lift, climb to the same saddle through the forest along the western side of the ski area.)

Head southwest from here for 1.7 mile, keeping to the top of the broad ridge. Hogback Mountain is the highpoint. Skiing is possible in many directions. Go glade exploring or yo-yo ski a favorite gully. Retrace the approach to return to White Pass.

Goat Rocks

Start Point: North Fork Tieton River Road, 3,300 feet, or Tieton Sno-Park, 3,040 feet

High Point: Old Snowy Mountain, 7,930 feet

Best Time: April to June

Extended Tour: 17 miles

Skiing Time: 14 hours

Skill Level: Advanced

Difficulties: High avalanche potential; routefinding required; permit/fee area

Maps: USGS Old Snowy Mtn., Pinegrass Ridge, White Pass, 1:24,000

Goat Rocks is the glaciated massif visible to the southeast from the Muir Snowfield. This area accumulates large amounts of snow. As late as Memorial Day, the area is still locked in the grip of winter—lucky for us!

The Goat Rocks tour is a comfortable 3-day trip with uncommon views of Mounts Adams, Rainier, and Saint Helens.

Drive US 12 to 7.5 miles east of White Pass to Clear Lake Road (Forest Road No. 1200). Drive this road to the North Fork Tieton River Road's end (16 miles).

Walk, ski, bike, or hitch a ride to road's end 5 miles upriver near 3,300 feet. The trail starts at the southwest side of the parking area and heads southwest for 300 yards to a trail junction.

At the trail junction, take the rightmost fork and begin climbing through timber for 0.9 mile. Near 3,700 feet, a trail heads right (northwest) uphill. Continue southwest in a climbing traverse, around a buttress, and in 1.5

miles (near 3,900 feet) cross a major stream. The route continues southwest, then west to reach Tieton Pass (4,820 feet) in another 1.7 mile.

From Tieton Pass, climb steeply southwest for 0.3 mile around a hill, then contour due south for 0.5 mile to Lutz Lake, which will probably be frozen. McCall Basin lies just to the southwest. Drop into the basin and continue southwest, scouting for a good place to camp.

From the center of the basin, head due south for 0.4 mile, skiing up a narrow draw into a nearly level upper basin (5,260 feet). Once in the upper basin, climb west-southwest for 0.6 mile, and then climb up the most convenient route to Old Snowy (1.4 miles, 7,930 feet). Good skiing may be found to the east in the direction of Ives Peak, and back down along the line of ascent. Retrace the approach to your car.

Alternative Route: A good way to approach this area in midwinter is to ride the chair lift at White Pass, then make a high traverse to Tieton Pass and McCall Basin.

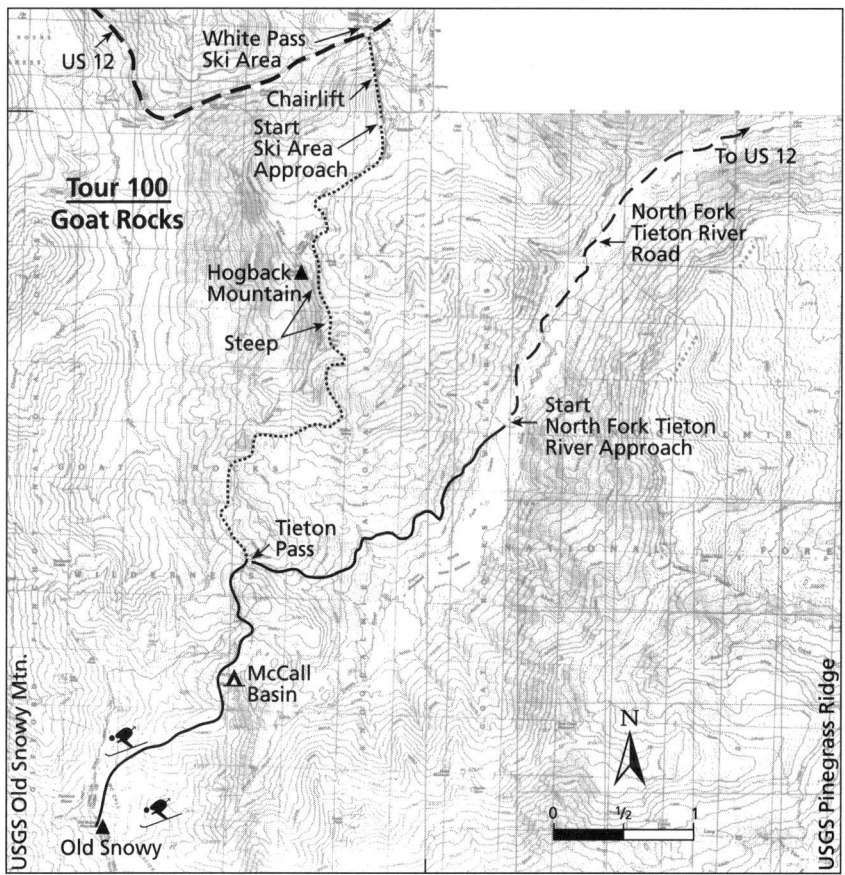

McCall Basin, with Old Snowy visible in the top left background (Photo by Rainer Burgdorfer)

Mount Adams

Start Point: Timberline Forest Camp, 6,300 feet
High Point: Mount Adams Summit, 12,310 feet
Best Time: April to June
Overnight: 8 miles
Skiing Time: 10 hours
Skill Level: Advanced
Difficulties: Low avalanche potential; routefinding required; permit/fee area
Maps: USGS 7.5 minute series, Mount Adams West; Mount Adams East

The southern shoulder of Mount Adams enables skiers to ascend the entire mountain without setting foot on crevassed terrain. The 4-mile-long ridge offers the hardy skier a 6,000-foot run! The only obstacle to complete enjoyment of this tour is exhaustion: after climbing to the summit, or even the false summit, few skiers will be at the top of their form. The United States Forest Service (USFS) has instituted registration and summit fee requirements for climbers, in

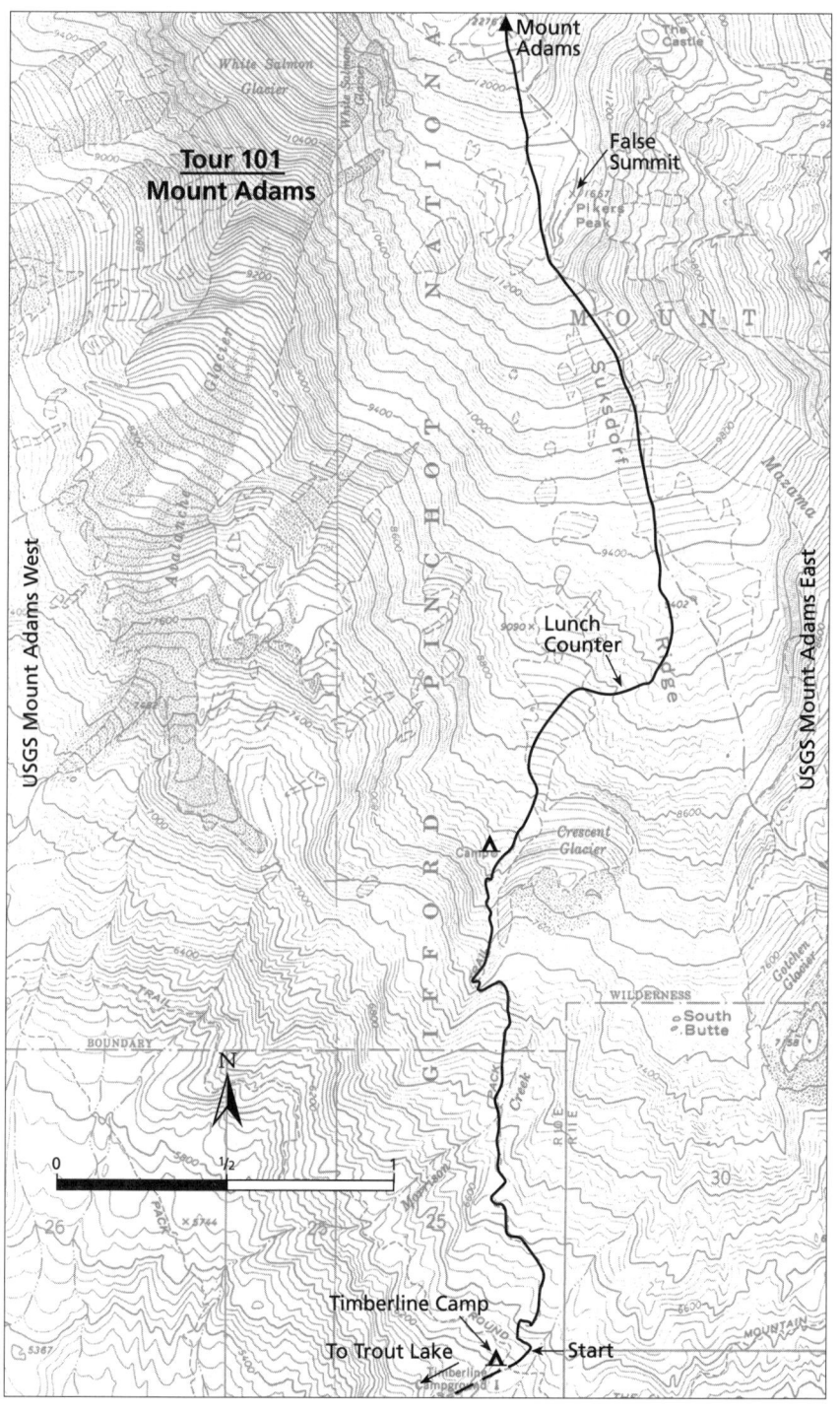

**Tour 101
Mount Adams**

Mount Adams

False Summit

Lunch Counter

USGS Mount Adams West

USGS Mount Adams East

N

0   1/2   1

Timberline Camp

To Trout Lake

Start

Mount Adams (Photo by William C. Shigley)

addition to the Sno-Park fee requirement. Call the ranger station for road conditions. This tour was made for snowboarders!

Drive Interstate 80 to the city of Hood River. Cross the Columbia River to the town of Bingen (pronounced *Binjen*), and drive north on State Route 141. This highway follows the White Salmon River through rolling ponderosa to the town of Trout Lake. Register and pay at the ranger station, then drive State Route 141 north for 1.4 miles to a fork. Turn right to Mount Adams Recreation Area. Drive for 0.6 mile and turn left on Road 80. Drive past Morrison Creek Campground to Timberline Camp at road's end (6,000 feet).

From Timberline Camp, head north and slightly east to the start of the south ridge, sometimes called Suksdorf Ridge (really!). Climb this ridge 2.3 miles due north to the Lunch Counter, a shoulder near 9,000 feet.

Near 9,700 feet, the slope steepens to the false summit (11,700 feet). The true summit lies just over the next hill, about 600 feet higher. Descend by reversing the approach.

Alternative Route: An astonishing descent can be made in the southwest chutes, the shallow gullies west of the south ridge but east of the avalanche glacier. The longest of these gullies is 30° steep, 30 feet wide in places, and

3,000 feet long (3, 3, 3). Near the bottom, exit left where convenient and traverse south back to Timberline Camp. Planning your return route, and following that plan, are vital to a timely return!

Mount *102* Saint Helens

Start Point: Marble Mountain Sno-Park, 2,640 feet

High Point: Mount Saint Helens, 8,300 feet

Best Time: January to May

Day Trip: 8 miles

Skiing Time: 8 hours

Skill Level: Advanced

Difficulties: High avalanche potential; routefinding required; permit/fee area

Maps: Green Trails No. 346S, Mount Saint Helens

Mount Saint Helens is an ideal winter tour because it is accessible, large, and wonderful. It is a good tour for snowboarders—gullies and wind scoops make perfect half pipes, and you can descend the fall line for much of the way. Take snowshoes. Take money, too—the USFS has instituted a summit fee ($15) in addition to the Sno-Park fee. (A separate summer Trail Use Permit is required after the Sno-Park season.)

Exit Interstate 5 at Woodland and head east on State Route 503 to Cougar. Five miles west of Cougar is Jack's Restaurant and Store. Purchase your permits here. Continue east on State Route 503 to Forest Road 83 and follow it to Marble

Mount Saint Helens from the trail (Photo by Craig Miller)

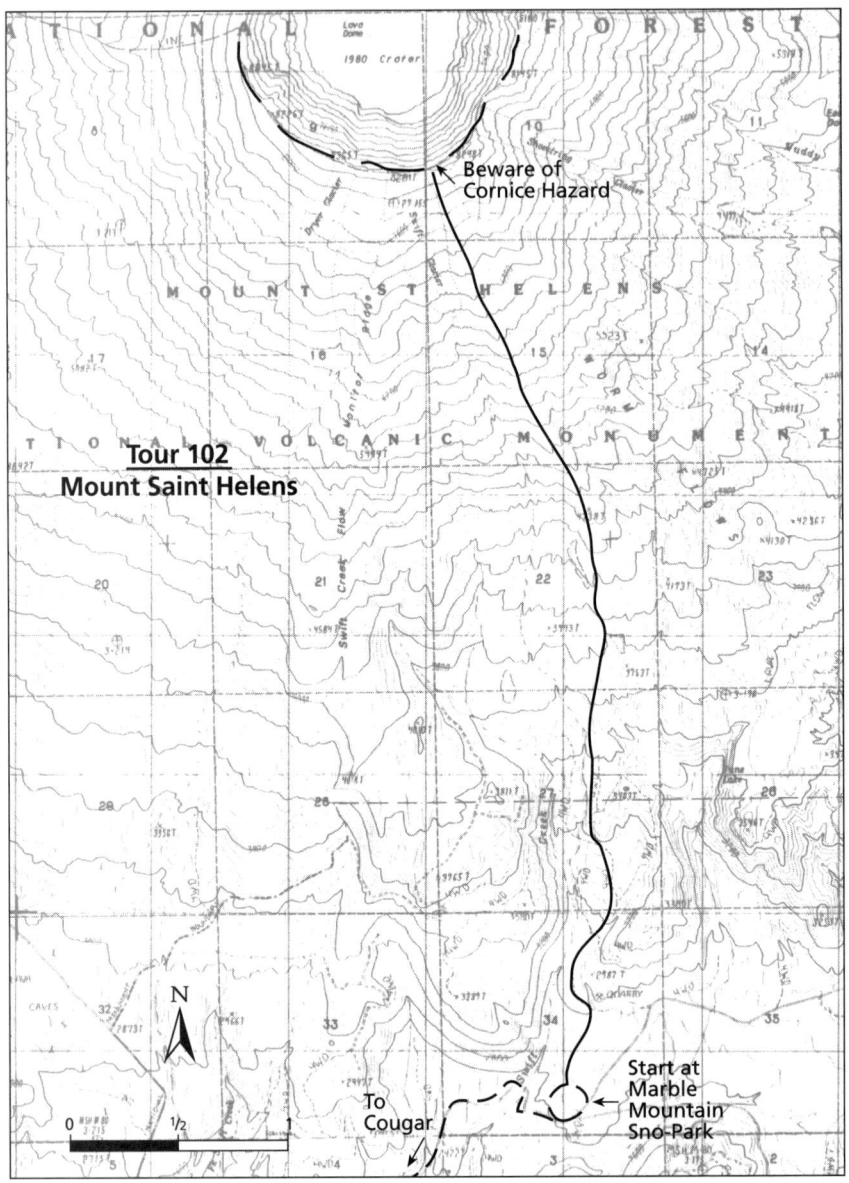

Mountain Sno-Park. Plan on arriving early so you can find a place to park.

From the Sno-Park, follow Trail No. 244 along the east bank of Swift Creek to its junction with Trail No. 216 near 3,700 feet. From here, climb north. Just go. Stop when you get within 50 feet or so of the summit rim. An early start may allow you to take advantage of sun-warmed corn snow. Reverse the route to return to your car.

Appendix A:
Reflections on Equipment, Clothing, Accessories, and Technique

Modern alpine touring equipment weighs (and costs) about the same as Nordic touring gear. The costs and performance of both types of equipment are so similar that the choice between them is simply a choice of idiom.

Boots. Alpine touring boots resemble alpine downhill boots except that they are lighter in weight, have plenty of forward flex, and have a lug sole for better off-ski traction. A cross-country downhill boot (not a telemark racing boot) suffices for Nordic ski mountaineering. Snowboarders seem to be divided on whether to choose "hard" boots or "soft" boots. A custom boot fitting is a worthwhile luxury for hard and alpine touring boots.

Skis and Boards. Alpine touring skis are (ideally) lighter and shorter, but not necessarily wider, than alpine downhill skis. They should have a general-purpose flex. Nordic mountaineering skis are wider than track-running skis, have metal edges, sidecut to assist in carving turns, and little or no wax pocket (generally, skins are used for climbing). For both skis and snowboards, a general recreational or "cruising" flex is recommended for backcountry touring. Both tip and tail should be moderately flexible and torsionally rigid. Slalom or racing flexes are inappropriate for backcountry touring because their specialized construction is unsuited to a wide range of snow conditions, ranging from powder to ice. Many skiers prefer a ski that is about head height, plus or minus a few centimeters. Longer snowboards tend to be seen in the backcountry, again with a medium flex.

Climbing Aids. The most efficient means of ascending a snow slope on skis is with the aid of climbing skins. Skins are long pieces of fabric with synthetic bristles on one side, with the "hair" all pointing in the same direction. Skins attach to ski bottoms with straps or adhesive. Although the method of attachment may vary, look for a system that keeps the ski edges exposed and the skins firmly attached, especially on steep traverses. Positive fasteners at either end are very desirable. Silicone treatments can reduce the water absorbency of skins in warmer weather. Very cold weather sometimes causes skin adhesive to lose its tack. In that case, prior to your next climb, warm the skins by wrapping them around your waist under your parka. They'll regain their tack quickly. In very wet conditions, use a chamois or cotton cloth to dry the adhesive side for better adhesion to your skis. Strap-on skins work better under these conditions.

It is not uncommon to encounter hard-frozen snow in early morning that thaws to perfect corn by early afternoon. Crampons and ice axes can ease ascents under these conditions, especially with modern telemark and alpine touring boots. Make certain that crampons fit before the tour commences. In deep snow, snowshoes tend to be the climbing tool of choice for snowboarders. Smaller models are more convenient, although they offer less flotation.

Bindings. Modern alpine touring bindings allow the skier to ski comfortably on flat or uphill terrain as well as downhill runs. This flexibility is achieved by hinging the binding at the toe and allowing the heel of the boot to rise slightly while in "touring mode." For an alpine-style descent, lock your heels down and go! Most touring bindings aren't designed for lift skiing and don't offer all six release angles, as conventional alpine bindings do. (The DIN standard for touring bindings is different than for alpine bindings.) Alpine touring bindings are typically available only at ski mountaineering outlets.

Nordic bindings come in a wide variety of styles, not all of them interchangeable. Cable bindings and releasable Nordic bindings are heaviest, but tend to provide the most stable platform. Carry replacement parts in your repair kit for binding components that might break or get lost.

Poles. Strong alpine-style poles are adequate for ski touring. Pick ones with large, sturdy baskets and be sure to carry extra baskets. Track skiing or Nordic racing poles are too long. Remove your hands from wrist loops while skiing through trees, brush, or avalanche areas.

Special touring poles with self-arrest grips and the ability to convert into avalanche probes are useful, and should be considered as standard equipment for serious tours. Whatever pole system you use, practice using your poles for self-arrest in case of a slip on steep slopes. See Vic Bien's *Mountain Skiing* for an excellent discussion of this technique. Do not ski downhill with an ice ax in your hand because of the danger of self-impalement.

Ski Restraints. In North American ski areas, skiers are required to use ski brakes or runaway straps. Runaway straps are essential in the backcountry where a runaway ski could fall into a crevasse or off a cliff. A real problem arises, however, when you are skiing in avalanche terrain. No one ever expects to get caught, but if you are, wearing runaway straps may cause you to be injured by your skis. One possible solution is "powder cords," 5- to 8-foot cords attached to the skis, tied to you, and tucked inside your gaiters. If you crash, the skis are retained. If you get caught in an avalanche, the cords permit some distance between you and your skis.

Kneepads. These should be seriously considered by inveterate telemarkers, especially in low-snow conditions where the trailing knee comes into contact with concealed rocks, stumps, and other terrain features. Kneepads provide protection against needlessly disabling injuries.

Clothing. While clothing is a personal matter, general principles do apply. Cotton has no place in the ski mountaineer's wardrobe (except as sweatbands and handkerchiefs) because of its drastically reduced insulating power when wet. Layered clothing, starting with a polypropylene or other non-absorbent layer, provides effective temperature and moisture control. Front-opening upper garments tend to be more versatile than pullover garments. Suspenders prevent pants from slipping, thereby preventing crotch failure. You should always—even on short day trips—bring enough clothing to safely spend the night outdoors if necessary.

Some skiers wear two pairs of thick wool socks, while others wear a thin "sliding layer" and a thick pair to prevent blisters. Still others report satisfactory results with synthetics such as polypropylene. Feet should not feel constricted—the resulting loss of circulation will guarantee cold feet. Vapor-barrier socks are claimed to keep your feet warmer longer. Antiperspirant (not deodorant) on your feet eliminates sweating for 12 to 16 hours, resulting in warmer feet in cold weather. It should be applied daily for the duration of the tour.

High gaiters are essential for keeping snow out of socks and boots. For extremely cold weather, insulated "super gaiters," covering the entire boot, help keep your feet toasty. On overnight trips, fleece-lined "P-booties" are more comfortable than ski boots while lounging around camp, or for that quick trip outside the tent. For the latter, non-skid soles help reduce the chance of an unexpected slip.

In cold weather, the first layer of clothing should be a synthetic layer for both leg and body covering. Zippered turtlenecks will give you ventilation when you are overheated. This "underwear" is available in various weights designed for different degrees of cold.

The next layer, often omitted in warmer conditions, should be a synthetic fleece layer. Side zippers on the legs of fleece allow you to put them on without removing your skis. Jackets offer more ventilation than pullovers do. Armpit zippers on some models provide additional ventilation.

The top layer should be a snow-shedding waterproof and vapor-permeable layer. Jumpsuits are warmer than separates, but lack the flexibility needed to keep the skier cool and dry while maintaining a vigorous pace.

In mild conditions, many skiers simply ski in athletic tights. High performance bicycle clothing has much in common with effective backcountry ski wear.

A light silk or polypropylene balaclava and a heavier wool or pile hat, with ear and neck protection, suffice for the head. Make sure that your hat is compatible with the hood on your jacket.

Light gloves, heavier mittens of wool or pile, and mitten shells will protect the skier's hands in most conditions found in the Cascades.

Many of the tours described in this book are excellent spring or summer trips. Summer temperatures are often quite temperate, and skiers frequently make their ascents in shorts and T-shirts. In this case, it is essential to wear clothing to protect against abrasions from falls or against sunburn. Conditions can change rapidly from sweltering heat to blowing snow; a trail may lead from a warm, sunny south side to an icy east-facing gully. The key to effective use of clothing is maintaining a state of dynamic equilibrium: keep your body fed and watered, dry, and at a comfortable temperature.

Impedimenta. Backcountry travelers are on their own. While the feeling of independence in untracked terrain is one of the special treats of ski mountaineering, this independence requires that skiers carry with them the capability to feed, shelter, and warm themselves and, under certain circumstances, to effect self-rescue.

A pack suitable for ski touring should be soft (or internal frame) and roomy, equipped with a waist belt and with ski-carrying patches on its sides. Packs designed especially for snowboarders make the uphill haul much easier. There should be a convenient place to carry your snow shovel. A pack that is too small becomes a chore to repack after a lunch or clothing break. Your first-aid kit should be accessible without unpacking your pack.

The following items should be in or on your pack for *every* tour:

1. Extra clothing, wrapped in plastic to keep it dry.
2. Extra food, enough for an emergency meal.
3. Extra glasses and sunglasses or goggles.
4. Knife.
5. Waterproof matches. Butane lighters are wonderful—until a snow-flake dampens the striker wheel. Carry both!
6. Chemical firestarter for wet wood. Above timberline, a stove and a small pot are essential.
7. First-aid kit, with a heavy emphasis on treating bleeding-type injuries. *Medicine for Mountaineering* is a good reference source.
8. Headlamp with spare bulbs and batteries.
9. Topographic maps. (This guidebook doesn't count.) Spray both sides of your topos with several coats of a clear acrylic spray enamel to render them flexible and waterproof.
10. Compass. An altimeter is useful, both for navigation and weather observations on longer trips. GPS can take some of the guesswork out of routefinding.
11. Wide-mouth water bottle and water.
12. An appetizing lunch, including plenty of high energy, high-nutrition food. The mountains are no place to restrict your caloric intake.
13. Sunscreen, including lip coating. Minimum SPF 15.
14. Two large plastic garbage sacks (or a bivy bag) for emergency bivouacs.
15. Garbage bag(s) for carrying out litter.
16. Personal hygiene articles.

Besides your preferred mountain travel equipment, the following gear should be carried on backcountry trips:

▲ Avalanche transceiver (one transceiver for each person or dog). Batteries should be fresh, and all units must be compatible. One way to ensure functioning is to have one person, with "beeper" set on receive, stand at the trailhead at the start of the tour and have the rest of the party pass in single file. Allow enough distance to enable the receiver to discriminate between beepers. Practice!

- ▲ Unbreakable snow shovel. (A two-year warranty does little good if your partner has to wait until the manufacturer sends you a replacement.) One shovel per person.
- ▲ Avalanche probe poles. One set per pair of skiers. Minimum two sets per party.
- ▲ Ski wax and scraper; a wax assortment for likely conditions; also, wax remover for late-season trips to remove pollen from running surfaces.
- ▲ Repair kit that includes picture-hanging wire, spare screws and bolts for bindings, extra bindings, extra ski-pole baskets, screwdrivers, pliers or Vise-grip™, duct tape, 5-minute epoxy, heavy string or cord, heavy-duty sewing needle and thread, and stove parts.
- ▲ A spare set of skins.

Some of the tours in this guide involve ascents of glaciers or short sections of steep terrain (alpine skiing). Useful equipment includes the following:

- ▲ Ice ax.
- ▲ Crampons. Take crampons whenever a tour has a mandatory steep section. You can never tell when something will be icy. Make certain they have been adjusted before you leave on the tour.
- ▲ Rope (40 to 50 meters of 9mm rope for two to three persons), one climbing harness per person, snow pickets, one or two ice screws, prusik slings, carabiners and pulleys, and wands (for marking the route on glaciers or above timberline—remove your markers as you leave).

Practice and discuss the use of these items with your party prior to setting out on a "bold" tour. Taking part in an alpine travel course is strongly recommended.

TOURING TECHNIQUES

Learning to Ski Unpacked Snow. The most efficient way to master skiing unpacked snow is to become technically proficient in skiing or snowboarding fundamentals. The easiest, fastest way to reach this goal is through qualified, competent instruction. Take lessons from instructors certified by Professional Ski Instructors of America (PSIA). If one instructor doesn't work for you, get another one. This works! Skiing the unpacked edges of intermediate runs in ski areas is an efficient way to gain practice at turning in the type of snow encountered in the backcountry. Short forays into the woods adjacent to ski areas are a good way to start the process of becoming a backcountry skier. Skiers should never ski closed runs and never ski solo out-of-bounds. Telemark skiers will derive tremendous benefit from learning groomed-trail cross-country skiing, including racing.

Routefinding. When skiing, choose a route that winds around obstacles instead of going directly over them. Look for the easiest, not necessarily the shortest, route. Such a route requires the least energy output and will often minimize avalanche hazards (with exceptions). Avoid very steep hills. Generally, you are better off picking a route that minimizes the overall slope angle.

If some in the party have skins and others are using waxless skis or wax for traction, have someone with skins break trail. The trailbreaker should make certain that the track is gentle enough for the others to follow easily. Uphill kick turns can reduce steep-hill anxiety. In the event you find yourself in an extremely steep traverse, you can increase your feeling of security by putting both poles together and bracing yourself on the uphill side, then stepping confidently to safety. If you slip, you can use the two poles together for self-arrest (like an ice ax).

Avoid this risky situation by looking and planning ahead. Some slopes are so steep that it becomes more efficient simply to remove skis and climb on foot. Hold one ski in each hand and ram their tails into the snow with each step while allowing the poles to dangle from the wrist. Or, put the skis onto your pack for long climbs. Attempting to remove skis in the middle of a steep hill is an invitation to disaster. When kicking steps, the trailbreaker should adjust the step height so that the smallest or least fit person in the party can comfortably climb along.

On the descent, "impossible snow" can sometimes be avoided by careful route selection: the lee sides of windswept ridges often hold pockets of powder (but watch for and avoid windslab conditions). Sometimes the snow stays soft much longer on forested slopes than it does on open, windswept slopes (see Mount Margaret, Tour 68). Sun-warmed slopes offer pleasant corn snow, but the same run can turn icy minutes after falling into shadow (see Mount Saint Helens, Tour 102). If conditions are truly un-skiable, it may be safer to simply doff the skis or snowboard and hike out—falling at the conclusion of every turn does little for your spirits, technique, or physical well-being.

STAYING WELL IN THE BACKCOUNTRY

The first principle of safety is to be observant. Be aware of your own body and equipment, of your party, of the weather, of the mountain terrain and its snow cover and its history. Be an active observer.

Stay Dry. Staying dry is essential for keeping warm in winter woods. Wet clothing is always uncomfortable, and sometimes life-threatening. Do not assume that, because you are planning to ski out shortly, it's all right to get wet. You may unexpectedly be forced to bivouac and find yourself in a real emergency.

Don't Overheat. Cold weather survival depends on not overheating. As you begin to warm up during the first part of the tour, unzip your jacket and armpit zippers and remove your hat, shell garments, and sweater to minimize perspiration. Slow the pace to keep from becoming drenched with sweat. Be sure, however, that removing hats or ear protection does not expose your nose, cheeks, or ears to frostbite. Remember to drink plenty of fluids to replenish losses.

Avoid Cold Injuries. When the wind blows or rain and snow begins to fall, put on shell garments to keep fuzzy sweaters, mittens, and hats dry. Move more slowly to reduce heat output and perspiration.

Avoid becoming chilled. Once chilled, it is harder for your body to rebuild energy. Chill and exhaustion can lead to hypothermia, a potentially fatal lowering of the body's core temperature. Carrying a small stove to "brew up" can significantly increase your comfort level and safety margin.

Symptoms of hypothermia include uncontrolled shivering, disorientation, and loss of appetite. Hypothermia is, and must be treated, as a life-threatening emergency. Warm liquids, dry clothing, and warm air must be administered to the conscious victim immediately. Research has shown that breathing heated air is the fastest, safest way to increase body temperature. One way of administering warm air is to have the conscious victim breathe the water vapor from a pan of hot water (careful!).

Very cold weather brings with it mixed blessings. Snow conditions tend to be better and insulation tends to stay drier, but the dangers of frostnip and frostbite (not to mention temperature gradient [TG] snow) increase drastically. Frostnip is a superficial cold injury to extremities, which is easily treated by simply warming the afflicted area. Frostbite is a serious injury in which the body part is actually frozen, with resulting cellular damage. Immediate evacuation and medical care *by those experienced in frostbite treatment* are called for in case of frostbite. Under no circumstances should the frozen body part be thawed or rubbed while in the field.

Cold injuries are easily prevented by making certain boots and mittens are warm and don't fit too snugly, that faces are covered during very cold or windy conditions, and that mittens are well mended and secured. For warmth, wear mittens instead of gloves. Wear a light pair of gloves under your mittens, in case delicate tasks require mitten removal. Some skiers secure their mittens with cords to prevent loss. Having the wind whisk your mitten away becomes serious if you have no extras!

An important part of cold-injury prevention is proper nourishment. Eat! Drink plenty of fluids and avoid dehydrated foods. It is very easy to get dehydrated in very cold weather. Dehydration leads to chemical imbalance, making production of body heat less efficient, which leads to frostnip, and so on.

Are your feet very cold and getting colder? Put on more clothing and have a snack. Pick up the pace a bit to generate more heat. Put an another hat, or put your hood on. If you find that you are not properly equipped for the tour, borrow clothing from your companions, descend to a lower elevation, and abandon the tour immediately. Playing the tough guy or silent sufferer only jeopardizes your health and the pleasures of the tour.

Avoid Heat Injuries. Spring and summer bring longer days, corn snow, and sunny weather, perfect conditions for excellent tours—and heat and radiation injuries. (Experienced skiers realize that sunburn is a hazard in winter as well as in summer.) Shield yourself with clothing, quality mountaineering sunglasses or goggles, and sunscreening agents and lip balm with SPF greater than 15.

Preventive measures for heat injuries include drinking plenty of water or electrolyte-replacement drinks, eating a balanced diet, wearing proper clothing, and maintaining a comfortable rate of travel.

Avoid Critter Hazards. The Center for Disease Control warns that backcountry rodents can be presumed to carry hantavirus. Avoid shelters and huts where you see evidence of mice, and avoid contact with rodent feces.

Giardia must be presumed to be endemic to the Cascades. Bring clean water with you (two quarts of water per person on warm days or on strenuous tours is not too much). If you choose to find water as you go, boil or chemically treat it before use. Some filters claim to remove giardia. Replenishing your water bottle from freshly fallen snow is one way to keep from running out of water while on the move.

Cougar and bear have not shown themselves to be significant hazards to skiers in North America. Keeping your distance and maintaining a large profile seem to be effective techniques for discouraging cougar and black bear attacks; the animals seem to be interested in easy meals (with exceptions). Grizzlies appear to be inherently more aggressive than other species. With U.S. Fish and Wildlife intent on repopulating Washington's wilderness with these animals, the likelihood of actually meeting one en route may increase. Capsicum repellant, properly deployed, may be an effective deterrent. Taking a class in the use of pepper spray is strongly suggested.

Bivouac in an Emergency. Sometimes it is better to spend a night out than to force a hike out in the dark while tired. When it becomes evident that you must spend an unexpected night out, decide on a suitable bivouac site immediately, before nightfall, if possible. Take inventory of your equipment and your immediate surroundings. Is there plenty of accessible firewood? Is it feasible to dig a snow cave? Do you have a functioning stove with fuel? How much fuel? Do you have a sleeping bag or a bivouac sack? Answers to these questions will determine how you should best prepare for the night.

Plan how you will use your resources. If you have plenty of firewood, you could build and tend a fire all night; you would be warm, although you might not get any sleep. An emergency is the only time that a fire in an alpine or subalpine forest is justified. If wood is not available, look for a site that is out of the wind, perhaps in a thicket of alpine dwarf firs. Windproof the shelter with snow blocks or dig a snow cave. Avoid becoming wet or exhausted while making your home.

Try to locate or melt enough drinking water to get through the night. Don't eat snow; melt it first. Put on all your clothes, loosen your ski boots or remove them entirely, and huddle together for warmth. Put your feet in your rucksack or sit on it. Contact lens wearers should remove their lenses to keep them from freezing. Eat frequently to keep up your energy throughout the night. Don't be afraid—plenty of others have spent nights out in the open and survived in fine shape.

Move out at first light, being extra careful not to get hurt or lost; with lowered reserves, you are even more susceptible to poor decision-making or injury. Keep your spirits up! Years from now, this experience will become part of the stories you can share around camp.

Appendix B:
Recommended Reading

Avalanches

Daffern, Tony. *Avalanche Safety for Skiers and Climbers*, 2d ed. Seattle: The Mountaineers, 1999.

LaChapelle, Edward R. *The ABC of Avalanche Safety*, 2d ed. Seattle: The Mountaineers, 1985.

McClung, David, and Peter Schaerer. *The Avalanche Handbook*, 2d ed. Seattle: The Mountaineers, 1993.

Perla, Ronald I. *Modern Avalanche Rescue*, USDA.

Perla, Ronald I., and M. Martinelli. *Avalanche Handbook A89*, USDA, revised 1978.

Renner, Jeff. *Northwest Mountain Weather: Understanding and Forecasting for Backcountry Use*. Seattle: The Mountaineers, 1992.

Routes

Beckey, Fred. *Cascade Alpine Guide: Climbing and High Routes*, 2d ed., vols. 1–3. Seattle: The Mountaineers, 1987, 1989, 1995.

Kirkendall, Tom, and Vicky Spring. *Cross-Country Ski Trails of Washington's Cascades and Olympics*, 2d ed. Seattle: The Mountaineers, 1995.

Portman, Sally. *Ski Touring Methow Style*. Lynnwood: Washington Trails Association, 1986.

Spring, Ira, and Harvey Manning. *50 Hikes in Mount Rainier National Park*, 4th ed. Seattle: The Mountaineers, 1999.

_____. *100 Hikes in Washington's North Cascades National Park Region*, 2d ed. Seattle: The Mountaineers, 1994.

Skiing and Ski Mountaineering

Barnett, Steve. *Cross-Country, Downhill and Other Nordic Mountain Skiing Techniques*, 3d ed. Seattle: Pacific Search Press, 1983 (out of print).

Bien, Vic. *Mountain Skiing*. Seattle: The Mountaineers, 1982 (out of print).

Gillette, Ned, and John Dostal. *Cross-Country Skiing*, 3d ed. Seattle: The Mountaineers, 1988.

The Mountaineers. *Mountaineering: The Freedom of the Hills*, 6th ed. Seattle: The Mountaineers, 1997.

Parker, Paul. *Free-Heel Skiing*, 2d ed. Seattle: The Mountaineers, 1995.

Van Tilburg, Christopher. *Backcountry Snowboarding*. Seattle: The Mountaineers, 1998.

First Aid

American Outdoor Safety League. *Emergency/Survival Handbook.* Seattle: The Mountaineers, 1987.

Carline, Jan D., Martha J. Lentz, and Steven C. Macdonald. *Mountaineering First Aid: A Guide to Accident Response and First Aid Care.* Seattle: The Mountaineers, 1996.

Lathrop, Theodore. *Hypothermia: Killer of the Unprepared.* Portland: Mazamas, 1972 (out of print).

Sabel, Gerald, ed. *First Aid: Quick Information for Mountaineering and Backcountry Use.* Seattle: The Mountaineers, 1988.

Weiss, Eric A. *Wilderness 911: A Step-by-Step Guide for Medical Emergencies and Improvised Care in the Backcountry.* Seattle: The Mountaineers, 1998.

Weiss, Hal. *Secrets of Warmth for Comfort or Survival.* Seattle: The Mountaineers, 1998.

Wilkerson, James A., ed. *Medicine for Mountaineering,* 4th ed. Seattle: The Mountaineers, 1992.

_____, ed. *Hypothermia, Frostbite and Other Cold Injuries: Prevention, Recognition, Pre-Hospital Treatment.* Seattle: The Mountaineers, 1986.

Appendix C:
Seasonal Cross-Reference

Use these tables to pick tours suitable for a given month. For example, if it is October, where are some places that are likely to offer good skiing? First, decide on a general region—say the Mount Baker area. Next, look in the top row for the current month, then trace down the appropriate column. The bullet indicates a tour that may be suitable for the given month, dependent on weather and snowpack conditions.

MOUNT BAKER HIGHWAY, SR 542

TOUR	JAN	FEB	MAR	APR	MAY	JUN	JUL	AUG	SEP	OCT	NOV	DEC
1. Tomyhoi Peak					*	*	*					
2. Goat Mountain			*	*	*	*						
3. Ruth Mountain					*	*	*	*				
4. Mount Ann	*	*	*	*								
5. Coleman Pinnacle	*	*	*	*	*	*				*	*	*
6. Sholes Glacier					*	*	*	*				
7. Herman Saddle	*	*	*	*	*	*				*	*	*
8. Chowder Ridge							*	*		*		
9. Skyline Divide					*	*	*				*	
10. Coleman Glacier				*	*	*				*	*	

NORTH CASCADES HIGHWAY, SR 20

TOUR	JAN	FEB	MAR	APR	MAY	JUN	JUL	AUG	SEP	OCT	NOV	DEC
11. Slate Peak					*	*	*					
12. Silver Star Mountain	*	*	*	*	*							
13. Delancey Ridge	*	*	*									
14. Early Winters					*	*	*					
15. Heather/Maple Passes					*	*	*				*	
16. Cutthroat Pass					*	*	*					
17. Névé Glacier	*	*	*	*	*	*						
18. Teebone Ridge	*	*	*	*	*							*
19. Eldorado					*	*	*					
20. Boston Basin					*	*	*					
21. Sahale Arm					*	*	*					
22. Snowking Mountain				*	*	*						

TOUR	JAN	FEB	MAR	APR	MAY	JUN	JUL	AUG	SEP	OCT	NOV	DEC
23. Sauk Mountain					*	*						
24. Mount Watson					*	*						
25. Bacon Peak					*	*	*					
26. Mount Shuksan		*	*	*	*	*						
27. Mount Baker: Boulder Glacier				*	*	*	*					
28. Mount Baker: Easton Glacier				*	*	*	*					
29. Park Butte			*	*	*							
30. Twin Sisters				*	*	*						

MOUNTAIN LOOP HIGHWAY AND SR 530

TOUR	JAN	FEB	MAR	APR	MAY	JUN	JUL	AUG	SEP	OCT	NOV	DEC
31. Glacier Peak					*	*						
32. Johnson Ridge					*	*						
33. Vesper Peak				*	*	*						
34. Green Mountain				*	*	*				*	*	
35. Dome Glacier				*	*	*	*					
36. Whitehorse Mountain		*	*	*	*							
37. Three Fingers				*	*	*						
38. Mount Pilchuck	*	*	*									

STEVENS PASS HIGHWAY, US 2

TOUR	JAN	FEB	MAR	APR	MAY	JUN	JUL	AUG	SEP	OCT	NOV	DEC
39. Big Snow Mountain			*	*	*	*						
40. Cowboy Mountain	*	*	*	*								*
41. Heather Ridge	*	*	*								*	*
42. Big Chief Mountain	*	*	*	*							*	*
43. Yodelin	*	*	*									
44. Union Peak	*	*	*	*								*
45. Jove Peak	*	*	*	*								*
46. Lichtenberg Mountain	*	*	*	*								*
47. Jim Hill Mountain	*	*	*	*								
48. Rock Mountain	*	*	*	*							*	*
49. Mount Mastiff				*	*							
50. Chiwaukum Mountains				*	*	*						
51. Alpine Lookout	*	*	*									
52. Mount Maude				*	*							
53. Chiwawa Mountain				*	*	*						
54. North Star Mountain				*	*	*						
55. Clark Mountain				*	*	*						
56. Big Jim Mountain		*	*	*	*							
57. Icicle Ridge	*	*										*

TOUR	JAN	FEB	MAR	APR	MAY	JUN	JUL	AUG	SEP	OCT	NOV	DEC
58. Dragontail Peak			*	*	*							
59. Cashmere Mountain	*	*	*	*	*	*						
60. Wedge Mountain	*	*	*	*								*

BLEWETT PASS HIGHWAY, US 97

TOUR	JAN	FEB	MAR	APR	MAY	JUN	JUL	AUG	SEP	OCT	NOV	DEC
61. Porcupine Creek	*	*	*	*	*							
62. Diamond Head	*	*	*									
63. Ingalls Peak					*	*	*					
64. Mount Stuart				*	*							

INTERSTATE 90

TOUR	JAN	FEB	MAR	APR	MAY	JUN	JUL	AUG	SEP	OCT	NOV	DEC
65. Mount Daniel			*	*	*							
66. Jolly Mountain	*	*	*	*								
67. Amabilis Mountain	*	*	*								*	
68. Mount Margaret	*	*	*								*	
69. Kendall Ridge	*	*	*								*	
70. Kendall Peak Lakes Basin	*	*	*								*	
71. Red Mountain	*	*	*	*								
72. Mount Snoqualmie	*	*	*	*								
73. Chair Peak Basin	*	*	*	*	*						*	
74. Silver Peak	*	*	*								*	
75. Humpback Mountain		*	*									
76. Granite Mountain	*	*	*	*								
77. McClellan Butte	*	*										

MOUNT RAINIER AND AREAS SOUTH

TOUR	JAN	FEB	MAR	APR	MAY	JUN	JUL	AUG	SEP	OCT	NOV	DEC
78. Norse Peak	*	*	*	*								
79. Union Creek	*	*	*	*								
80. Silver King	*	*	*	*								
81. Crystal Basin	*	*	*	*								
82. Chinook to Crystal	*	*	*	*							*	*
83. Naches Peak				*							*	
84. Yakima Peak				*							*	
85. Summerland				*	*	*			*	*		
86. Cowlitz Chimneys				*	*	*						
87. Interglacier				*	*	*						
88. Goat Island				*	*	*						

TOUR	JAN	FEB	MAR	APR	MAY	JUN	JUL	AUG	SEP	OCT	NOV	DEC
89. Burroughs Mountain				*	*	*					*	
90. Carbon Glacier	*	*	*	*	*	*						
91. Russell Glacier					*	*						
92. Puyallup Cleaver				*	*	*						
93. Sunset Park				*	*	*						
94. Van Trump Park	*	*	*	*							*	
95. Tatoosh Range	*	*	*	*	*						*	
96. Muir Snowfield	*	*	*	*	*	*			*	*	*	
97. Nisqually Glacier	*	*	*	*								
98. Paradise Glacier	*	*	*	*	*	*						
99. White Pass	*	*	*	*								*
100. Goat Rocks					*	*	*					
101. Mount Adams					*	*						
102. Mount Saint Helens	*	*	*	*	*							

Appendix D:
Sources of Weather and Snow Information

Information about NOAA Weather Radio
Website: www.nws.noaa.gov/nwr/index.html

National Weather Service
National Oceanic and Atmospheric Administration (NOAA)
Website: www.nws.noaa.gov

Northwest Avalanche Center
Phone: (206) 526-6677
Website: www.seawfo.noaa.gov/nwac.html

Washington State Weather Information
Interactive Weather Information Network
Website: iwin.nws.noaa.gov/iwin/wa/wa.html

WeatherPhone
National Weather Service
Call the Seattle Times Information Line, (206) 464-2000, then enter
Menu Code Number 9904 for the current forecast for the Cascade
and Olympic Mountains

Index

About the Author

Rainer Burgdorfer is a backcountry skiing guru in the Pacific Northwest. A resident of Seattle, he has been exploring the slopes, faces, and valleys of the Cascades on skis and on foot for more than 30 years. He's taught backcountry skiing and safety for years. He also is a mountaineer and has climbed throughout Washington and California and participated in mountain rescues.

THE MOUNTAINEERS, founded in 1906, is a nonprofit outdoor activity and conservation club, whose mission is "to explore, study, preserve, and enjoy the natural beauty of the outdoors. . . . " Based in Seattle, Washington, the club is now the third-largest such organization in the United States, with 15,000 members and five branches throughout Washington State.

The Mountaineers sponsors both classes and year-round outdoor activities in the Pacific Northwest, which include hiking, mountain climbing, ski-touring, snowshoeing, bicycling, camping, kayaking and canoeing, nature study, sailing, and adventure travel. The club's conservation division supports environmental causes through educational activities, sponsoring legislation, and presenting informational programs. All club activities are led by skilled, experienced volunteers, who are dedicated to promoting safe and responsible enjoyment and preservation of the outdoors.

If you would like to participate in these organized outdoor activities or the club's programs, consider a membership in The Mountaineers. For information and an application, write or call The Mountaineers, Club Headquarters, 300 Third Avenue West, Seattle, Washington 98119; (206) 284-6310.

The Mountaineers Books, an active, nonprofit publishing program of the club, produces guidebooks, instructional texts, historical works, natural history guides, and works on environmental conservation. All books produced by The Mountaineers are aimed at fulfilling the club's mission.

Send or call for our catalog of more than 300 outdoor titles:

 The Mountaineers Books
1001 SW Klickitat Way, Suite 201
Seattle, WA 98134
800-553-4453
mbooks@mountaineers.org
www.mountaineersbooks.org

Other titles you may enjoy from The Mountaineers:

FREE-HEEL SKIING: Telemark and Parallel Techniques for All Conditions, 2d Edition, *Paul Parker*
This fully revised, classic guide is the definitive manual on free-heel skiing. Parker is a veteran instructor with over 20 years experience in Nordic and Alpine disciplines and offers advice for all levels of expertise.

BACKCOUNTRY SNOWBOARDING, *Christopher Van Tilburg*
This is the first book to introduce snowboarders to the techniques and concerns of backcountry snowboarding. Fully illustrated with color photos throughout, this book covers everything the advanced freerider needs for safe ascent and descent.

SNOWSHOE ROUTES—WASHINGTON, *Dan A. Nelson*
The most comprehensive guidebook to prime winter hiking in Washington. Provides complete details on a prime selection of 81 diverse snowshoe routes.

WILDERNESS 911: A Step-by-Step Guide for Medical Emergencies and Improvised Care in the Backcountry, *Eric A. Weiss, M.D.*
This book provides quick-access wilderness medicine from *BACKPACKER* magazine experts. Covers the injuries and incidents most likely to happen in the backcountry.

WILDERNESS NAVIGATION: Finding Your Way Using Map, Compass, Altimeter, and GPS, *Bob Burns and Mike Burns*
A guide to navigating both on the trail and in the backcountry. Includes the most reliable and easy-to-learn methods of navigation yet devised.

CONDITIONING FOR OUTDOOR FITNESS: A Comprehensive Training Guide, *David Musnick, M.D., and Mark Pierce, A.T.C.*
The most comprehensive guide to conditioning, fitness, and training for all outdoor activities. Chapters on specific sports, including hiking, climbing, biking, paddling, and skiing, with information on cross-training.

THE AVALANCHE HANDBOOK, 2d Edition, *David McClung and Peter Schaerer*
This fully revised and rewritten edition continues as the unrivaled resource for comprehensive information on avalanches and snow safety. Includes the latest information, techniques, and research on understanding and surviving avalanches.

100 CLASSIC HIKES IN™ WASHINGTON: North Cascades, Olympics, Mount Rainier & South Cascades, Alpine Lakes, Glacier Peak, *Ira Spring and Harvey Manning*
A full-color guide to Washington's finest trails. The essential classic for hiking this picturesque state including maps, photos, and full details you need to plan the perfect trip.